MORE THAN WORDS

ALSO BY MARIO M. CUOMO

Diaries of Mario M. Cuomo
Forest Hills Diary
Lincoln on Democracy (editor)
The Cuomo Commission Report (editor)
The Real New York

·

MORE

than

WORDS

·

St Martin's Press / New York

DESIGN   BY   JAYE   ZIMET

Frontispiece photograph courtesy Don Pollard

Library of Congress Cataloging-in-Publication Data
Cuomo, Mario Matthew.
      More than words / Mario Cuomo.
         p.   cm.
      ISBN 0-312-11385-4
         1. New York (State)—Politics and government—1951–   2. United
      States—Politics and government   1981–1989.   3. United States—
Politics and government—1989–1993.   I. Title.
      [F125.3.C86A5   1994]
      974.7'043—dc20   94-18982
                                                                CIP

First Paperback Edition: August 1994
10   9   8   7   6   5   4   3   2   1

To Matilda,

who has given me so much

more than I deserve

Contents

CONTENTS

PART III

1990 – 1994

ACKNOWLEDGMENTS

This book represents in a significant way the input of many public servants, friends, and family who have joined me in pursuit of a better New York . . . and beyond. I am enormously grateful to them all.

The speech of man is like embroidered tapestries, since like them this too has to be extended in order to display its patterns, but when it is rolled up it conceals and distorts them.
—Plutarch

Politics had nothing to do with the formation of my basic values. They were not derived from campaign platforms nor from arguments between Truman and Dewey or Kennedy and Nixon. Throughout my youth and for most of my professional life as a lawyer, I was only mildly interested in politics. The things I came to believe most deeply I learned from the sweaty example of my immigrant parents' struggle to build a life for themselves and their children, from the Sisters of Charity at little St. Monica's Church and from an absorbing love affair with Our Lady of the Law. They were simple values: the dignity of hard work; respect for family; respect for law and order; a shameless, bold patriotism; a recognition of the overriding importance of education; a gratitude for God's nature and a feeling of responsibility for it.

The unadorned Christian ethic which my parents lived by seemed exactly right to me, even as a basis for the government that ruled and guided us all. While recognizing that we were too weak to live by this ethic perfectly, we were nevertheless called upon to try to do good things for other people. Prudently, without ignoring our obligations to ourselves, we tried, realistically but insistently, to arrange a package of justice, charity, and mercy that would be available to all we could touch. I did not need courses in political science or esoteric tracts to teach me what the role of our government should be. We were entitled to all the government we needed, but only the government we needed.

Government should, then, work to assure us opportunity while insisting we bear individual responsibility for providing all we can for ourselves. Government should also protect our liberty—our right to live securely and to express ourselves freely so long as we deny no one else the same right. Government should see to it that the productive remain productive and, indeed, grow stronger, but there are two major groups that deserve more of government's efforts than they are receiving. The first consists of those who work for a living because they have to, people not poor enough to be desperate but not rich enough to be worry-free. The second is those people who are struggling to make it but, for whatever reason, cannot.

For two decades as a lawyer, I tried applying these basic principles to the small circle of my own family and, beyond that, to the larger community, through a series of confrontations with government in court and outside of it on behalf of individuals and small groups who, I believed, had been dealt with wrongly by government. That brought me some public notice but only partial satisfaction. I became convinced that the only way I could help change things would be to become part of the political system and push for my values from within.

Now, after some time in government, I have the good feeling that comes from knowing we have been able to do some useful things. At the same time, however, I have the continuing frustration of knowing we are still far from the solid and vitalizing ideals implanted by my own family, the good nuns of St. Monica, and the splendid legal system that keeps us intact.

That is why I agreed to publish this collection of speeches: because they state ideas and principles that I believe in deeply, and describe dreams that have still not been adequately realized in our incomplete miracle of a democracy.

Each of these speeches might have been written better by other writers. Unfortunately, however, I have found that I am not capable of delivering an important speech even reasonably well unless its content, style, and language are mostly my own, so that the option of simply having an excellent writer produce a speech ready for delivery is unavailable to me. And the reason I did not write most of them better myself is that except in two cases, the Democratic Convention and the Notre Dame speeches in 1984, I simply was not able to give them the time and effort a better speech would have required.

The truth is that writing a good speech is such a demanding process that throughout my public life I have avoided that painful experience by speaking extemporaneously whenever possible.

There are advantages to that kind of communication. Spontaneity is one. Audience contact is another. Because you're not tied to a text, your eyes scan the audience and you can detect signs of agreement that encourage you to elaborate effective points. Or you see impatient fidgeting, the sidelong glances of disapproval, and occasionally, the sure sign of abject failure—eyes closed, chin on chest, a customer not only declaring "no sale," but making it clear he or she is no longer shopping. Alerted, the speaker can then change pace, improvise, move on to a more interesting proposition. It's easier to engage the audience when you have both eyes in direct contact with the people you're addressing, both arms drawing pictures in the air, adding punctuation, fighting off the glaze.

It's more fun, too. It has an adventurous quality that one misses when the assignment is just to read a prepared text. That sense of adventure is nourished by the recollection of extemporaneous efforts that have misfired—sometimes disastrously. Every speech is subject to that danger: the casual blunder that escapes the lips before the brain has calculated its capacity for damage. Like a president addressing a friendly crowd during a presidential campaign and trying to express his gratitude for its exuberant and encouraging welcome. He departed from his text for only one sentence: "Gee, thanks for that marvelous . . . *recession!*"

And even if the blunder is not your own, extemporaneous comments are more apt to produce ambiguities, because they have not had the benefit of rehearsal before actual delivery. Talking to a group of business leaders in New York, I put the prepared text aside and began to speak freely. I wanted to make the point that if we were bold enough with our policies and did some exciting things, we could succeed dramatically . . . even be number one again! For some reason, one of my brain cells, the one that stores the memory of favorite childhood poems, suddenly sparked and there came to my lips the old poem by Leigh Hunt. "Like Abou Ben Adhem," I said, "we will lead all the rest!"

One of the men in the audience turned to the woman next to him and said, "That's not like the governor. . . . What does he mean by 'a boob and Adam'? It sounds dirty to me."

There are of course other disadvantages to the extemporaneous speech. There is the chance one will neglect to make a vital point or fail to impart a significant piece of information or even be perceived as showing disrespect. I recall my translator in Milan explaining to

me, after a full day of speeches to the business and political communities of that great industrial city, that my failure to use texts
throughout the day had become a subject of unfavorable comment
by the people I was trying so hard to impress. They felt that because
I did not have a full written text, I had not considered them worthy
of the effort it takes to prepare.

So, at least some of the time, one is obliged to undergo the
tedium and occasional agony of preparing in advance a complete
speech, with all the words in place, and then delivering them as
close to verbatim as possible.

Writing speeches is always difficult for me and it's almost as difficult
to describe how I go about doing it. There are no set formulas or
fail-proof techniques that I am aware of; I suppose different people
use different methods.

For me, the vital thing is that there is something important I
want to say. That was the case in 1984 when I wrote the Notre
Dame speech to reply to the charge that my political position on
abortion was morally untenable for a Catholic politician. I never
wanted more to be able to express clearly my ideas and feelings. I
thought about what to write for days. I talked about it; wrote notes
on scratch paper; read about "fetuses," studied Aristotle and Aquinas.
I read from books and articles on theology, one after the other,
dozens of them, and when there were so many notes in so many
places that I began to feel inundated, I organized them by subject
matter: "Church teachings," "Supreme Court," "Courtney Murray,"
each title on the top of five-by-eight index cards containing excerpts,
quotes, ideas. I wound up with forty-three stacks of cards.

The next step was an outline. I won't even try to write without
one, not since Father Newman's high school English class at St.
John's Prep in 1948. Forty-five years of outlines produce a tough
habit to break.

Now the piece began to take shape: an introduction, presentation of the subject to be discussed, description of the issues, positions on the issues, my arguments, the answers, my rebuttals. I
wrote for a week and produced scores of yellow pad pages, then
boiled them all down to a more workable size, closer in length to
what the finished product would be.

All of this while I was paying virtually no attention to the exact words I would use: at this stage I was concentrating on ideas, without trying to be precise or pretty about the way they were described. That could come later: first I had to be sure of what I meant to say; then I would worry about how to say it.

After a couple of weeks, I knew what I wanted to say. I had gone over it several times with Peter Quinn and Bill Hanlon of my staff, two bright, clever, gifted thinkers and writers, both of them profoundly Catholic and just as troubled as I was by the task of agonizing over the powerful, almost paralyzing issues raised by the abortion question. We wrote, discussed, debated, and finally decided.

There was left the last task: finding the right words. This is when we began to think more carefully about another fundamental question raised by every speech: who exactly is the audience?

In this regard the Notre Dame speech was different from most I've done. Normally, the nature of the audience would be the first thing I would measure. Before beginning the process, I would try to ascertain the expectations of the group I was addressing. But here I knew what I wanted to say before I knew to whom it would be said. The issue had been forced early in 1984 by public statements from high Catholic church officials who argued that a Catholic politician had no choice but to advocate the Catholic hierarchy's position on abortion, in effect insisting that the whole population live by our Catholic beliefs.

I concluded I had no choice but to speak, even before I knew what I would say or when.

Having decided on the substance of my message, I was now ready to deal with the fundamental question raised by the exact nature of the audience. Who were they? A few hundred students, priests, nuns, brothers, and citizens of Indiana on the Notre Dame campus present in the room and armed with some specific knowledge of the issue? Or the television viewers across the country who would see it and hear it . . . overall less expert than the people in the room? Or both groups?

The choice makes a difference. The best way to address the television audience is to look directly at the camera, but then you lose contact with the people in the room. I chose to talk to the people in the room, ignoring the camera. The eventual result, I'm told, was predictable; the appearance proved to be more effective at Notre Dame than it was on television.

Having chosen the audience, I set about to find the exact words.

One thing is clear about that process: the possibilities are infinite. Picking the right words, quotes, metaphors, humor, one-liners, punctuation, order, could go on forever if you let it. The work is finished only when you choose to end it because you decide you're out of time. For the Notre Dame speech that was after four or five weeks; for most speeches it is much less than that.

Finally, I was satisfied with the product. It had a beginning, a middle, and an end. It was organized. It was clear. It said something I believed was important, and it was honest.

When I walked into the hall on the Notre Dame campus I was confident I had a worthwhile message; the only issue left was whether I would deliver it well to the people in the hall. The music must fit the lyrics. A poor delivery can kill a great speech; a great delivery can improve a mediocre one.

My guess is it would be about as hard to teach a person when to do what during a speech as to teach a person how to sing. Maybe harder. I've never learned the rules, if there are any, and there have been times that I have felt awkward and inappropriate. For the most part, however, I've discovered over the years that as long as I am strongly committed to the message I am trying to deliver, my mind and voice and body will find ways to help people understand what I'm trying to say.

In delivering speeches there are times for gestures and dramatic voice changes and stories and jokes . . . and there are times for none of those things. It seemed to me the Notre Dame speech didn't lend itself to histrionics or drama the way some might; it was more like a lecture than a keynote or a fund-raiser. What it needed was a clear, careful rendition—staying true to the prepared text. That's what I believe I was able to give it.

As I look back over the speeches I selected for this volume, I note that most of the things I was trying to say revolved around the small cluster of basic ideas that have resonated with me for most of my adult life. Perhaps the most fundamental are those dealing with the starting question in political dialogue: "What is the role of government?" More than once my answer was simply, paraphrasing Lincoln, "We should have all the government we need but only the government we need." That comes about as close to a slogan as I like to get. In various addresses, I have interpreted that simple phrase to mean that government has a positive role that goes far beyond the obvious function of protecting us from foreign and domestic threats to our existence. Government should also assist the private sector to create a prosperous economy, and help those who cannot participate in that economy because they are somehow unable to, and have no one else but government to help them.

Most of the other generalities I feel most comfortable with appear in one or more of these speeches. They include the rule of law; insistence on a sense of responsibility; the rejection of the melting pot for the mosaic view of our multiculturalism; the need for seeing our disparate society as a family; the belief that work is better than welfare; and the idea that "economic growth" is the provider of the American dream.

I confess that I am always a little uneasy about using these sweeping ideas because I am so painfully aware that in governing, as elsewhere, the devil is in the details, and that's where policy is made.

The generalities work nicely in speeches, especially inaugurals or convention speeches—but they don't work for statutes. Making the laws people live by requires specific decisions that involve real consequences to real people. Is a "bailout" of an auto manufacturer in an attempt to save 3,700 jobs in Tarrytown, New York, an offense to the principle of free enterprise? Is a welfare benefit to help a young mother feed her newest child born out of wedlock, no matter how many others she's had, appropriate help to the needy or a wrongful conversion of the hard-earned wealth of the taxpayers? Is abortion a matter of constitutionally protected political liberty or should we treat it as murder?

So, in various places throughout these speeches, a reader can find reminders that ideology is certainly worth talking about, but specific ideas tied down to the Procrustean bed of reality are what really matter. There is, as I said in the Yale speech, a world of difference between the poetry of campaigns and the prose of governance. Perhaps it should be required that a label stating that be affixed to every political speech that is delivered. If you agree, please consider that I have now affixed my label.

—MARIO CUOMO
EXECUTIVE MANSION
ALBANY, NEW YORK

MORE THAN WORDS

P A R T   I

—

1 9 7 4 — 1 9 8 6

This was my first political speech. I was seeking the office of lieutenant governor in 1974. The New Democratic Coalition was the extreme liberal wing of the Democratic party, and this group was not comfortable with hearing its views challenged by other Democrats. It was, after all, a period of high confidence for them. Watergate had made Republicans and Conservatives (a party new in New York) vulnerable, and indeed, the elections later that year created a new tidal wave of Democratic power in New York and beyond. But I felt strongly about what I took to be a new political elitism that was chasing the old middle-class, ethnic core of the Democratic constituency out of the party.

I think the history since then is on my side of the argument. Six years later, Ronald Reagan became president by luring the "working stiffs" into his conservative circle, telling them they had been abandoned by the Democrats as he had been after Truman. Even today some of the ideas in this speech are still developing. Thus I called for a "shifting of the cost of education from the real estate tax" to "a more progressive source like the income tax." That idea has only now begun to attract attention in New York, as I write this note, in 1993.

I have no real expectancy that any large number of you will vote for me. Indeed, most of you have no fair basis for making a judgment on my candidacy.

On the other hand, I may, by whatever currently unpredictable confluence of circumstances, survive the rigors of the campaign and become the candidate of our party for the office of lieutenant governor. Should that happen, I'd like my candidacy to be acceptable to a large number, if not all, of you. That will probably require that you know a good deal more about me than I can tell you today, but I'll do what I can.

I'll leave my years of experience in public affairs, and my specific positions on the whole range of major issues, to the brochures, literature, and other meetings from now until the primaries. But I would like to talk to you today about a single pervasively significant question: what is the constituency we seek to represent as the Democratic party?

As I see it, our basic constituency is that whole spectrum of people from the desperately poor welfare mother in South Jamaica through the nearly comfortable middle-class worker of Clinton County, as well as the enlightened affluent.

The less affluent part of the constituency is described principally not by color, sex, ethnic origin, or religion, but by economic class and the problems peculiar to economic condition.

It's a broad and at times sharply diverse constituency.

We must serve—first and foremost—those without power or property. No matter how out of fashion that may be regarded this political season, our greatest energies must go to the areas of greatest need.

But at the same time it's wrong for us to overlook that other major segment of our constituency, the so-called middle class: the worker, blue-collar or white-collar, of whatever skin color, who labors hard, lives modestly, asks little, and gets less in return. The individual not poor enough for welfare nor rich enough to be worry-free. The men and women who work for a living *not* because a psychiatrist says it's a good way for them to fill the interval between birth and eternity. The individual whom John Dos Passos dubbed the "working stiff." The small businessman, young professional. They voted for Roosevelt and Lehman and Kennedy. As Catholics, they voted for Lehman, and as Jews, they voted for Kennedy. As blacks, they voted for both of them. They were and are the backbone of our work force, the stabilizing influence in our society. The hope of the future.

And they *were* the strength of our party.

Then we lost them.

For some reason they felt alienated by a new Democratic party which they thought neither understood nor related to them. They were made to feel voiceless, powerless, and frustrated. So they became Republicans or conservatives.

We must bring them back to our party.

Without them, we can neither win nor regard ourselves as

entitled to win. They must be heard and served and they can be, simultaneously with their poor brothers and sisters—with fairness to both groups.

Many of the problems they share in common. And many of our programs serve them both. The effort to break down corporate power, the pushing of a substantial governmental assumption of campaign financing, the reconstituting of our regulatory agencies, tax reform, a shifting of the cost of education from the real estate tax. These are the relatively easy areas for us.

But there are much more difficult questions.

Like busing and scatter-site housing and minority employment in the unions.

The flash points.

The cutting edges.

Where the two groups collide, interests compete, tempers are frayed, and fears arise.

This is the real challenge for our party. To find a way to harmonize the competing interests. To serve the poor without crushing the middle class. And while doing this . . . to make clear to the middle class that it isn't our intention to crush them.

It can be done—if we remember what Burke and Webster and John F. Kennedy tried to teach: that social truths in these hard areas are not painted in pure black and white, that while principles may never be compromised, issues may.

If we can remember that neither the nation, the city, nor the state is governed simply by glittering general propositions, but that the work of government is done by nailing down our highest aspiration to the Procrustean bed of reality. By applying those generalizations to the hard reality of real people with real concerns and real fears.

If we have the humility and decency to remember that all the angels seldom stand on one side of a particular issue. And that in the subtle conflict situations, not every resistance to what seems a good idea is bigotry and not every new liberal idea is infallible.

If we remember that while cowardice and equivocation are not virtues, conciliation and compassion are.

If we have the strength and the courage and the reasonableness to find the middle ground where some enmity will surely be earned from both sides, but the greater good is served.

5

If we can have the restraint not to torment the middle class with arrogant and insensitive rhetoric, nor to patronize the poor with artificial and academic sociological propositions to which they themselves attach no real value.

This is not easy to articulate: it must be seen and lived. It's largely a matter of style and emphasis requiring, at times, an exquisite delicacy of judgment and, always, an unrelenting desire to do—to accomplish good—rather than just to ennoble ourselves by saying good.

It can be done. More importantly, it must be done, and it must be done by us. Because the alternative is not only to lose the election, but to leave these dangerous problems to the callousness of a Republican party that thrives on polarizing people, that exploits fear and hate. A Republican party that will seduce the middle class by pandering to its worst instincts in these dangerous situations and then, with the heavy hammer forged out of the coalition of rich and middle class, will beat the poor into even greater submission.

This group had a distinguished and honorable genesis. As a Democrat, I'm grateful to you for having led the way on Vietnam, for having taken the progressive road, for having opened the party process so that outsiders like myself might reasonably consider running for office.

I'm familiar with the New Democratic Coalition platform as set out in 1972. There are aspects of it with which I'm not in accord. But I believe those dissents to be, overall, not dominant. Unless the New Democratic Coalition requires a total and slavish acceptance of every utterance of its platform committee, I believe we are compatible. I ask you for the opportunity to prove that.

Thank you.

My first speech as governor described two basic ideas that are still at the heart of my beliefs—government's necessary and proper role in doing what we cannot do for ourselves individually, which I called "progressive pragmatism," and the idea of society as a family. I was surprised by a much more favorable response than I had anticipated, including a letter of praise from former president Richard Nixon. I was not surprised when the Reagan administration continued to advance their policy of social Darwinism, propounding a new ethic in place of the idea of government as family: "God helps those whom God had helped, and if He has left you out who are we to presume on His judgment?"

This is a beautiful celebration, of our state, of our superb system of government, and of our extraordinary good fortune.

I am grateful that we have been allowed to share it.

Permit me a special word of gratitude to three people:

• to the one most effective instrument of our success, who shares this inauguration with me, Matilda;

• to the man who has led this state for eight years and to whom I owe a special debt for having given me my first opportunity to serve the people of the state of New York, as secretary of state in 1975, Governor Hugh Carey;

• and to an institution among public officials, who cannot be with us physically today, but who has been with me from the beginning of what appeared then to be an impossible pursuit, a man of strength, stature, and splendid style, the mayor of the city of Albany, Erastus Corning.

I would be less than honest if I did not admit to some small personal satisfaction at having won two elections [primary and general]. Especially since I am all too familiar with what it feels like not to win.

But I would be less than intelligent if I didn't recognize that the outcome was not so much a personal vindication as it was the judgment of the people of New York as to the body of principles and programs which we advanced as the reason and justification for my candidacy.

Throughout the campaign, I spoke insistently on what we believe our government must do over the next four years. I hope the next four years will show that I did not speak idly or cynically.

We will go forward with the program of jobs and justice that I described in the campaign and that I believe the people of this state generally regard as a fair appraisal of what we need: A criminal justice system that is a firmer, surer, more effective vehicle of deterrence; a new emphasis on high technology, agribusiness, domestic manufacturing; a responsible approach to our fiscal difficulties; an infrastructure program that will rebuild our state's physical strength while we put to work unemployed New Yorkers; a continuing emphasis on educational excellence; reformation of our system of regulating utilities; reorganization of the operating agency for mass transit in the twelve counties of our metropolitan New York region.

We will go forward with these and the other elements of our program for New York that I have urged for all of this year.

Part of that program will be our message to Washington.

We will say to our president and the present administration that we have no intention of using Washington as a scapegoat for all of our failures and difficulties, or as an excuse for not doing for ourselves, as a state, everything we can.

On the other hand, we will not allow the national administration to escape responsibility for its policies. We will continue to point out what we believe is the massive inequity of the new redistribution of national wealth—a redistribution that moves our nation's resources from the vulnerable Northeast and Midwest to the affluent or at least less troubled parts of the nation. We will point out what we believe is the cruelty and economic recklessness of the unemployment those policies produce. And the mistake of an excessive multiplication of nuclear weapons that denies us the resources we need to put people back to work and to lift others out of wheelchairs.

Because we meant what we said in the campaign, all of these positions will be part of the flesh and blood—the programs and policies—of this administration. You will see them described in detail a few days from now in the State of the State Message. And again in the budget that will be presented to the legislature and the people of the state.

For now, however, allow me to speak a few words about what I hope will be the *soul* of this administration.

The philosophy of a government is the pattern revealed by the lines that connect hundreds of decisions government makes on a day-to-day basis. Over the course of our history these lines have often meandered and formed unclear images. The last few years, however, have raised sharp and profound questions about government's purpose and role. These questions are being discussed at all levels and are operating to affect the policies that touch the lives of our people. In the debate, the Empire State's view of government's ultimate rationale will have special significance. This is the way I see it: This state has always led the way in demonstrating government's best uses. Overall it has pursued a course of progressive pragmatism. For more than fifty years, without dramatic deviation for whatever party happened to be in power, New York has proven that government can be a positive force for good. It still can be.

I believe government's basic purpose is to allow those blessed with talent to go as far as they can—on their own merits. But I believe that government also has an obligation to assist those who, for whatever inscrutable reason, have been left out by fate: the homeless, the infirm, the destitute. To help provide those necessary things which, through no fault of their own, they cannot provide for themselves.

Of course, we should have *only* the government we need. But we must insist on *all* the government we need.

So, a technically balanced budget that fails to meet the reasonable needs of the middle class and poor would be the emblem of hypocrisy.

It has become popular in some quarters to argue that the principal function of government is to make instruments of war and to clear obstacles from the way of the strong. The rest—it is said—will happen automatically: the cream will rise to the top, whether the cream be well-endowed individuals or fortunate regions of the nation.

"Survival of the fittest" may be a good working description of the process of evolution, but a government of humans should elevate itself to a higher order, one which tries to fill the cruel gaps left by chance or by a wisdom we don't understand.

I would rather have laws written by Rabbi Hillel or Pope John Paul II than by Darwin.

I would rather live in a state that has chipped into the marble face of its capitol these memorable words of the great rabbi: "If I am not for myself—who is for me? And if I am for myself alone—what am I?" Or the words of our great pope: "Freedom and riches and strength bring responsibility. We cannot leave to the poor and the disadvantaged only the crumbs from the feast. Rather we must treat the less fortunate as guests."

A society as blessed as ours should be able to find room at the table—shelter for the homeless, work for the idle, care for the elderly and infirm, and hope for the destitute. To demand less of our government or ourselves would be to evade our proper responsibility. At the very least, the government of this generation should be able to do for those who follow us what has been done for us. And if my election proves anything, it proves how very much the system has been able to do for us.

Like all of us in this room today—and all of us in New York State except for our Native American brothers and sisters—I am the offspring of immigrants. My parents came some sixty years ago from another part of the world, driven by deprivation, without funds, education, or skills.

When my mother arrived at Ellis Island, she was alone and afraid. She carried little more than a suitcase and a piece of paper with the address of her laborer husband who had preceded her here in search of work.

She passed through all the small indignities visited on immigrants everywhere, in all ages. She was subjected to the hurried condescension of those who decide if others are good enough to be let in . . . or at least not quite bad enough to be kept out.

Like millions of others, my mother and father had provided

little other than a willingness to spend all their effort in honest toil. They asked only for the opportunity to work and to be protected in those moments when they would not be able to protect themselves.

Thanks to a government that was wise enough to help them without stifling them, and strong enough to provide them with an opportunity to earn their own bread, they survived.

They remained a people of modest means.

That they were able to build a family and live in dignity and see one of their children go from behind their little grocery store in South Jamaica where he was born to occupy the highest seat in the greatest state of the greatest nation in the only world we know is an ineffably beautiful tribute to the magnificence of this American democracy.

This is not a personal story. This is the story of all of us. What our imperfect but peerless system of government has done for these two frightened immigrants from Europe it has done for millions of others in different ways.

That experience is a source of pride and gratitude. But it must be more. It must serve as a challenge to all of us, as we face the future.

The achievement of our past imposes upon us the obligation to do as much for those who come after us.

It would be a desecration of our history to allow the difficulties of the moment, which pale when compared to those faced by our ancestors, to excuse our obligation to produce government that excels at doing what it is supposed to do.

We need not fear the challenge.

Underlying everything I believe about our government is my unshakable conviction that it is good enough to do what must be done, and much more.

For all our present travail—the deficits; the stagnant economy; the hordes of homeless, unemployed, and victimized; the loss of spirit and belief—for all of this, I believe we are wise enough to address our deficits without taxing ourselves into bankruptcy, strong enough to reconcile order with justice, brave enough to bring opportunity and hope to those who have neither.

We can, and we will, refuse to settle for survival, and certainly not just survival of the fittest!

I believe we can balance our lives and our society even as we manage to balance our books.

We can—if those who today stand on platforms built by our forebears' pain and are warmed by the applause earned by their courage remember who we are and where we came from and what we have been taught.

Those who made our history taught us above all things the idea of family, mutuality, the sharing of benefits and burdens, fairly, for the good of all.

It is an idea essential to our success.

And no family that favored its strong children or that, in the name of evenhandedness, failed to help its vulnerable ones would be worthy of the name.

And no state, or nation, that chooses to ignore its troubled regions and people while watching others thrive can call itself justified.

We must be the family of New York, feeling one another's pain, sharing one another's blessings, reasonably, equitably, honestly, fairly, without respect to geography or race or political affiliation.

Those who made our history taught us more. By their willingness to sweat for a lifetime just to give their children more than they had themselves, they taught us the virtue of hard work.

These things I pledge as I begin my term: that I have learned what they had to teach, that if we do not succeed it will not be because we have divided one part of this state from the other or dealt unfairly with any person or region, or forgotten that we are a family.

Nor will it be because we have failed to expend all the strength and effort that we might have.

This will be a government as hardworking and realistic as the thousands of families and businesses struggling to survive a national economy more distressed than at any time since the 1930s.

I have no illusions about the difficulty of converting these noble aspirations into hard reality. It will be a fierce test of our resolve.

But if the risks we face are great, the resources we command are greater: a rich good earth; water, that ties us together, replenishes us, feeds our capacity to grow; an education system matched by few other states or nations; an intricate, irreplaceable weave of roads and rails; the world's largest banks, financial institutions, communications systems, and markets.

And more than all of this, our marvelous people—the offspring of Native Americans, Africans, Europeans, Asians, people from the North and from the South. The children of those who refused to stop reaching, building, and believing.

We are the sons and daughters of giants, and because we were born to their greatness, we are required to achieve.

We begin to meet that obligation today—all of us together.

So, good people of the Empire State, I ask all of you, whatever your political beliefs, whatever your region, whatever you think of me as an individual, to help me keep the moving and awesome oath I just swore before you and before God.

Pray that we all see New York for the family that it is.

That all of us sworn into office today give New York the leadership it deserves.

That I might be the state's good servant and God's, too.

Thank you and Happy New Year to all of us.

This speech for my daughter Maria's commencement from Iona College in New Rochelle, New York, is one of my favorites. It gave me a chance to express to her and my other children the pain that I and some other parents feel at concluding that our imperfections have made us less credible to the children we love. A number of the parents in the group went out of their way to tell me they agreed. I used a device here that I tried again once or twice later, literally telling the students that, while I didn't mind their eavesdropping, I wanted to talk directly to their parents, and then starting all over again addressing their parents, grandparents, and other family. It has worked well.

This is your day, a time for celebrating the culmination of your hard work, for rejoicing with your family and friends, with the people who've sustained you and supported you and, when necessary, put up with you. You've done well, you deserve to feel proud. Congratulations.

And it's a special day for me, also. Special, first of all, because Iona is a special college. It is named, the Brothers tell me, after a monastery founded by the followers of an Irish Saint called Columba. Now I've encountered many extraordinary things in my career, people from every background imaginable, but I've never encountered an Irishman named Columba. Not even an O'Columba. I think, perhaps, what we have here is another case of that legendary Irish hospitality which surrounds the stranger with such warmth he or she ends up feeling Irish. Apparently, it happened to San Columba.

And I'm sure, in some measure, it's happened to the Italians, Hispanics, Poles, blacks, Germans, and Asians who've come here to Iona, who've been taught and nurtured and inspired by the Irish

Christian Brothers, who've gone away marked by their faith and their love.

Before all else, the Irish are a people of words. They regard them the way the French regard love and Italians regard food—passionately. There are so many examples. It was an Irishman who gave me the best advice I've ever been given about the art of delivering a commencement speech. Father Flynn was the president of my alma mater, St. John's, and the first time I was ever asked to speak at a graduation, I asked him how I should approach it.

"Commencement speakers," said Father Flynn, "should think of themselves as the body at an old-fashioned Irish wake. They need you in order to have the party, but nobody expects you to say very much."

That's advice I intend to remember today.

Instead of speaking to you as a public official invited to deliver the required platitudes, let me speak in my real capacity here today—as the proud father of a graduate. And speaking as a parent, let me confess to you graduates a reluctance to stand here and try to lecture or instruct you, a reluctance to try to pretend to teach you lessons that we, your predecessors, learned only very poorly.

I think the people sitting behind you graduates—your parents and grandparents—understand me. Probably, they can relate to what I'm saying a good deal more easily than you can. So if you don't mind, I'd like to talk to *them* for a few minutes.

Ladies and gentlemen, I think I understand how you feel. I've felt it before and I do again today.

It's a great day. It almost makes up for all the years of toil, anxiety, and desperate prayer.

The kids, they think *they* had it tough. But how we've suffered through the last four years of schooling, and before that. Remember when they were in high school? They were having a good time. Meanwhile, our doubts were tormenting us . . . especially on weekends.

I can hear us now! "They're out again, tonight. They should

15

have been home by midnight and now it's nearly one o'clock. I wonder if they are in a car and drinking. Did you see their friends? Where are they from? What a bunch. They look like pot smokers, God forbid!"

Remember what we were thinking? "I know they're growing up, but I wonder if they know anything. Can they protect themslves? Are they getting a little too sophisticated? Will they stay out of trouble? Will their grades be good enough to get them into college?"

Well, they did make it to college, and a good one at that, and were we relieved!

Of course by now they were getting older and better able to make their own way. And there was less cause for us to be maternalistic or paternalistic. But we were, anyway. No matter how wise we thought we were, no matter how blasé we made them think we were, and no matter how deeply we believed in him or her, always there were the fears and cautions: "God, don't let them hurt themselves."

Yes, always there were the concerns, and even on occasion the tears, ones they weren't permitted to see because it would embarrass and irritate them.

But now, *after* it all, here they are.

They made it, and we are proud of them . . . and we made it. It's a good feeling, and we will all enjoy it, as we should.

But at the end of the party, the thoughts crowded out of mind by the gratitude and joy of this day will return. The concerns, the desire to help, to teach, because we know that now, for them, comes the real beginning of their lives. The need to make the difficult choices: to marry, or not; to work, or not; at this, at that.

Those are tough choices, but there is an even harder one: they will have to decide soon the ultimate question—whether or not to live for *something* or simply go from experience to experience, concerned about nothing more than the few material scraps they can gather.

They'll have to deal with the most fundamental question of all:

Why do we make the effort? *Why* do we work? *Why* do we try? For sustenance? For family? For money? For pleasure? For power?

I know that you are thinking—good parents and grandparents, loved ones of the graduates—what I'm thinking: "We've been through it all, at least most of it, or a lot of it. There's so much ahead that they ought to know about. So many temptations they should ignore. So much we can tell them about how to begin answering these hard questions."

We have the *obligation* to tell them, to reduce as much as possible the pain of their learning only from their own blunders. But do we have the right? Can we, who found the ultimate truth so elusive for so long, tell them with confidence now of the futility of gathering up riches and the things of the world?

It's clear to us that all the newly won power over space and time, the conquest of the forces of nature, the fulfilling of age-old challenges, have not made us any happier or surer of ourselves.

We have built rockets and spaceships and shuttles; we have harnessed the atom; we have dazzled a generation with a display of our technological skills. But we still spend millions of dollars on aspirin and psychiatrists and tissues to wipe away the tears of anguish and uncertainty that result from our confusion and our emptiness.

Most of us have never had it so good. We have achieved levels of affluence and comfort unthought of two generations ago. Nor have we ever complained so bitterly about our problems.

The closed circle of pure materialism is clear to us now—aspirations become wants, wants become needs, and self-gratification becomes a bottomless pit. All around us we have seen success in this world's terms become ultimate and desperate failure. Teenagers and college students, raised in affluent surroundings and given all the material comforts our society can offer, commit suicide. Entertainers and sports figures achieve fame and wealth but find the world empty and dull without the solace or stimulation of drugs. Men and women rise to the top of their professions after years of struggling. But despite their apparent success, they are driven nearly mad by a frantic search for diversions, new mates, games, new experiences—anything to fill the diminishing interval between their existence and eternity.

We know because we've been there. But do we have the right

to tell these graduates that the most important thing in their lives will be their ability to believe in believing? And that without that ability sooner or later they will be doomed to despair?

Do you think they would believe us if we told them today what we know to be true? That after the pride of obtaining a degree and maybe later another degree; and after their first few love affairs; that after earning their first big title, their first shiny new car, and traveling around the world for the first time and having had it all, they will discover that none of it counts unless they have something real and permanent to believe in.

Tell me, ladies and gentlemen, are we the ones to tell them what their instructors have tried to teach them for years?

That the philosophers were right. That Saint Francis, Buddha, Mohammed, Maimonides all spoke the truth when they said the way to serve yourself is to serve others, and that Aristotle was right, before them, when he said the only way to assure yourself happiness is to learn to give happiness.

Don't you remember that we were told all this when we were younger? But nevertheless, we got caught up in the struggle and the sweat and the frustration and the joy of small victories, and forgot it all. Until recently when we began to look back.

How simple it seems now. We thought the Sermon on the Mount was a nice allegory and nothing more. What we didn't understand until we got to be a little older was that it was the whole answer, the whole truth. That the way, the only way, to succeed and to be happy is to learn those rules so basic that a shepherd's son could teach them to an ignorant flock without notes or formulae.

We carried Saint Francis's prayer in our wallets for years and never learned to live the message.

Do we have the right now to tell them that when Saint Francis begged the Lord to teach him to want to console instead of seeking to be consoled, to teach him to want to love instead of desiring to be loved, that he was really being intensely selfish? Because he knew the only way to be fulfilled and pleased and happy was to give instead of trying to get.

We have for a full lifetime taught our children to be go-getters. Can we now say to them that if they want to be happy they must be go-givers?

I wonder if we can, in good conscience, say these things to

them today when we ourselves failed so often to practice what we would preach?

I wonder if we—who have fought, argued, and bickered and so often done the wrong thing to one another—are the ones to teach them love.

How do we tell them that one ought not to be discouraged by imperfection in the world and the inevitability of death and diminishment? How do we tell them when they lose a child, or are crippled, or know that they will themselves die too soon that God permits pain and sickness and unfairness and evil to exist, only in order to permit us to test our mettle and to earn a fulfillment that would otherwise not be possible?

How can we tell our children *that* when we have ourselves so often cried out in bitter despair at what we regarded to be the injustice of life and when we have so often surrendered?

How can we tell them that it is their *duty* to use all that they have been given to make a better world, not only for themselves and their families, but for all who live in this world, when it was our generation that permitted two great wars and a number of smaller ones. Our generation that made the world a place where the great powers are so alienated from one another that they can't even play together in an Olympics.

Do we have the right to tell them, as our teachers told us, that they have an obligation in justice to participate in politics and government? Can we without shame say to them that our system of democracy works well only when there is involvement by all? That in our democracy the policies that become law, the rules of justice, the treatment of individuals, are the responsibility of *each* citizen? That you get what you deserve out of our system, and that indifference deserves nothing good? When we ourselves have chosen to sit at home on so many Election Days muttering grim remarks about the politicians who appear on the television set, instead of doing what we could to change things, for the better.

Would they believe us if we said these things?.

Would we be able to explain the embarrassment of our own failures?

Do you blame me, ladies and gentlemen, for being reluctant to deliver to them the message that is traditional on Commencement Day?

• • •

But maybe, ladies and gentlemen, this problem is not as great as I've made it out to be.

I've been taking a closer look at these graduates. They are actually taller, stronger, smarter than we were, smart enough maybe to take our mistakes as their messages, to make our weaknesses their lessons, and to make our example, good and not so good, part of their education.

I think I see in their eyes a depth of perception that perhaps we didn't have. A sense of truth, deeper and less fragile than ours.

As you talk to them you get the feeling that they are certainly mature enough to see the real problems of our society: the need for peace, the need to keep pure the environment God offered us, the need to provide people the dignity of earning their own way.

Indeed, as I think about it, I have to conclude that these young people before me today are the best reason for hope that this world knows.

I see them as believers and doers who will take what we will pass on to them so clumsily and make it something better than we have ever known. Honoring us by their works, but wanting to be better than we have been.

I tell you, ladies and gentlemen, looking at them now, closer and harder than I have before, I have a feeling about these people that makes me want to live long enough to see and be part of the world they will create.

Now, ladies and gentlemen, parents and grandparents, I would like to tell them, the graduates, all of this, and I know that if we thought they wouldn't be embarrassed by hearing it, we would all be telling them about how proud we are of them and how much we believe in them and their future. But again maybe we don't have to tell them; maybe they know. Maybe they can tell just by seeing the love in our eyes today.

Congratulations, ladies and gentlemen, on the good children you have cared for and raised.

DEMOCRATIC NATIONAL CONVENTION

KEYNOTE ADDRESS,

"A TALE OF TWO CITIES"*

JULY 16, 1984

MOSCONE CENTER, SAN FRANCISCO, CALIFORNIA

This speech, one of the first national convention speeches to be carried around the world by CNN, had repercussions for me for years after it was delivered. It instructed me forever on the awesome power of television. I hear this address and read about it even today. When I do, I feel again the regret of knowing that it didn't appear to have made much of a difference, judging by the outcome of the election, which was, of course, another Reagan victory. Eventually—but not until eight years later, in 1992— it became clear we were right in San Francisco: the poor were getting poorer, the middle class was being battered, and the American dream was vanishing, except for a small, but growing, group of extremely successful people at the top of the economic ladder. It was indeed a "Tale of Two Cities."

On behalf of the Empire State and the family of New York, I thank you for the great privilege of being allowed to address this convention.

Please allow me to skip the stories and the poetry and the temptation to deal in nice but vague rhetoric.

Let me instead use this valuable opportunity to deal with the questions that should determine this election and that are vital to the American people.

Ten days ago, President Reagan admitted that although some people in this country seemed to be doing well nowadays, others were unhappy, and even worried, about themselves, their families, and their futures.

*This speech was originally called "A Case for the Democrats in 1984: A Tale of Two Cities."

The president said he didn't understand that fear. He said, "Why, this country is a shining city on a hill."

The president is right. In many ways we *are* "a shining city on a hill."

But the hard truth is that not everyone is sharing in this city's splendor and glory.

A shining city is perhaps all the president sees from the portico of the White House and the veranda of his ranch, where everyone seems to be doing well.

But there's another part of the city, the part where some people can't pay their mortgages and most young people can't afford one, where students can't afford the education they need and middle-class parents watch the dreams they hold for their children evaporate.

In this part of the city there are more poor than ever, more families in trouble, more and more people who need help but can't find it.

Even worse: there are elderly people who tremble in the basements of the houses there.

There are people who sleep in the city's streets, in the gutter, where the glitter doesn't show.

There are ghettos where thousands of young people, without an education or a job, give their lives away to drug dealers every day.

There is despair, Mr. President, in faces you never see, in the places you never visit in your shining city.

In fact, Mr. President, this nation is more a "Tale of Two Cities" than it is a "shining city on a hill."

Maybe if you visited more places, Mr. President, you'd understand.

Maybe if you went to Appalachia, where some people still live in sheds, and to Lackawanna, where thousands of unemployed steel workers wonder why we subsidized foreign steel while we surrender their dignity to unemployment and to welfare checks; maybe if you stepped into a shelter in Chicago and talked with some of the homeless there; maybe, Mr. President, if you asked a woman who'd been denied the help she needs to feed her children because you say we need the money to give a tax break to a millionaire or to build a missile we can't even afford to use, maybe then you'd understand.

Maybe, Mr. President.

But I'm afraid not.

Because, the truth is, this is how we were warned it would be.

President Reagan told us from the beginning that he believed in a kind of social Darwinism. Survival of the fittest. "Government can't do everything," we were told. "So it should settle for taking care of the strong and hope that economic ambition and charity will do the rest. Make the rich richer and what falls from their table will be enough for the middle class and those trying to make it into the middle class."

The Republicans called it trickle-down when Hoover tried it. Now they call it supply-side. It is the same shining city for those relative few who are lucky enough to live in its good neighborhoods.

But for the people who are excluded—locked out—all they can do is to stare from a distance at that city's glimmering towers.

It's an old story. As old as our history.

The difference between Democrats and the Republicans has always been measured in courage and confidence.

The Republicans believe the wagon train will not make it to the frontier unless some of our old, some of our young, and some of our weak are left behind by the side of the trail.

The strong will inherit the land!

We Democrats believe that we can make it all the way with the whole family intact.

We have. More than once.

Ever since Franklin Roosevelt lifted himself from his wheelchair to lift this nation from its knees. Wagon train after wagon train. To new frontiers of education, housing, peace. The whole family aboard. Constantly reaching out to extend and enlarge that family. Lifting them up into the wagon on the way. Blacks and Hispanics, people of every ethnic group, and Native Americans—all those struggling to build their families and claim some small share of America.

For nearly fifty years we carried them to new levels of comfort, security, dignity, even affluence.

Some of us are in this room today only because this nation had that confidence.

It would be wrong to forget that.

So, we are here at this convention to remind ourselves where we come from and to claim the future for ourselves and for our children.

Today our great Democratic party, which has saved this nation from depression, from fascism, from racism, from corruption, is called upon to do it again . . . this time to save the nation from confusion and division, from the threat of eventual fiscal disaster, and, most of all, from a fear of a nuclear holocaust.

In order to succeed, we must answer our opponent's polished and appealing rhetoric with a more telling reasonableness and rationality.

We must win this case on the merits.

We must get the American public to look past the glitter, beyond the showmanship . . . to reality, to the hard substance of things. And we will do that not so much with speeches that sound good as with speeches that are good and sound.

Not so much with speeches that bring people to their feet as with speeches that bring people to their senses.

We must make the American people hear our "Tale of Two Cities."

We must convince them that we don't have to settle for two cities, that we can have one city, indivisible, shining for *all* its people.

We will have no chance to do that if what comes out of this convention—what is heard throughout the campaign—is a babel of arguing voices.

To succeed we will have to surrender small parts of our individual interests, to build a platform we can *all* stand on, at once, comfortably, proudly singing out the truth for the nation to hear, in chorus, its logic so clear and commanding that no slick commercial, no amount of geniality, no martial music will be able to muffle it.

We Democrats must unite so that the entire nation can. Surely the Republicans won't bring the convention together. Their policies divide the nation . . . into the lucky and the left out, the royalty and the rabble.

The Republicans are willing to treat that division as victory. They would cut this nation in half, into those temporarily better off and those worse off than before, and call it recovery.

We should not be embarrassed or dismayed if the process of unifying is difficult, even at times wrenching.

Unlike any other party, we embrace men and women of every color, every creed, every orientation, every economic class. In our family are gathered everyone from the abject poor of Essex County in New York to the enlightened affluent of the gold coasts of both ends of our nation. And in between is the heart of our constituency. The middle class. The people not rich enough to be worry-free but not poor enough to be on welfare. Those who work for a living because they have to. White-collar and blue-collar. Young professionals. Men and women in small business desperate for the capital and contracts they need to prove their worth.

We speak for the minorities who have not yet entered the main stream.

For ethnics who want to add their culture to the mosaic that is America.

For women indignant that we refuse to etch into our governmental commandments the simple rule: "Thou shalt not sin against equality," a commandment so obvious it can be spelled in three letters: ERA.

For young people demanding an education and a future.

For senior citizens terrorized by the idea that their only security—their *Social* Security—is being threatened.

For millions of reasoning people fighting to preserve our environment from greed and stupidity and fighting to preserve our very existence from a macho intransigence that refuses to make intelligent attempts to discuss the possibility of nuclear holocaust with our enemy. Refusing because they believe we can pile missiles so high that they will pierce the clouds and the sight of them will frighten our enemies into submission.

We're proud of this diversity. Grateful we don't have to manufacture its appearance the way the Republicans will next month in Dallas, by propping up mannequin delegates on the convention floor.

But we pay a price for it.

The different people we represent have many points of view. Sometimes they compete and then we have debates, even arguments. That's what our primaries were about. But now the primaries are over and it is time to lock arms and move into this campaign together.

•   •   •

If we need any inspiration to make the effort to put aside our small differences, all we need to do is to reflect on the Republican policy of divide and cajole and how it has injured our land since 1980.

The president has asked us to judge him on whether or not he's fulfilled the promises he made four years ago. I accept that. Just consider what he said and what he's done.

Inflation is down since 1980. But not because of the supply-side miracle promised by the president. Inflation was reduced the old-fashioned way, with a recession, the worst since 1932. More than 55,000 bankruptcies. Two years of massive unemployment. Two hundred thousand farmers and ranchers forced off the land. More homeless than at any time since the Great Depression. More hungry, more poor—mostly women—and a nearly 200 billion dollar deficit threatening our future.

The president's deficit is a direct and dramatic repudiation of his promise to balance our budget by 1983. That deficit is the largest in the history of this universe, more than three times larger than the deficit in President Carter's last year. It is a deficit that, according to the president's own fiscal advisor, could grow as high as 300 billion dollars a year, stretching "as far as the eye can see."

It is a debt so large that as much as one-half of our revenue from the income tax goes to pay the interest on it each year. It is a mortgage on our children's futures that can only be paid in pain and that could eventually bring this nation to its knees. Don't take my word for it. . . . I'm a Democrat.

Ask the Republican investment bankers on Wall Street what they think the chances are this recovery will be permanent. If they're not too embarrassed to tell you the truth, they'll say they are appalled and frightened by the president's deficit. Ask them what they think of our economy, now that it has been driven by the distorted value of the dollar back to its colonial condition—exporting agricultural products and importing manufactured ones.

Ask those Republican investment bankers what they expect the interest rate to be a year from now. And ask them what they predict for the inflation rate then.

How important is this question of the deficit?

Think about it: What chance would the Republican candidate

have had in 1980 if he had told the American people that he intended to pay for his so-called economic recovery with bankruptcies, un-employment, and the largest government debt known to humankind? Would American voters have signed the loan certificate for him on Election Day? Of course not! It was an election won with smoke and mirrors . . . with illusions. It is a recovery made of the same stuff.

And what about foreign policy?

They said they would make us and the whole world safer. They say they have.

By creating the largest defense budget in history, one even they now admit is excessive. By escalating to a frenzy the nuclear arms race. By incendiary rhetoric. By refusing to discuss peace with our enemies. By the loss of 279 young Americans in Lebanon in pursuit of a plan and a policy no one can find or describe.

We give monies to Latin American governments that murder nuns, and then lie about it.

We have been less than zealous in our support of the only real friend we have in the Middle East, the one democracy there, our flesh-and-blood ally, the state of Israel.

Our policy drifts with no real direction, other than an hysterical commitment to an arms race that leads nowhere . . . if we're lucky. If we're not . . . could lead us to bankruptcy or war.

Of course we must have a strong defense!

Of course Democrats believe that there are times when we must stand and fight. And we have. Thousands of us have paid for freedom with our lives. But always—when we've been at our best—our pur-poses were clear.

Now they're not. Now our allies are as confused as our enemies.

Now we have no real commitment to our friends or our ideals . . . to human rights, to the refuseniks, to Sakharov, to Bishop Tutu and the others struggling for freedom in South Africa.

We have spent more than we can afford. We have pounded our chests and made bold speeches. But we lost 279 young Americans in Lebanon and we are forced to live behind sandbags in Washington.

How can anyone believe that we are stronger, safer, or better?

That's the Republican record.

That its disastrous quality is not more fully understood by the

American people is attributable, I think, to the president's amiability and the failure by some to separate the salesman from the product.

It's now up to us to make the case to America. And to remind Americans that if they are not happy with all the president has done so far, they should consider how much worse it will be if he is left to his radical proclivities for another four years unrestrained by the need once again to come before the American people.

If July brings back Ann Gorsuch Burford . . . what can we expect of December?

Where would another four years take us?

How much larger will the deficit be?

How much deeper the cuts in programs for the struggling middle class and the poor to limit that deficit? How high the interest rates? How much more acid rain killing our forests and fouling our lakes?

What kind of Supreme Court? What kind of court and country will be fashioned by the man who believes in having government mandate people's religion and morality?

The man who believes that trees pollute the environment, that the laws against discrimination go too far. The man who threatens Social Security and Medicaid and help for the disabled.

How high will we pile the missiles?

How much deeper will be the gulf between us and our enemies?

Will we make meaner the spirit of our people?

This election will measure the record of the past four years. But more than that, it will answer the question of what kind of people we want to be.

We Democrats *still* have a dream. We *still* believe in this nation's future.

And this is our answer—*our* credo:

We believe in *only* the government we need, but we insist on all the government we need.

We believe in a government characterized by fairness and *reasonableness*, a reasonableness that goes beyond labels, that doesn't distort or promise to do what it knows it can't do.

A government strong enough to use the words "love" and "compassion" and smart enough to convert our noblest aspirations into practical realities.

We believe in encouraging the talented, but we believe that

while survival of the fittest may be a good working description of the process of evolution, a government of humans should elevate itself to a higher order, one which fills the gaps left by chance or a wisdom we don't understand.

We would rather have laws written by the patron of this great city, the man called the "world's most sincere Democrat"—Saint Francis of Assisi—than laws written by Darwin.

We believe, as Democrats, that a society as blessed as ours, the most affluent democracy in the world's history, that can spend trillions on instruments of destruction, ought to be able to help the middle class in its struggle, ought to be able to find work for all who can do it, room at the table, shelter for the homeless, care for the elderly and infirm, hope for the destitute.

We proclaim as loudly as we can the utter insanity of nuclear proliferation and the need for a nuclear freeze, if only to affirm the simple truth that peace is better than war because life is better than death.

We believe in firm but fair law and order, in the union movement, in privacy for people, openness by government, civil rights, and human rights.

We believe in a single fundamental idea that describes better than most textbooks and any speech what a proper government should be. The idea of family. Mutuality. The sharing of benefits and burdens for the good of all. Feeling one another's pain. Sharing one another's blessings. Reasonably, honestly, fairly—without respect to race, or sex, or geography, or political affiliation.

We believe we must be the family of America, recognizing that at the heart of the matter we are bound one to another, that the problems of a retired schoolteacher in Duluth are *our* problems. That the future of the child in Buffalo is *our* future. The struggle of a disabled man in Boston to survive, to live decently, is *our* struggle. The hunger of a woman in Little Rock *our* hunger. The failure anywhere to provide what reasonably we might, to avoid pain, is *our* failure.

For fifty years we Democrats created a better future for our children, using traditional Democratic principles as a fixed beacon, giving us direction and purpose, but constantly innovating, adapting to new realities: Roosevelt's alphabet programs, Truman's NATO and the GI Bill of Rights, Kennedy's intelligent tax incentives and the Alliance for Progress, Johnson's civil rights, Carter's human rights and the nearly miraculous Camp David peace accord.

Democrats did it . . . and Democrats can do it again.

We can build a future that deals with our deficit.

Remember, fifty years of progress never cost us what the last four years of stagnation have. We can deal with that deficit intelligently, by shared sacrifice, with all parts of the nation's family contributing, building partnerships with the private sector, providing a sound defense without depriving ourselves of what we need to feed our children and care for our people.

We can have a future that provides for all the young of the present, by marrying common sense and compassion.

We *know* we can, because we did it for nearly fifty years before 1980.

We can do it again. If we do not forget. Forget that this entire nation has profited by these progressive principles. That they helped lift up generations to the middle class and higher, gave us a chance to work, to go to college, to raise a family, to own a house, to be secure in our old age, and, before that, to reach heights that our own parents would not have dared dream of.

That struggle to live with dignity is the real story of the shining city. It's a story I didn't read in a book, or learn in a classroom. I saw it, and lived it. Like many of you.

I watched a small man with thick calluses on both hands work fifteen and sixteen hours a day. I saw him once literally bleed from the bottoms of his feet, a man who came here uneducated, alone, unable to speak the language, who taught me all I needed to know about faith and hard work by the simple eloquence of his example. I learned about our kind of democracy from my father. I learned about our obligation to each other from him and from my mother. They asked only for a chance to work and to make the world better for their children and to be protected in those moments when they would not be able to protect themselves. This nation and its government did that for them.

And that they were able to build a family and live in dignity and see one of their children go from behind their little grocery store on the other side of the tracks in South Jamaica where he was born, to occupy the highest seat in the greatest state of the greatest nation in the only world we know is an ineffably beautiful tribute to the democratic process.

And on January 20, 1985, it will happen again. Only on a much grander scale. We will have a new president of the United States, a Democrat born not to the blood of kings, but to the blood of immigrants and pioneers.

We will have America's first woman vice president, the child of immigrants, a New Yorker, opening with one magnificent stroke a whole new frontier for the United States.

It will happen—*if we make it happen.*

I ask you—ladies and gentlemen, brothers and sisters—for the good of all of us, for the love of this great nation, for the family of America, for the love of God. Please, make this nation remember how futures are built.

RELIGIOUS BELIEF AND PUBLIC MORALITY:

A CATHOLIC GOVERNOR'S PERSPECTIVE*

SEPTEMBER 13, 1984

UNIVERSITY OF NOTRE DAME,

SOUTH BEND, INDIANA

Preparing the words I would deliver at the University of Notre Dame was more like writing an academic paper than writing a speech. It is the piece of work that took more of me than any other. As I noted in my introduction to this book, I labored over it for weeks. It produced one of the first full and candid debates of the difficult question as to the proper role of religious belief in the public forum, focused specifically on abortion and Catholics. I've been told it helped turn the discussion toward a more constructive phase. The truth is, since 1984, the discussion has been more reasonable, and whatever part in that development this speech had, the change relieves and gratifies me.

I would like to begin by drawing your attention to the title of this lecture: "Religious Belief and Public Morality: A Catholic Governor's Perspective." I was not invited to speak on "church and state" generally. Certainly not "Mondale versus Reagan." The subject assigned is difficult enough. I will not try to do more than I've been asked.

It's not easy to stay contained. Certainly, although everybody talks about a wall of separation between church and state, I've seen religious leaders scale that wall with all the dexterity of Olympic athletes. In fact, I've seen so many candidates in churches and synagogues that I think we should change Election Day from Tuesdays to Saturdays and Sundays.

*A paper prepared for delivery to the Department of Theology at the University of Notre Dame.

I am honored by this invitation, but the record shows that I am not the first governor of New York to appear at an event involving Notre Dame. One of my great predecessors, Al Smith, went to the Army–Notre Dame football game each time it was played in New York.

His fellow Catholics expected Smith to sit with Notre Dame; protocol required him to sit with Army because it was the home team. Protocol prevailed. But not without Smith noting the dual demands on his affections. "I'll take my seat with Army," he said, "but I commend my soul to Notre Dame!"

Today I'm happy to have no such problem: both my seat and my soul are with Notre Dame. And as long as Father McBrien doesn't invite me back to sit with him at the Notre Dame–St. John's basketball game, I'm confident my loyalties will remain undivided.

In a sense, it's a question of loyalty that Father McBrien has asked me here today to discuss. Specifically, must politics and religion in America divide our loyalties? Does the "separation between church and state" imply separation between religion and politics? Between morality and government? Are these different propositions? Even more specifically, what is the relationship of my Catholicism to my politics? Where does the one end and other begin? Or are the two divided at all? And if they're not, should they be?

Hard questions.

No wonder most of us in public life—at least until recently—preferred to stay away from them, heeding the biblical advice that if "hounded and pursued in one city," we should flee to another.

Now, however, I think that it is too late to flee. The questions are all around us, and answers are coming from every quarter. Some of them have been simplistic, most of them fragmentary, and a few, spoken with a purely political intent, demagogic.

There has been confusion and compounding of confusion, a blurring of the issue, entangling it in personalities and election strategies, instead of clarifying it for Catholics, as well as others.

Today I would like to try to help correct that.

I can offer you no final truths, complete and unchallengeable. But it's possible this one effort will provoke other efforts—both in support and contradiction of my position—that will help all of us understand our differences and perhaps even discover some basic agreement.

In the end, I'm convinced we will all benefit if suspicion is replaced by discussion, innuendo by dialogue, if the emphasis in our debate turns from a search for talismanic criteria and neat but simplistic answers to an honest, more intelligent attempt at describing the role religion has in our public affairs, and the limits placed on that role.

And if we do it right—if we're not afraid of the truth even when the truth is complex—this debate, by clarification, can bring relief to untold numbers of confused, even anguished Catholics, as well as to many others who want only to make our already great democracy even stronger than it is.

I believe the recent discussion in my own state has already produced some clearer definition. In early summer, an impression was created in some quarters that official church spokespeople would ask Catholics to vote for or against specific candidates on the basis of their political position on the abortion issue. I was one of those given that impression. Thanks to the dialogue that ensued over the summer—only partially reported by the media—we learned that the impression was not accurate.

Confusion had presented an opportunity for clarification, and we seized it. Now all of us are saying one thing, in chorus, reiterating the statement of the National Conference of Catholic Bishops that they will not "take positions for or against political candidates" and that their stand on specific issues should not be perceived "as an expression of political partisanship."

Of course the bishops will teach—they must—more and more vigorously and more and more extensively. But they have said they will not use the power of their position, and the great respect it receives from all Catholics, to give an imprimatur to individual politicians or parties.

Not that they couldn't if they wished to—some religious leaders do; some are doing it at this very moment.

Not that it would be a sin if they did—God doesn't insist on political neutrality. But because it is the judgment of the bishops, and most of us Catholic laypeople, that it is not wise for prelates and politicians to be tied too closely together.

I think that getting this consensus was an extraordinarily useful achievement.

Now, with some trepidation, I take up your gracious invitation to continue the dialogue in the hope that it will lead to still further clarification.

Let me begin this part of the effort by underscoring the obvious. I do not speak as a theologian; I do not have that competence. I do not speak as a philosopher; to suggest that I could would be to set a new record for false pride. I don't presume to speak as a "good" person except in the ontological sense of that word. My principal credential is that I serve in a position that forces me to wrestle with the problems you've come here to study and debate.

I am by training a lawyer and by practice a politician. Both professions make me suspect in many quarters, including among some of my own coreligionists. Maybe there's no better illustration of the public perception of how politicians unite their faith and their profession than the story they tell in New York about "Fishhooks" Mc-Carthy, a famous Democratic leader on the Lower East Side and right-hand man to Al Smith.

"Fishhooks," the story goes, was devout. So devout that every morning on his way to Tammany Hall to do his political work, he stopped into St. James Church on Oliver Street in downtown Manhattan, fell on his knees, and whispered the same simple prayer: "O, Lord, give me health and strength. We'll steal the rest."

"Fishhooks" notwithstanding, I speak here as a politician. And also as a Catholic, a layperson baptized and raised in the pre–Vatican II church, educated in Catholic schools, attached to the church first by birth, then by choice, now by love. An old-fashioned Catholic who sins, regrets, struggles, worries, gets confused, and most of the time feels better after confession.

The Catholic church is my spiritual home. My heart is there, and my hope.

There is, of course, more to being a Catholic than a sense of spiritual and emotional resonance. Catholicism is a religion of the head as well as the heart, and to be a Catholic is to say, "I believe," to the essential core of dogmas that distinguishes our faith.

The acceptance of this faith requires a lifelong struggle to understand it more fully and to live it more truly, to translate truth into experience, to practice as well as to believe.

That's not easy: applying religious belief to everyday life often presents difficult challenges.

It's always been that way. It certainly is today. The America of the late twentieth century is a consumer society, filled with endless distractions, where faith is more often dismissed than challenged, where the ethnic and other loyalties that once fastened us to our religion seem to be weakening.

In addition to all the weaknesses, dilemmas, and temptations that impede every pilgrim's progress, the Catholic who holds political office in a pluralistic democracy—who is elected to serve Jews and Muslims, atheists and Protestants, as well as Catholics—bears special responsibility. He or she undertakes to help create conditions under which *all* can live with a maximum of dignity and with a reasonable degree of freedom; where everyone who chooses may hold beliefs different from specifically Catholic ones, sometimes contradictory to them; where the laws protect people's right to divorce, to use birth control, and even to choose abortion.

In fact, Catholic public officials take an oath to preserve the Constitution that guarantees this freedom. And they do so gladly. Not because they love what others do with their freedom, but because they realize that in guaranteeing freedom for all, they guarantee *our* right to be Catholics: *our* right to pray, to use the sacraments, to refuse birth control devices, to reject abortion, not to divorce and remarry if we believe it to be wrong.

The Catholic public official lives the political truth most Catholics through most of American history have accepted and insisted on: the truth that to assure our freedom we must allow others the same freedom, even if occasionally it produces conduct by them which we would hold to be sinful.

I protect my right to be a Catholic by preserving your right to believe as a Jew, a Protestant, or nonbeliever, or as anything else you choose.

We know that the price of seeking to force our beliefs on others is that they might someday force theirs on us.

This freedom is the fundamental strength of our unique experiment in gov-

ernment. In the complex interplay of forces and considerations that go into the making of our laws and policies, its preservation must be a pervasive and dominant concern.

But insistence on freedom is easier to accept as a general proposition than in its applications to specific situations. There are other valid general principles firmly embedded in our Constitution, which, operating at the same time, create interesting and occasionally troubling problems. Thus the same amendment of the Constitution that forbids the establishment of a state church affirms my legal right to argue that my religious belief would serve well as an article of our universal public morality. I may use the prescribed processes of government—the legislative and executive and judicial processes—to convince my fellow citizens, Jews and Protestants and Buddhists and nonbelievers, that what I propose is as beneficial for them as I believe it is for me; that it is not just parochial or narrowly sectarian but fulfills a human desire for order, peace, justice, kindness, love, any of the values most of us agree are desirable even apart from their specific religious base or context.

I am free to argue for a governmental policy for a nuclear freeze not just to avoid sin, but because I think my democracy should regard it as a desirable goal.

I can, if I wish, argue that the state should not fund the use of contraceptive devices not because the pope demands it, but because I think that the whole community—for the good of the whole community—should not sever sex from an openness to the creation of life.

And surely I can, if so inclined, demand some kind of law against abortion not because my bishops say it is wrong, but because I think that the whole community, regardless of its religious beliefs, should agree on the importance of protecting life—including life in the womb, which is at the very least potentially human and should not be extinguished casually.

No law prevents us from advocating any of these things: I am free to do so.

So are the bishops. And so is Reverend Falwell.

In fact, the Constitution guarantees my right to try. And theirs. And his.

But should I? Is it helpful? Is it essential to human dignity? Does it promote harmony and understanding? Or does it divide us so

37

fundamentally that it threatens our ability to function as a pluralistic community?

When should I argue to make my religious value your morality? My rule of conduct your limitation?

What are the rules and policies that should influence the exercise of this right to argue and promote?

I believe I have a salvific mission as a Catholic. Does that mean I am in conscience required to do everything I can as governor to translate *all* my religious values into the laws and regulations of the state of New York or the United States? Or be branded a hypocrite if I don't?

As a Catholic, I respect the teaching authority of the bishops.

But must I agree with everything in the bishops' pastoral letter on peace and fight to include it in party platforms?

And will I have to do the same for the forthcoming pastoral on economics even if I am an unrepentant supply-sider?

Must I, having heard the pope renew the church's ban on birth control devices, veto the funding of contraceptive programs for non-Catholics or dissenting Catholics in my state?

I accept the church's teaching on abortion. Must I insist you do? By law? By denying you Medicaid funding? By a constitutional amendment? If so, which one? Would that be the best way to avoid abortions or to prevent them?

These are only some of the questions for Catholics. People with other religious beliefs face similar problems.

Let me try some answers.

Almost all Americans accept some religious values as a part of our public life. We are a religious people, many of us descended from ancestors who came here expressly to live their religious faith free from coercion or repression. But we are also a people of many religions, with no established church, who hold different beliefs on many matters.

Our public morality, then—the moral standards we maintain for everyone, not just the ones we insist on in our private lives—depends on a consensus view of right and wrong. The values derived from religious belief will not—and should not—be accepted as part of the public morality unless they are shared by the pluralistic community at large, by consensus.

That values happen to be religious values does not deny them acceptability as a part of this consensus. But it does not require their acceptability, either.

The agnostics who joined the civil rights struggle were not deterred because that crusade's values had been nurtured and sustained in black Christian churches. Those on the political left are not perturbed today by the religious basis of the clergy and laypeople who join them in the protest against the arms race and hunger and exploitation.

The arguments start when religious values are used to support positions which would impose on other people restrictions they find unacceptable. Some people *do* object to Catholic demands for an end to abortion, seeing it as a violation of the separation of church and state. And some others, while they have no compunction about invoking the authority of the Catholic bishops in regard to birth control and abortion, might reject out of hand their teaching on war and peace and social policy.

Ultimately, therefore, the question whether or not we admit religious values into our public affairs is too broad to yield a single answer. Yes, we create our public morality through consensus and in this country that consensus reflects to some extent religious values of a great majority of Americans. But no, all religiously based values don't have an a priori place in our public morality.

The community must decide if what is being proposed would be better left to private discretion than public policy; whether it restricts freedoms, and if so to what end, to whose benefit; whether it will produce a good or bad result; whether overall it will help the community or merely divide it.

The right answers to these questions can be elusive. Some of the wrong answers, on the other hand, are quite clear. For example, there are those who say there is a simple answer to *all* these questions; they say that by history and practice of our people we were intended to be—and should be—a Christian country in law.

But where would that leave the nonbelievers? And whose Christianity would be law, yours or mine?

This "Christian nation" argument should concern—even frighten—two groups: non-Christians and thinking Christians.

39

I believe it does.

I think it's already apparent that a good part of this nation understands—if only instinctively—that anything which seems to suggest that God favors a political party or the establishment of a state church is wrong and dangerous.

Way down deep the American people are afraid of an entangling relationship between formal religions—or whole bodies of religious belief—and government. Apart from constitutional law and religious doctrine, there is a sense that tells us it's wrong to presume to speak for God or to claim God's sanction of our particular legislation and his rejection of all other positions. Most of us are offended when we see religion being trivialized by its appearance in political throw-away pamphlets.

The American people need no course in philosophy or political science or church history to know that God should not be made into a celestial party chairman.

To most of us, the manipulative invoking of religion to advance a politician or a party is frightening and divisive. The American people will tolerate religious leaders taking positions for or against candidates, although I think the Catholic bishops are right in avoiding that position. But the American people are leery about large religious organizations, powerful churches, or synagogue groups engaging in such activities—again, not as a matter of law or doctrine, but because our innate wisdom and democratic instinct teaches us these things are dangerous.

Today there are a number of issues involving life and death that raise questions of public morality. They are also questions of concern to most religions. Pick up a newspaper and you are almost certain to find a bitter controversy over any one of them: Baby Jane Doe, the right to die, artificial insemination, embryos in vitro, abortion, birth control . . . not to mention nuclear war and the shadow it throws across all existence.

Some of these issues touch the most intimate recesses of our lives, our roles as someone's mother or child or husband; some affect women in a unique way. But they are also public questions, for all of us.

Put aside what God expects—assume, if you like, there is no God—then the greatest thing still left to us is life. Even a radically secular world must struggle with the questions of when life begins, under what circumstances it can be ended, when it must be protected, by what authority; it, too, must decide what protection to extend to the helpless and the dying, to the aged and the unborn, to life in all its phases.

As a Catholic, I have accepted certain answers as the right ones for myself and my family, and because I have, they have influenced me in special ways, as Matilda's husband, as a father of five children, as a son who stood next to his own father's deathbed trying to decide if the tubes and needles no longer served a purpose.

As a governor, however, I am involved in defining policies that determine *other* people's rights in these same areas of life and death. Abortion is one of these issues, and while it is one issue among many, it is one of the most controversial and affects me in a special way as a Catholic public official.

So let me spend some time considering it.

I should start, I believe, by noting that the Catholic church's actions with respect to the interplay of religious values and public policy make clear that there is no inflexible moral principle which determines what our *political* conduct should be. For example, on divorce and birth control, without changing its moral teaching, the church abides by the civil law as it now stands, thereby accepting—without making much of a point of it—that in our pluralistic society we are not required to insist that *all* our religious values be the law of the land.

Abortion is treated differently.

Of course there are differences both in degree and quality between abortion and some of the other religious positions the church takes: abortion is a "matter of life and death," and degree counts. But the differences in approach reveal a truth, I think, that is not well enough perceived by Catholics and therefore still further complicates the process for us. That is, while we always owe our bishops' words respectful attention and careful consideration, the question whether to engage the political system in a struggle to have it adopt certain articles of our belief as part of public morality is not a matter of doctrine: it is a matter of prudential political judgment.

Recently, Michael Novak put it succinctly. "Religious judgment and political judgment are both needed," he wrote. "But they are not identical."

My church and my conscience require me to believe certain things about divorce, birth control, and abortion. My church does not order me—under pain of sin or expulsion—to pursue my salvific mission according to a precisely defined political plan.

As a Catholic I accept the church's teaching authority. While in the past some Catholic theologians may appear to have disagreed on the morality of some abortions (it wasn't, I think, until 1869 that excommunication was attached to all abortions without distinction), and while some theologians still do, I accept the bishops' position that abortion is to be avoided.

As Catholics, my wife and I were enjoined never to use abortion to destroy the life we created. We thought church doctrine was clear on this. Life or fetal life in the womb should be protected, even if five of nine justices of the Supreme Court and my neighbor disagree with me. A fetus is different from an appendix or a set of tonsils. At the very least, even if the argument is made by some scientists or some theologians that in the early stages of fetal development we can't discern human life, the full potential of human life is indisputably there. That—to my less subtle mind—by itself should demand respect, caution, indeed . . . reverence.

But not everyone in our society agrees.

And those who don't—those who endorse legalized abortions—aren't a ruthless, callous alliance of anti-Christians determined to overthrow our moral standards. In many cases, the proponents of legal abortion are the very people who have worked with Catholics to realize the goals of social justice set out in papal encyclicals: the American Lutheran Church, the Central Conference of American Rabbis, the Presbyterian Church in the United States, B'nai B'rith Women, the Women of the Episcopal Church. These are just a few of the religious organizations that don't share the church's position on abortion.

Certainly, we should not be forced to mold Catholic morality to conform to disagreement by non-Catholics, however sincere or severe their disagreement. Our bishops should be teachers, not pollsters. They should not change what we Catholics believe in order to ease our consciences or please our friends or protect the church from criticism.

But if the breadth, intensity, and sincerity of opposition to church teaching shouldn't be allowed to shape our Catholic morality, it can't help but determine our ability—our realistic, political ability—to translate our Catholic morality into civil law, a law not for the believers who don't need it but for the disbelievers who reject it.

And it is here, in our attempt to find a political answer to abortion—an answer beyond our private observance of Catholic morality—that we encounter controversy within and without the church over how and in what degree to press the case that our morality should be everybody else's, and to what effect.

I repeat, there is no church teaching that mandates the best political course for making our belief everyone's rule, for spreading this part of our Catholicism. There is neither an encyclical nor a catechism that spells out a political strategy for achieving legislative goals.

And so the Catholic trying to make moral and prudent judgments in the political realm must discern which, if any, of the actions one could take would be best.

This latitude of judgment is not something new in the church, not a development that has arisen only with the abortion issue. Take, for example, the question of slavery. It has been argued that the failure to endorse a legal ban on abortions is equivalent to refusing to support the cause of abolition before the Civil War. This analogy has been advanced by the bishops of my own state.

But the truth of the matter is few, if any, Catholic bishops spoke for abolition in the years before the Civil War. It wasn't, I believe, that the bishops endorsed the idea of some humans owning and exploiting other humans; Pope Gregory XVI, in 1840, had condemned the slave trade. Instead it was a practical political judgment that the bishops made. They weren't hypocrites; they were realists. At the time, Catholics were a small minority, mostly immigrants, despised by much of the population, often vilified and the object of sporadic violence. In the face of a public controversy that aroused tremendous passions and threatened to break the country apart, the bishops made a pragmatic decision. They believed their opinion would not change people's minds. Moreover, they knew that there were Southern Catholics, even some priests, who owned slaves. They concluded that under the circumstances arguing for a constitutional amendment against slavery would do more harm than good, so they were silent. As they have been, generally, in recent years, on the question of birth control. And as the church has been on even more controversial issues in the past, even ones that dealt with life and death.

What is relevant to this discussion is that the bishops were making judgments about translating Catholic teachings into public policy, not about the moral validity of the teachings. In so doing they grappled with the unique political complexities of their time. The decision they made to remain silent on a constitutional amendment to abolish slavery or on the repeal of the Fugitive Slave Law wasn't a mark of their moral indifference: it was a measured attempt to balance moral truths against political realities. Their decision reflected their sense of complexity, not their diffidence. As history reveals, Lincoln behaved with similar discretion.

The parallel I want to draw here is not between or among what we Catholics believe to be moral wrongs. It is in the Catholic response to those wrongs. Church teaching on slavery and abortion is clear. But in the application of those teachings—the exact way we translate them into action, the specific laws we propose, the exact legal sanctions we seek—there was and is no one, clear, absolute route that the church says, as a matter of doctrine, we must follow.

The bishops' pastoral letter, "The Challenge of Peace," speaks directly to this point. "We recognize," the bishops wrote, "that the Church's teaching authority does not carry the same force when it deals with technical solutions involving particular means as it does when it speaks of principles or ends. People may agree in abhorring an injustice, for instance, yet sincerely disagree as to what practical approach will achieve justice. Religious groups are entitled as others to their opinion in such cases, but they should not claim that their opinions are the only ones that people of good will may hold."

With regard to abortion, the American bishops have had to weigh Catholic moral teaching against the fact that we are a pluralistic country where our view is in the minority, acknowledging that what is ideally desirable isn't always feasible, that there can be different political approaches to abortion besides unyielding adherence to an absolute prohibition.

This is in the American-Catholic tradition of political realism. In supporting or opposing specific legislation the church in this country has never retreated into a moral fundamentalism that will settle for nothing less than total acceptance of its views.

Indeed, the bishops have already confronted the fact that an absolute ban on abortion doesn't have the support necessary to be placed in our Constitution. In 1981, they put aside earlier efforts to describe a law they could accept and get passed, and supported the Hatch amendment instead.

Some Catholics felt the bishops had gone too far with that action, some not far enough. Such judgments were not a rejection of the bishops' teaching authority: the bishops even disagreed among themselves. Catholics are allowed to disagree on these technical political questions without having to confess.

Respectfully, and after careful consideration of the position and arguments of the bishops, I have concluded that the approach of a constitutional amendment is not the best way for us to seek to deal with abortion.

I believe that legal interdicting of all abortions by either the federal government or the individual states is not a plausible possibility and, even if it could be obtained, it wouldn't work. Given present attitudes, it would be Prohibition revisited, legislating what couldn't be enforced and in the process creating a disrespect for law in general. And as much as I admire the bishops' hope that a constitutional amendment against abortion would be the basis for a full, new bill of rights for mothers and children, I disagree that this would be the result.

I believe that, more likely, a constitutional prohibition would allow people to ignore the causes of many abortions instead of addressing them, much the way the death penalty is used to escape dealing more fundamentally and more rationally with the problem of violent crime.

Other legal options that have been proposed are, in my view, equally ineffective. The Hatch amendment, by returning the question of abortion to the states, would have given us a checkerboard of permissive and restrictive jurisdictions. In some cases people might have been forced to go elsewhere to have abortions and that might have eased a few consciences, but it wouldn't have done what the church wants to do—it wouldn't have created a deep-seated respect for life. Abortions would have gone on, millions of them.

Nor would a denial of Medicaid funding for abortion achieve our objectives. Given *Roe v. Wade,* it would be nothing more than an attempt to do indirectly what the law says cannot be done directly; worse, it would do it in a way that would burden only the already disadvantaged. Removing funding from the Medicaid program would not prevent the rich and middle class from having abortions. It would not even assure that the disadvantaged wouldn't have them; it would only impose financial burdens on poor women who want abortions.

Apart from that unevenness, there is a more basic question. Medicaid is designed to deal with health and medical needs. But the arguments for the cutoff of Medicaid abortion funds are not related to those needs. They are moral arguments. If we assume health and medical needs exist, our personal view of morality ought not to be considered a relevant basis for discrimination.

We must keep in mind always that we are a nation of laws—when we like those laws and when we don't.

The Supreme Court has established a woman's constitutional right to abortion. The Congress has decided the federal government should not provide federal funding in the Medicaid program for abortion. That, of course, does not bind states in the allocation of their own state funds. Under the law, the individual states need not follow the federal lead, and in New York I believe we *cannot* follow that lead. The equal protection clause in New York's constitution has been interpreted by the courts as a standard of fairness that would preclude us from denying only the poor—indirectly, by a cutoff of funds—the practical use of the constitutional right given by *Roe v. Wade.*

In the end, even if after a long and divisive struggle we were able to remove all Medicaid funding for abortion and restore the law to what it was, if we could put most abortions out of our sight, return them to the back rooms where they were performed for so long, I don't believe our responsibility as Catholics would be any closer to being fulfilled than it is now, with abortion guaranteed by the law as a woman's right.

The hard truth is that abortion isn't a failure of government. No agency or department of government forces women to have abortions, but abortion goes on. Catholics, the statistics show, support the right to abortion in equal proportion to the rest of the population. Despite the teaching in our homes and schools and pulpits, despite the sermons and pleadings of parents and priests and prelates, despite all the effort at defining our opposition to the sin of abortion, collectively we Catholics apparently believe—and perhaps act—little differently from those who don't share our commitment.

Are we asking government to make criminal what we believe to be sinful because we ourselves can't stop committing the sin?

The failure here is not Caesar's. This failure is our failure, the failure of the entire people of God.

Nobody has expressed this better than a bishop in my own state, Joseph Sullivan, a man who works with the poor in New York City, is resolutely opposed to abortion, and argues, with his fellow bishops, for a change of law. "The major problem the church has is internal," the bishop said last month in reference to abortion. "How do we teach? As much as I think we're responsible for advocating public policy issues, our primary responsibility is to teach our own people. We haven't done that. We're asking politicians to do what we haven't done effectively ourselves."

I agree with the bishop. I think our moral and social mission as Catholics must begin with the wisdom contained in the words: "Physician, heal thyself." Unless we Catholics educate ourselves better to the values that define—and can ennoble—our lives, following those teachings better than we do now, unless we set an example that is clear and compelling, then we will never convince this society to change the civil laws to protect what we preach is precious human life.

Better than any law or rule or threat of punishment would be the moving strength of our own good example, demonstrating our lack of hypocrisy, proving the beauty and worth of our instruction.

We must work to find ways to avoid abortions without otherwise violating our faith. We should provide funds and opportunity for young women to bring their child to term, knowing both of them will be taken care of if that is necessary; we should teach our young men better than we do now their responsibilities in creating and caring for human life.

It is this duty of the church to teach through its practice of love that Pope John Paul II has proclaimed so magnificently to all peoples. "The Church," he wrote in *Redemptor Hominis* (1979), "which has no weapons at her disposal apart from those of the spirit, of the word and of love, cannot renounce her proclamation of 'the word . . . in season and out of season.' For this reason she does not cease to implore . . . everybody in the name of God and in the name of man: Do not kill! Do not prepare destruction and extermination for each other! Think of your brothers and sisters who are suffering hunger and misery! Respect each other's dignity and freedom!"

The weapons of the word and of love are already available to us; we need no statute to provide them.

I am not implying that we should stand by and pretend indifference to whether a woman takes a pregnancy to its conclusion or aborts it. I believe we should in all cases try to teach a respect for life. And I believe with regard to abortion that, despite Roe v. Wade, *we can, in practical ways. Here, in fact, it seems to me that all of us can agree.*

Without lessening their insistence on a woman's right to an abortion, the people who call themselves "pro-choice" can support the development of government programs that present an impoverished mother with the full range of support she needs to bear and raise her children, to have a real choice. Without dropping their campaign to ban abortion, those who gather under the banner of "pro-life" can join in developing and enacting a legislative bill of rights for mothers and children, as the bishops have already proposed.

While we argue over abortion, the United States' infant mortality rate places us sixteenth among the nations of the world. Thousands of infants die each year because of inadequate medical care. Some are born with birth defects that, with proper treatment, could be prevented. Some are stunted in their physical and mental growth because of improper nutrition.

If we want to prove our regard for life in the womb, for the helpless infant, if we care about women having real choices in their lives and not being driven to abortions by a sense of helplessness and despair about the future of their child, then there is work enough for all of us. Lifetimes of it.

In New York, we have put in place a number of programs to begin this work, assisting women in giving birth to healthy babies. This year we doubled Medicaid funding to private-care physicians for prenatal and delivery services.

The state already spends 20 million dollars a year for prenatal care in outpatient clinics and for inpatient hospital care.

One program in particular we believe holds a great deal of promise. It's called New Avenues to Dignity, and it seeks to provide a teenage mother with the special services she needs to continue with her education, to train for a job, to become capable of standing on her own, to provide for herself and the child she is bringing into the world.

My dissent, then, from the contention that we can have effective and enforceable legal prohibitions on abortion is by no means an argument for religious quietism, for accepting the world's wrongs because that is our fate as "the poor banished children of Eve."

Let me make another point. Abortion has a unique significance but not a preemptive significance. Apart from the question of the efficacy of using legal weapons to make people stop having abortions, we know our Christian responsibility doesn't end with any one law or amendment. That it doesn't end with abortion. Because it involves life and death, abortion will always be a central concern of Catholics. But so will nuclear weapons. And hunger and homelessness and joblessness, all the forces diminishing human life and threatening to destroy it. The "seamless garment" that Cardinal Bernardin has spoken of is a challenge to all Catholics in public office, conservatives as well as liberals.

We cannot justify our aspiration to goodness simply on the basis of the vigor of our demand for an elusive and questionable civil law declaring what we already know, that abortion is wrong.

Approval or rejection of legal restrictions on abortion should not be the exclusive litmus test of Catholic loyalty. We should understand that whether abortion is outlawed or not, our work has barely begun: the work of creating a society where the right to life doesn't end at the moment of birth; where an infant isn't helped into a world that doesn't care if it's fed properly, housed decently, educated adequately; where the blind or retarded child isn't condemned to exist rather than empowered to live.

The bishops stated this duty clearly in 1974, in their statement to the Senate subcommittee considering a proposed amendment to restrict abortions. They maintained such an amendment could not be seen as an end in itself. "We do not see a constitutional amendment as the final product of our commitment or of our legislative activity," they said. "It is instead the constitutional base on which to provide support and assistance to pregnant women and their unborn children. This would include nutritional, prenatal, child birth and post-natal care for the mother, and also nutritional and pediatric care for the child through the first year of life. . . . We believe that all of these should be available as a matter of right to all pregnant women and their children."

The bishops reaffirmed that view in 1976, in 1980, and again this year when the United States Catholic Committee asked Catholics to judge candidates on a wide range of issues—on abortion, yes, but also on food policy, the arms race, human rights, education, social justice, and military expenditures.

The bishops have been consistently pro-life in the full meaning of that term, and I respect them for that.

The problems created by the matter of abortion are complex and confounding. Nothing is clearer to me than my inadequacy to find compelling solutions to all of their moral, legal, and social implications. I, and many others like me, are eager for enlightenment, eager to learn new and better ways to manifest respect for the deep reverence for life that is our religion and our instinct. I hope that this public attempt to describe the problems as I understand them will give impetus to the dialogue in the Catholic community and beyond, a dialogue which could show me a better wisdom than I've been able to find so far.

It would be tragic if we let that dialogue become a prolonged, divisive argument that destroys or impairs our ability to practice any part of the morality given us in the Sermon on the Mount, to touch, heal, and affirm the human life that surrounds us.

We Catholic citizens of the richest, most powerful nation that has ever existed are like the stewards made responsible over a great household: from those to whom so much has been given, much shall be required. It is worth repeating that ours is not a faith that encourages its believers to stand apart from the world, seeking their salvation alone, separate from the salvation of those around them.

We speak of ourselves as a body. We come together in worship as companions, in the ancient sense of that word, those who break bread together, and who are obliged by the commitment we share to help one another, everywhere, in all we do and, in the process, to help the whole human family. We see our mission to be "the completion of the work of creation."

This is difficult work today. It presents us with many hard choices.

The Catholic church has come of age in America. The ghetto walls are gone, our religion no longer a badge of irredeemable foreignness. This newfound status is both an opportunity and a temptation. If we choose, we can give in to the temptation to become more and more assimilated into the larger, blander culture, abandoning the practice of the specific values that made us different, worshiping whatever gods the marketplace has to sell while we seek to rationalize our own laxity by urging the political system to legislate on others a morality we no longer practice ourselves.

Or we can remember where we come from, the journey of two millennia, clinging to our personal faith, to its insistence on constancy and service and on hope. *We can live and practice the morality Christ gave us, maintaining his truth in this world, struggling to embody his love, practicing it especially where that love is most needed, among the poor and the weak and the dispossessed. Not just by trying to make laws for others to live by, but by living the laws already written for us by God, in our hearts and our minds.*

We can be fully Catholic, proudly, totally at ease with ourselves, a people in the world, transforming it, a light to this nation. Appealing to the best in our people, not the worst. Persuading, not coercing. Leading people to truth by love. And still, all the while, respecting and enjoying our unique pluralistic democracy. And we can do it even as politicians.

Mostly this speech dealt with the counterproductive tendency we have to exalt glib ideology over good ideas, a subject I referred to in my first speech in 1974, and will probably continue to discuss for the rest of my career. Here I talked about it in terms of the poetry of campaigns dissolving into the prose of governance. I've heard "poetry and prose" and "progressive pragmatism" a number of times since then. That does not please me because of any personal pride as an author of the phrases—no one can be sure who said things first. But it is comforting to receive from time to time reassurance that others like these same ideas.

John Kennedy once said he had the best of all possible worlds, a Harvard education and a Yale degree.

I can't boast of either.

But in honor of my alma mater, I'd like to wish you the best of all possible worlds: a Yale education and a St. John's basketball team.

Yale is, of course, where the thinking of so many famous Americans was nurtured and developed: Archibald MacLeish, Cole Porter, Thornton Wilder.

In fact, Yale's intellectual tradition reaches far back in time . . . back past the progressive ideas of this century or the last, back even past the Puritanism of colonial America . . . to the ideas of William F. Buckley, Jr.

When the invitation to come here arrived, I took the time to read a little about that tradition. I came across a sermon of the

Reverend Timothy Dwight to the class of 1798, in which he cautioned the early Elis against the fleshpots of New Haven.

"You must not be seen," Reverend Dwight warned the class of '98, "wagering at horseraces, betting at cockpits, winning at gaming-tables, dancing wantonly, attending duels, rioting at the board of intemperance, drinking deep at the midnight debauch, or stealing to infamous enjoyments in houses outside this college."

I'd like to note for the record that I haven't seen a horserace or a gaming-table or a cockpit—or even a duel—since I arrived here.

Yes, the Reverend Dwight would be proud tonight. . . .

. . . Tomorrow night . . . I'm not so sure.

But Yale has far more to be proud of than the probity of its student body. This is one of the premier universities in the United States—indeed in the world. It is an institution whose graduates routinely go on to positions of great influence.

You are the elite of your generation and will undoubtedly take an important role in shaping the future of this country. Some of you may actually run for political office, a decision your family may find hard to accept.

I say this from experience.

In my own case, I set out to be a lawyer and had a successful practice in New York City before, at about age forty, I decided that with all this country had given to my family, it was time to try to give something back.

I decided to run for office.

I talked the decision over with my family. Finally, I told my father, an immigrant who'd sweated all his life to give his children the chance he'd never had.

"Papa," I said, "this is my chance to try to repay the system for all it's done for you and Momma and all of us—to help the other people who are still looking for their chance."

Papa just shook his head.

"Mario," he said, "you gonna be in the politics!"

"Yes, Papa."

"But, Mario, how you gonna do that? Alla your life you've been honest."

Well, despite my father's fears and a more or less general misimpression, I've found no more corruption or greed in politics than anywhere else in the human condition. Maybe less.

I've found that most of those I know who are committed to this vocation work long hours for far less than they'd make in the private sector. Many—perhaps most—give everything they have to the struggle to improve people's lives.

That leads me to the first point I want to make. It's simple but, I think, important.

Perhaps the biggest problem with our politics today is that not enough people are involved. It's appalling that only about half the people eligible to vote even bother to, and some of us who vote know more about the Super Bowl lineup than we do about the issues.

This isn't good for the nation or the nonvoters.

Our representative democracy depends for its efficacy on the participation of its people. It's a system that rewards involvement and punishes aloofness: those hurt the most are the ones who can't, or won't, get involved.

So, as people particularly well qualified to make a contribution, I urge you to consider getting as actively involved as possible.

Now, I know this is good advice. But beyond this encouragement to get involved I'm not sure what I can offer in the way of political wisdom.

Actually, I've come here to Yale expecting to be as much a student as a teacher, to listen and learn from our dialogue. Certainly, I didn't come here to Connecticut as a candidate for any political office. . . . . I think Governor Bill O'Neill is doing a terrific job.

Nor did I come to tell you my formula for winning elections. Recently—at least on the national level—we Democrats seem to have lost that formula. In fact, we've become a little like the characters in one of my favorite "Peanuts" cartoons.

Picture Linus and Charlie Brown sitting on a fence. Linus turns and says, "You know what they say, Charlie Brown: 'Win some; lose some.' "

For a moment Charlie Brown is lost in reflection. Then he says, "Gee, wouldn't that be great."

Finally, I am not here as a *de facto* or *de jure* spokesperson for my party, empowered to proclaim a new philosophy for Democrats!

The party has an abundance of both candidates and speakers, and if a new philosophy is to be articulated, I'll leave that to others. As a matter of fact, when they describe what that philosophy should be, I'll like to be in the audience, because I can't even think of a new philosophy.

The philosophy I believe in—and that I hope was accepted by the people of New York when they elected me in 1982—I described at San Francisco and Notre Dame.

Let me be careful here: By saying I don't see the need for a new philosophy—that is, for a new set of basic emphases and principles—I'm not implying we shouldn't be looking for new ways to apply our philosophy. We must. Always.

Ultimate objectives and commitments remain the same, but their application to changing realities requires flexibility and adaptation. That's the real challenge of politics, not only admitting an obligation to promote new economic growth or expand opportunities for women and the disadvantaged or help young people go to college, but *doing* it in real and concrete ways, with *new* programs and *new* ideas. That certainly is the challenge for a governor.

In response to it, in my state we've implemented a broad range of new ideas. Our New Avenues to Dignity program gives young mothers on welfare a chance to finish their education and have a career. We've created new centers for innovation that will spur the growth of high tech in the state. We're setting up new "High Schools of Excellence" to give our brightest children the finest education possible.

We've created a series of programs to end dependency, not encourage it. The school-to-employment program, the employment assistance program, the work incentive program are all helping people get off the welfare roll and onto the private-sector payroll.

In New York, as in the nation, nearly 90 percent of the people receiving public assistance are women and their children, so we've put a special emphasis on making it possible for these women to find a private-sector job and hold it.

In economic development, housing, agriculture, health care, we're finding new ways to give meaning to our basic principle that government can help people without suffocating them.

And where government involvement or regulation hinders rather than helps we're going ahead with reasonable deregulation.

In banking, insurance, telecommunications, we're seeking less government, not more.

The bottom line is this: programs and policies change; our principles *don't*.

And so, if I were invited back to give another keynote or to speak at Notre Dame, I wouldn't feel the need to say anything novel. What I'd say is that the principles I believe in are working. So I don't see any reason for abandoning them simply because the Republican candidate won a presidential election.

Think about it. If losing the election were a reason for changing what I believe in, wouldn't I find myself in a situation that, in some small way, resembles the one which faced the great Italian astronomer Galileo?

Galileo, as you know, described the world as he saw it, a world that circled the sun in constant orbit. Many people had trouble accepting this. They were taught the Earth was the center of the universe and never moved. Galileo challenged their perception of the universe and, they believed, challenged the basis of their faith. So, with the help of the Inquisition, they forced Galileo to kneel before their tribunal and retract his assertion that the Earth moved. They made him say the Earth was stationary because God had created it that way.

Galileo knelt and spoke the words they forced him to speak: he denied the Earth orbited the sun. But as he arose, those around him heard him say in a quiet voice, *"E pur si muove."*

"But still it moves."

Despite the events of last November, I haven't changed the underlying tenets of my political philosophy, *"E pur si muove."*

Why should I? As governor of New York I'll continue to seek new ways to improve our state, but why should I seek new principles?

The major intervening event since the Democratic convention was the overwhelming victory of President Reagan. Not the overwhelming victory of the Republican philosophy in the Senate or in the House of Representatives, but the overwhelming victory of President Reagan.

Now, let's have some fun.

We know that he has the heart and mind of a Republican. But let's face it: he tried very hard not to sound that way in his enormously successful campaign. You never heard him cite President Coolidge or Hoover or Nixon or Ford or even Dwight Eisenhower. Instead he quoted Democrats; Franklin Roosevelt, Harry Truman, John Kennedy.

He kept telling us that he'd keep the "social safety net" in place. He even pledged himself to maintain Social Security, and to help America's small farmers and steelworkers, the people untouched by economic recovery.

He didn't say in the campaign, "I've already made the poor pay; now it's the turn of the middle class."

He didn't tell us *that* . . . until after the election, until he presented his budget.

In the campaign, he was so casual about his deficit that it was hard, on this question at least, to distinguish him from a stereotypical "New Deal liberal." And tax reform was, of course, a plank in the Democratic platform.

So one could argue that President Reagan didn't want to challenge the Democratic philosophy, that he preferred selling his personality. One could argue that. But I won't.

Let me assume instead that the last election was a struggle over philosophies and that we couldn't get 51 percent of the people to agree with our Democratic philosophy. Does that mean we should put aside the firmly held convictions, beliefs, and principles of a lifetime? Unless we invented those principles just to win an election, we cannot justify ourselves in discarding them now, because we lost one.

What would that be except proof that we never believed in our principles in the first place? And after we'd adjusted our principles to reflect the outcome in the electoral college, after we described a philosophy we thought a majority wanted to hear, what would we do if we lost the *next* election?

Would we work on still another set of principles? Another philosophy?

Should we admit the foundations of our political beliefs are so many reeds to be shaken by the winds of political popularity, or even an electoral hurricane?

It seems to me there comes a point where the eagerness to change can become an intent to pander, an intent not to lead, but simply to win.

The unfortunate fact for those of us who prefer winning is that what is right is sometimes not popular, or at least not likely to get you elected, that sometimes the price of saying what you believe is to be rejected.

Remember Lincoln. He, after all, lost his senatorial election to Stephen Douglas. Lincoln didn't then devote his energies to swinging the Republican party over to the doctrine of popular sovereignty as the basis for deciding on the extension of slavery.

Hubert Humphrey didn't recant after his loss in 1968.

Nor did Barry Goldwater in 1964.

Nor did the fledgling politician who supported Goldwater in that Republican debacle, a former head of the Screen Actors Guild who would be twice elected governor of California before losing his bid to lead the Republicans against Jimmy Carter in 1976.

Indeed, when you consider that, at that time, less than 20 percent of the electorate formally identified themselves as Republicans, Ronald Reagan's success seems a pretty good practical argument for constancy amid diversity.

It seems to me that in politics, as in love, there is a great deal to be said for that quality, for sticking by your principles in good times and in bad—for better or for worse—in sickness and in health, even when you're down in the polls.

The problem is that sticking by your principles requires that you *explain* your principles, and in this age of electronic advocacy this process can often be tedious and frustrating. This is especially so when you must get your message across in twenty-eight-second celluloid morsels, when images prove often more convincing than ideas.

Almost a quarter of a century ago, in 1962, John Kennedy spoke here at Yale and called attention to what was then an emerging tendency in our politics.

President Kennedy said, "We cannot understand and attack our contemporary problems . . . if we are bound by traditional labels and worn-out slogans of an earlier era. But the unfortunate fact of the matter is that our rhetoric has not kept pace with the speed of social and economic change. Our political debates, our public discourse—our current domestic and economic issues—too often bear little or no relation to the actual problems the United States faces."

President Kennedy's words haven't lost their validity. On the contrary, they've taken on a new urgency.

Labels are no longer a *tendency* in our politics. In this electronic age, they *are* our politics. Instead of Lincoln-Douglas debates that last for three hours, the most subtle and complex truths are contested in a clash of twenty-eight-second Technicolor movies.

Consider for a moment what this means. Consider trying to describe your position on "Star Wars" or the deficit or tax reform or import quotas or the death penalty or abortion in fifty words or less, in the space of less than half a minute of television time . . . even with music.

But it's done all the time, with the result that we pigeonhole by stereotypes: we settle for caricatures instead of candidates.

Some are "soft on crime," others "hard" on it.

Some are "realistic," others "bleeding hearts."

Some are "pro-defense," others "antidefense."

And the ultimate labeling—the final avoidance of analysis and subtlety—is when we simply settle for a one-word summary of an entire philosophy.

We call candidates "conservatives" or "liberals," and when we do, we believe we've described everything they hold about the environment, human rights, foreign policy, defense spending, the country's past, present, and future.

The temptation is great: labels make life easier. Most of us don't have time to watch C-Span or read the *National Review*—or the *New Republic*—or George Will or David Broder.

We're busy studying for a chemistry final, playing with our

children, watching "Dallas" or "Dynasty." And the labels save us time: they're a shortcut, a kind of substitute for thought, the way a good commercial is.

The only problem is that with political candidates we can't get our money back if the contents don't match the packaging.

Take President Reagan, for example. Despite some slick disguising in the last campaign, everybody thinks of him as a conservative. Conservatives are of course against big government, but he's given us the biggest government in our history. And he wants to give government the authority to dictate a woman's choice on abortion, and how and where children should pray.

Before all else, conservatives believe in free enterprise. He's for free enterprise and letting the market decide . . . except when Continental Illinois Bank loses in the game of competition.

And the president is against deficits as a simple matter of conservative principle. But he's given us the biggest deficits in the history of the world; he's spilled more red ink in four years than liberals—or conservatives—spilled in the fifty years before.

Some people, who are aware that the traditional labels don't tell the whole story, think the solution might be to expand the list. They do so on the assumption that we could avoid some of the present contradictions by expanding the nomenclature.

Some suggest we add categories like "libertarian" and "populist."

I'd like to see that.

With a lineup of Republicans, Democrats, conservatives, liberals, libertarians, and populists, I'd run on the bottom of the ballot under the designation "None of the Above." I guarantee I'd win.

In truth, I've faced this labeling process more than once. In running for governor I was Mario Cuomo, the representative, as one local paper put it, of "the old liberalism."

People expected the programs and policies I spoke about to conform to their image of liberalism, and when they didn't—when I said things about crime that didn't sound "liberal" enough or when I talked about the pain we'd have to face in balancing the state budget—some of my supporters got upset. They warned me that I was blurring my image, turning off that little light that should go on in the voters' heads whenever they heard my name.

So I began prefacing my speeches with the explanation that what I was going to say might not be entirely what people expected to hear.

The problem, I said, was we'd all become so accustomed to images that maybe what we needed was a whole new political party, with an entirely new approach—a platform with only one promise: "reasonableness."

I said let's call the new party the "Common Sense party," take a profile of Thomas Paine as its symbol, and when people insisted on a slogan—on one phrase to flash on the TV screen under Paine's profile—they could have "Progressive Pragmatism."

What would progressive pragmatism mean?

That would depend on the question.

If the liberals asked what progressive pragmatism said about the role of government in our society, we'd answer, "It says we should have *all* the government we need."

If the conservatives asked, we'd answer, "It says we should have *only* the government we need."

To the yuppies, independents, and the supporters of "None of the Above," we'd say, "We believe in *only* the government we need, but we insist on *all* the government we need."

After we got elected, we'd tackle problems without regard for the shibboleths of right or left. And if the political scientists began drawing lines between individual decisions, trying to detect a pattern for predicting what we'd do in the future—in effect, a label to stereotype us with—we'd renounce progressive pragmatism and start over with a whole new slogan: "*Neo*—progressive pragmatism."

The object of this exercise wouldn't be to deny our principles or to confuse people about where we stood, but to make them think about a basic political truth. That truth is: we campaign in poetry. But when we're elected, we're forced to govern in prose.

And when we govern—as distinguished from when we campaign—we come to understand the difference between a speech and a statute.

It's here that the noble aspirations, neat promises, and slogans of a campaign get bent out of recognition or even break as you try to nail them down to the Procrustean bed of reality.

Consider, for example, the difference between President Reagan's recent State of the Union Address and his proposed budget.

The State of the Union was a magnificent piece of political theater, eloquent and uplifting. On the other hand, the budget is drab, harsh, even draconian.

The State of the Union indicated that although the budget was a problem, it's one "we'll grow our way out of." But the budget slashes away at the middle class in an effort to reduce a deficit in danger of spinning out of control.

The State of the Union talks about restoring traditional family values. But the budget subverts the economic stability of millions of poor and middle-class families, denying them the aid for housing, education, food, and mass transit they depend on.

Is there a way to avoid these contradictions? Is there a way to bridge the yawning credibility gap between what we promise and how we perform? Between the simplistics of campaigning and the complexities of governing?

I think there is.

I think you begin by being clear about what you believe, both during the campaign and after it, stating as directly and concisely— over and over again—the principles that shape your politics, that are its soul.

In New York we try to do it—constantly, in speeches and community forums all over the state, in the budget as much as in the State of the State Address.

What are those principles, as we see them in New York?

We start with Lincoln's simple definition of government as the means by which the people do "what needs to be done but which they cannot by individual effort do at all, or do so well by themselves."

We are agreed that the maintenance of our systems of public education, public health, public schools, public transit, public safety—our courts and schools and roads and police—are all the proper responsibility of government.

We know that what gives government the resources to do these things is the free-enterprise system. We believe, therefore, that government must accommodate the producers of wealth; indeed, that it must encourage as many people as possible to pursue the honest rewards of imagination, ambition, and hard work.

But we recognize that even at its best the free-enterprise system won't be able to include everyone, that there'll always be those left out, the frail, the poor, the old, those without skills or hope, sometimes without even a roof over their heads.

We are confident that government can act progressively and pragmatically to help care for those who simply can't care for themselves.

And as well as recognizing the obligations of government we admit its limits. We are *not* confident about government's ability to configure our souls and consciences.

We don't want government telling us what our relationship with our God should be.

We sum up our view of ourselves as a community, as a government, with one word: "family."

This intelligent self-interest, this synergism, isn't an excuse for fiscal waste in government. It isn't a commitment to any one program or social policy, a specific pledge to retain old ideas or even endorse new ones.

It isn't a call to blind compassion.

It's a simple reaffirmation of what we are as a people. What we are capable of when we learn to draw on all of our strengths to deal with all of our vulnerabilities.

It teaches us that we fail unless we meet the challenge to balance our budgets without punishing the middle class or abandoning the poor.

In ten years of public service, I've found no reason to disavow these principles or revise them.

They've proven their worth in practice. From 1932 to 1980, they worked for a whole nation. And today they're working in New York.

We've been able in New York with these principles to begin the largest reconstruction program in our history, putting thousands of people to work. We've been able to do more for the disabled and unemployed than ever before, more for the homeless than any other state, indeed more than the federal government.

We've done it not with deficits and fiscal gimmicks, but with balanced budgets. Indeed, this year we'll even cut taxes.

In New York neither Republicans nor Democrats apologize for government: we use it intelligently, reasonably, proudly.

I subscribe to these principles because I've seen them work. I've seen them work both as governor and as the child of immigrants, people who couldn't speak the language, people whose one great hope was a better life for their children.

A government capable of compassion and common sense helped lift their children to the middle class and higher.

It did that for me.

And it helped make life better for millions of others, in cities and the rural South, on farms and in factories. With land grant colleges, the GI Bill, the TVA, the Civil Rights Act, the Occupational Safety Act, unemployment insurance, the minimum wage, FHA loans, Medicare, Medicaid, Social Security, Head Start, student loans, the National Highway Act, the Voting Rights Act, Fair Housing.

So even if all the polls and all the pundits said it was prudent to forget, that to deny these principles was the price of popularity, I would prefer to remember.

Not out of arrogance, but because I would prefer to believe in the hope my principles represented than to live with a future of shrunken aspirations.

I don't want to accept as destiny what we once believed it was in our power to change.

I don't accept that the price of progress for the majority of us is that government must forget the rest of us.

I don't believe that to have part of the nation become a "shining city on a hill," we must condemn the rest of the nation to deteriorating ghettos with more homeless, more hungry, more poor than at any time since the Great Depression.

I will not accept the proposition that we cannot afford to fight crime in the streets of our cities, or alleviate the needs of our elderly, or help the children of our struggling middle class to educate themselves, because all of our national wealth must go for the endless accumulation of missiles, the preservation of our large corporations from taxation, and for interest on the debt we amass in that profligacy.

I reject the proposition that we must choose between policies of the heart and policies of the head.

•   •   •

I know what the results of the last election were.

I know what 59 percent of the electorate appeared to believe for that moment. Surely that's significant.

And I understand how this defeat has created the temptation to be silent, to accept the victor's version of the truth.

But I hope I will be strong enough to know all of this and still be able to say, *"E pur si muove."*

Thank you.

Two ideas that I have dealt with extensively and for a long time appear here: how one uses government to apply Christianity to life in the world without offending those who do not share that Christianity; and the necessity to add enlightened self-interest to compassion as a motive for action if one hopes to get anything done politically in our current society. I've tried discussing these concepts a number of times in Catholic and Protestant churches, in synagogues and Jewish centers, and even at a Sikh temple in Queens. Sometimes I think I give these speeches because I feel I need to hear them.

The Westminster Presbyterian Church is a house of both prayer and works, of both the worship of God and the service of humanity, the two linked in everything you do.

Yours is an important example, a reminder to everyone of the compassionate heart of the Christian tradition, of the challenges we face in living our faith in the world.

We are, of course, from two parts of that Christian tradition. I am a Roman Catholic. You are Presbyterians. Our churches have certain similarities.

Our priests, or ministers of the Gospel, are celibate, but we call them Father. Your pastors are allowed to marry and have children, but you don't call them Fathers.

And you still have only one collection on Sunday.

There are, of course, some more substantial differences.

Doctrinally, at least in the past, one of the biggest differences between our traditions was the argument over free will. It's an argument, in all candor, I've never quite fully understood, although I've always sympathized with the view expressed in the story told about Andrew Jackson's deathbed.

Jackson was a fiery man, strong-willed and indomitable, his iron determination summed up by his nickname, "Old Hickory." As he lay dying, his family and friends gathered around his bed, and one of them, remembering Jackson's love for indulging in all the pleasures of this earth, said fearfully, "I doubt if Old Hickory will go to heaven."

To which Jackson's doctor answered, "He will if he *wants* to."

Without trying even to imagine that I have the smallest claim to any final wisdom on the theological question of free will—of sorting out God's role and our role in the achievement of salvation—I admit a certain respect for the opinion of that doctor on willpower.

I, too, believe willpower can make a difference.

I believe that by our own volition, freely, out of our Christian commitment, we can will not only to profess the faith, but to live it, to make our faith matter in this world, not just in the churches, but in the mean streets where people go hungry and homeless, without hope or love.

That's what you're doing here at Westminster Presbyterian, with your active involvement in giving people shelter, in feeding them, in joining with the other "focus churches" to touch and heal the wounds all around us.

That's what Bishop Tutu is doing in South Africa, choosing to risk imprisonment and perhaps even death by giving prophetic witness to his faith.

It's what three American nuns and a lay missionary did in El Salvador, dying on a back road because they refused to keep the Gospel to themselves, to limit their faith to the safety of the cloister.

This week, in fact, in a New York paper, there was a parable about two Christians in Northern Ireland, but a true parable, a story that really happened and that has meaning for us all.

It occurred in a small village outside the city of Derry, a place where ancient antagonisms are still fresh, where after three centuries of bitterness and resentment and conflict the hatreds are wide and deep.

Last Christmas, a Presbyterian clergyman named David Armstrong crossed that great divide. He extended an invitation to the local Catholic priest to pray in his church. And the priest came. And when people on both sides protested and objected, when finally his own elders pressured Reverend Armstrong to surrender his pastorship, he walked with some of his congregation to the Catholic church—a short distance in feet, a great distance in Northern Ireland—to embrace the priest, publicly; to stand with him, publicly; to sing a simple hymn: "Be Not Afraid."

Afterwards, when the media came to check on the existence of this miracle, one of Reverend Armstrong's followers asked a question of the TV interviewer. "If we Christians are silent," she said, "if we're too afraid to love, then what hope is there for us? Or for the world?"

What hope, indeed?

And as Christians, we are required to face that same challenge here today, everywhere, in everything we do. And as Christians, we always will.

We will because we are those who profess to follow a Savior who insisted on living among all the men and women his society rejected, the social outcasts, the poor, the lepers, the blind, and the religious outcasts as well, Samaritans, Romans, foreigners.

As imperfect as we are, sinners all, in claiming his name, in calling ourselves *Christians*, in looking to the prophets and teachers of Israel, we willingly assume special responsibilities for each other, for the world.

We know that if we *are* who we *say* we are, then we must love. Then we must reject the logic of the social Darwinists; then we must reject the theory that is the best solution to the problems of the Third World, that by turning off the television reports from Ethiopia or El Salvador or Northern Ireland we can turn off our moral involvement there.

And *some of us* believe—as the bishops of my own church have expressed in their recent proposal on the economy, as Reverend

Armstrong does—that our obligation to love isn't just an individual obligation, but a societal and governmental one as well.

That's not necessarily a popular political opinion, as the bishops are learning . . . and as Reverend Armstrong learned. Nor is it an easy or comforting thought for Christians. It increases our obligations. As the bishops point out, it places a heavy burden on all who recognize it. If we accept his proposition, then we can no longer protect ourselves from self-criticism by the knowledge that we have spent a life in prayer and churchgoing and avoidance of transgression. The quiet life of personal goodness, remote from the rest of the world, may then not be enough.

If we accept the proposition, then in the moment of our last reckoning, we will not be able to say: "But, Lord, we were never in Ethiopia. How could we have seen you hungry?" Or "Lord, when did we ever see you homeless? Was that really *you* huddled in a doorway in South Broadway?" "Lord, where we lived—in our nice suburb—I never saw anyone hungry. I saw no one without shelter, broken, and alone. Had I seen them, surely I would have cared for them!"

If we believe we have a Christian obligation not just individually, but as a people, a church, a community, a society—yes, even through our government—then it becomes difficult for any of us to excuse our failure to do good works by emphasizing our diligence in prayer and churchgoing.

For those of us who recognize the duty and the capacity to function collectively, there is a whole world of pain and imperfection that summons us, challenges us.

There is the cry of the prophets for justice, always in our ears. Even when we are weak and tired.

There is always Christ. His arms nailed open to the whole world. His life as man given for the whole world . . . calling us, reminding us.

Not easy to believe these things.

Today, of course, many people reject the idea of that collective responsibility, especially to the least among us. They say government is *not* a family that shares benefits and burdens. Instead, they say that government's only collective responsibility is to insist on a governmentally imposed mode of private behavior. We should use government to police private lives, and not to try to make social policy out of Jesus' command to compassion.

Morality, they say, is a public issue; charity, a private one.

Some reject the entire notion of governmental compassion. It impedes the evolution of society, they say. The only way to help the poor and the weak is to make the rich richer and the strong stronger, and as the strong ascend this world's ladder of success, they'll pull the rest of Creation with them.

Recently, these views appeared to be growing stronger in the United States. More and more, governmental compassion has been seen as weakness, as unrealistic, as an unfair redistribution of hard-won gains.

The evidence of this attitude is all around us, and at the same time the evidence of the need for compassion grows more and more obvious as well.

Thus today there are more poor people in this country than ever before—35 million people. Most of them women and children, 9 million of them added in the past four years alone. There are more hungry. More homeless. More socially disoriented.

All at the same time that we spend hundreds of billions of dollars on weapons we pray we will never have to use. At the same time that parts of our nation have achieved comfort, and smaller parts great affluence.

Some Americans feel that this extraordinary disparity presents a basic question: How do we link up our Christian belief in compassion with the actual policies of our society? How do those of us who believe we were born to love teach a whole society to do it collectively through its government? Or are we not required to try?

Those of us who believe that we cannot separate our religion from the rest of our lives, that we live in one world, not two, and that our charity cannot be limited to a once-a-week burst of generosity are presented with a further question: if we want to impress our convictions or rightness on the whole society, how do we go about it?

I think there are two ways basically. First, we can insist that people agree with us as a moral proposition. We can argue, passionately, that there is a moral obligation to be kind. That it's a sin for us not to feed the hungry and help the poor and to redistribute wealth to achieve those objectives.

Some of that is being done. I think, frankly, the bishops are doing that, and I certainly do not disapprove.

On the other hand, I'm a politician, not a priest, and as a politician, as one who fights in the front lines of the battle to create consensus, I think there is an additional approach, and often a more effective one. And that is to convince our brothers and sisters that even if they don't believe they are required to love as a matter of moral obligation, then helping the poor and the disadvantaged and those who need a bit of a start makes common sense, even in the most practical terms.

We can help people to understand that even if they don't feel an obligation to love, they ought to consider their own self-interest. We can teach them that everyone pays for unemployment. Those who earn and are comfortable are paying their taxes for the unemployed and those on welfare. And all of us—tangibly, palpably, practically—feel and are hurt by social disorientation.

We can help people to understand that if we bring children into this world and let them go hungry and uneducated, if we are indifferent to the drugs and squalor that surrounds them and the despair that it produces in them, then we, whose children have been raised in strength and decency, we, all of us in all of our communities, will reap the bitter harvest.

Yes, it will cost us even in material terms. We will have to pay to maintain a growing number of people at subsistence levels. We will spend more on jail cells and police, taking money we could have used to build schools and day-care centers to build prisons instead. We will live in fear: bars on our windows. Our suburban enclaves walled off from the cities they surround.

We should help people to ask themselves a simple question— that is: "If we turn our backs on the most vulnerable—the aged, the retarded, the disabled—then who will speak for us should we find ourselves weak or dependent?

"If we ignore the world's pain, the oppression and poverty of millions across the globe, then who will be safe when the whirlwind of violence grows and surrounds us?"

71

We should remind everyone that if we exploit the environment, poisoning God's earth, polluting the skies, fouling the waters, we will, all of us, punish and betray our own descendants.

We must strive to show the relevance of Jeremiah's ancient truth: that each of us will find our own good and welfare in the welfare of the whole community.

And so, maybe by arguing self-interest, we can teach the good uses of compassion.

In the end, of course, however we make the case to the rest of our society, we will know what our ultimate motivation is. We will know that we do it because we believe it's right and because it justifies us to do it.

There's been a lot of talk about religion and government the last year or so. Some of it has been tedious, some of it difficult. But in the long run, I think the dialogue has been beneficial. I believe it has pointed up the truth of an observation Mahatma Gandhi once made. Asked to describe the greatest strength of the Christian faith, Gandhi answered, "Jesus. . . . Jesus is its greatest strength." Asked to describe Christianity's greatest weakness, Gandhi answered, "Christians."

The accuracy of that analysis might hurt us, but it should also remind us of the reality we face in looking to Jesus as our justification. It should remind us how easy it is to claim his name . . . yet deny his cross.

It should remind us that if we are to cease being Christianity's greatest weakness, then we, as Christian citizens of the world's richest nation, face a hard choice.

That choice consists in this: We can swim with the tide in this nation and accept the idea that the best way to help the unfortunate is to help the fortunate, and hope that private charity will do the rest, knowing that it can't and it won't. Knowing it will never be enough to reach all those huddled against the cold in doorways, all those palsied children captured in their silent pain. . . . Never enough to reach all those who suffer.

Or we can resist and do the harder thing, and the better thing.

We can resist the tide of opinion that seeks to make the denial of compassion respectable. We can resist the present mood that would settle for the cheap grace of a morality that only condemns and does not comfort.

We can resist by affirming as our moral and political foundation the idea that we *are our* brother's keeper, all of us as a people . . . and, yes, as a government. That our responsibility to our brothers and sisters is greater than any *one* of us and that this responsibility doesn't end when people are out of the individual reach of our hand.

Yes, this is the harder thing, believing that as we express ourselves through our government, we have an obligation to love.

It can haunt us.

It can nag at us in moments of happiness and personal success, disturbing our sleep and giving us that sense of guilt and unworthiness that the modern age is so eager to deny. And it can accuse us—from the faces of the starving and the dispossessed and the wounded, faces that stare back at us from the front page of our newspapers, images from across the world that blink momentarily on our television screens.

"I was homeless," it says, "and you gave me theories of supply and demand.

"I was imprisoned and silenced for justice's sake, and you washed the hands of my torturers.

"I asked for bread, and you built the world's most sophisticated nuclear arsenal."

Yet, as people who claim Christ's name, who dare to call ourselves Christians, what choice do we really have but to hear that voice and to answer its challenge?

Jesus, himself, instructed us. Answering the question of a lawyer, in language to be understood by all, he said that the law and the prophets, their wisdom and vision and insight, their teaching about religious obligation and stewardship, were all contained in two commandments: "You shall love the Lord your God with all your heart, and with all your soul, and with all your mind. And you shall love your neighbor as yourself."

That is the law, as simply as it can be expressed—for both the stewards and those in their charge, for both the governed and those who govern them, for all who look to Christ's mercy, wherever they might find themselves.

We should all be thankful for that law and for the people like yourselves—people all over this globe—who are willing to live by it.

Thankful for those who ask themselves, "What will happen if we're too afraid to love?" and then answer that question by their examples, by their love.

Thank you for that example and for having me here today.

One of America's greatest institutions was a perfect site for the major point I wanted to make in this speech. Harvard represents intellectual and educational superiority. It represents America at its boldest and best. But our federal government, at this time, was telling America it should settle for less, that we weren't strong enough to get everyone onto the wagon on the way to security and success. As I saw it, the pundits behind the supply-side theory were willing to sacrifice much of the country, and that wasn't fair or necessary. We should aspire to much more. We were capable of much more. What better place to demonstrate that capability than Harvard?

It's an honor for me to be here, to be allowed to be a small part of the Harvard tradition.

This is a school with a reputation for greatness.

And like so many others, for as long as I can remember I've had a deep respect for that greatness, a respect that was almost . . . religious.

Let me explain.

I remember when I was very young, maybe twelve or so, one of the kids from my neighborhood had an older brother who was accepted here.

That neighborhood was in South Jamaica, in New York City, an immigrant neighborhood where going to college was rare and going to Harvard unheard of.

So, when the adults in the neighborhood spoke of this young man who'd been admitted here, they did it in reverential tones, in the serious voices usually reserved for people who'd had twins or entered the priesthood . . . or died.

I was so young at the time—just beginning service as an altar boy—I got a little confused. I guess in my confusion I heard my parents say, not that he'd been *accepted*, but that he'd been "*assumed into Harvard.*"

And when he finally left—when he went off to Cambridge—I thought, in truth, he had been "assumed," but instead of going to heaven or purgatory or limbo or some place closer to the tropics, God had taken him to this special abode called "Harvard," so special that the nuns who taught us religion never even talked about it.

Harvard, at least to my child's mind, became a kind of hidden paradise, an ethereal region where God took only the brightest and the best, where the brightest and the best were bathed in light and music and happiness, where they never knew disappointment or defeat and even the choirs of angels admired them.

I believed this for a long time.

And it wasn't till I grew up and got to know that distinguished Harvard alumnus and former professor Daniel Patrick Moynihan that I discovered I'd been right.

I discussed my childhood impression of Harvard with him.

Daniel Patrick only corrected me on a single detail. "You're wrong on only one point, Mario," he said. "God has no say in the deliberations of the Harvard admissions committee. How could he? God's neither an overseer nor a member of the faculty. Why, he's not even an alumnus."

In one form or another, you've probably heard a lot of stories like mine. God might not be a Harvard graduate—actually, how could he be? I know it to be a fact that he went to St. John's, where I went, but this is still a school that inspires reverence, even awe, an awe which expresses itself in many ways, sometimes as respect and admiration and other times, yes, in disdain, and worse.

Let's be frank about it. It might be hard for you to think about on this special day, but there are people in this country who despise Harvard and everything it stands for. To them, Harvard is a symbol of everything wrong with America, a perverse and corruptive force. The invention of sociological and intellectual devils. These people who feel this way even have a name for themselves. They call themselves . . . "Yalies."

Other people don't so much hate Harvard as misunderstand it.

They think all Harvard graduates look like Arthur Schlesinger and sound like Ted Kennedy.

Those are some of the perceptions, or misperceptions, of Harvard. But at bottom they're all rooted in one fact: Harvard is synonymous with excellence. Even the hard-core "Harvard haters" know that although they might not like what Harvard does, it does it better than anyplace else.

They can't deny the standard Harvard has set for the entire enterprise of American education, or the rigorous academic training that's made its sons and daughters leaders in every phase of our national life.

That tradition of excellence is irrefutable.

And it belongs to you, Harvard's newest graduates.

By getting into Harvard—and now by getting out—you've won a special distinction for yourselves, becoming living links in one of the oldest and finest of America's traditions.

Wherever you go, Harvard will go with you.

And even if you don't travel around with a scarlet letter "H" emblazoned on your sweater, or sound like you're from Boston, or order your clothes from L. L. Bean, people are going to discover soon enough where you went to school.

They'll know because of what you'll do, the learning and intellect you'll bring to bear on your work, the depth and breadth of your talents.

And they'll know from your ambition. To be recognized. To distinguish yourselves. To be successful. To measure up to Harvard's standards: to be the best.

That instinct to strive for personal success, that ambition, is a large part of the reason for this nation's extraordinary emergence and growth.

America was born in outrageous ambition, so bold as to be improbable.

The deprived, the oppressed, the impoverished, the powerless from all over the globe came here with little more than the desire

77

to realize themselves. They carved a refuge out of the wilderness and then, in two hundred years, built it into the most powerful nation on earth, a place that has multiplied success for generation after generation of its children.

I'm one of those children. I know the story, the desire, because I saw it in my own parents. They came from another part of the world, uneducated, friendless, destitute, but driven . . . with ambition. To succeed materially. Not in any grand or global way, but just for themselves and their family.

And they did.

They allowed their children to live at a level of security and assurance and comfort that they neither enjoyed—nor even understood—themselves.

That instinct is alive in you. It has been honed and refined by this great university, and it is alive in you.

If you choose, you will become the leaders of industry. The pioneers of science and medicine. The great teachers and deans. The brilliant lawyers and jurists. You will earn and wield influence. You will be comfortable in material things. In all likelihood you will eventually be wealthy.

And most of this nation will commend that success and respect you for your striving. And they should. It's your birthright as Americans.

But along with the ability to succeed, Harvard has given you something more. Harvard has taught you that there is more to the full life than M.B.As, Ph.D.s, IRAs, stocks and bonds. More than brass plaques on mahogany doors, and mortgages and deeds and European vacations and the sweet green of the exchequer.

Harvard has taught you that America's greatness has been more than a saga of rugged individuals and Lone Rangers, solitary sojourners who rode to the horizon, alone, seeking their own fortunes.

America's greatness has not been just in the strength and success of individuals, but in the ability of its leaders to teach compassion to its people, to create a collective generosity that pooled our strengths and used them to help the vulnerable, to try to fill the gaps created by some inscrutable fate.

America has always been more than J. P. Morgan and Henry Ford and Commodore Vanderbilt. It's always been the people—and the leaders they raised up—who've asked with Rabbi Hillel, "If I am not for myself—who is for me? But if I am for myself alone—what am I?"

America's greatness has always been more than Horatio Alger. It's been in America's achieving enormous strength and then opening its heart to the world, and saying with Pope John Paul, "Freedom and riches and strength bring responsibility. We cannot leave to the poor and the disadvantaged only the crumbs from the feast. Rather, we must treat the less fortunate as guests."

Think about it.

For fifty years, from the Great Depression on, America allowed millions of its children to rise from poverty and anonymity to affluence and fame. We used our strength to lift up those who without our help would never have been able to reach the first rung of the ladder of success. And we grew stronger with the strength these people brought us.

For fifty years, we prized words like "guts" and "grit" and "victory." But we weren't afraid to use other words like "heart" and "compassion" and even "love."

For fifty years, we thought of this nation as a family, those aboard the wagon train reaching out to all the others, striving always to leave no one behind at the side of the trail.

With our collective strength, we built hospitals and homes and schools, believing that the only way we could truly succeed—not just as individuals, but as a nation—was together.

We built an America of great expectations.

Of liberty and justice and opportunity for *all.*

We struggled to provide those things for everyone. For brown, black, and white. For every state and every region and every town.

We, the people, created a government that enabled us to do

together, as a country, what no one of us could do so well, or at all, by ourselves.

With that *government*, we reached out constantly to include the excluded: impoverished immigrants, the victims of slavery and prejudice, women, those who couldn't speak the language, people born blind, disabled.

We did it hesitantly at times, sometimes reluctantly. But gradually, inexorably, we moved always toward the light.

With the leadership of Harvard graduates named Roosevelt and Kennedy, we found new ways to help people off their knees so one day they could stand on their own two feet.

New ways to train the unemployed, to rebuild neighborhoods, to send the young to college, to save the environment, to care for the elderly, to bring hope and opportunity to those who'd tasted precious little of either.

We used the wealth of states like Massachusetts and New York to settle the West and irrigate its fields.

We built dams in the South and parks in the Northwest, invested in the Southwest, dredged the harbors of the East.

And we made it!

With our *government*, we made excellence more than the privilege of a lucky few, the possession of an elite. With the help of our *government*, the children of Ellis Island joined the descendants of Plymouth Rock in creating a society always struggling to be fair as well as free.

For fifty years, from 1932 on, we showed the world the shape of what could be.

America was always the future.

Then, we changed course.

We still used the language of opportunity. The music was the same. But the reality was different.

We decided that for fifty years we had been wrong. We had reached too high. We had aspired too grandly.

We had too much ambition.

Without admitting that it was a retreat, we withdrew from our position as world leader and said, "We've decided there's only enough room in the wagon train for some of us—the strongest and fittest of us."

Despite all the better mousetraps we've designed, despite all the wonderful stories of rags to riches, despite the examples of success and comfort—even exotic luxury—despite the bunting and the martial music, despite our Olympic medals, the truth is we've grown more timid. More afraid. Less confident. Not just more selfish as individuals, but less confident as a nation.

And all the cheering and all the flags and all the elegant speeches with proud references to "our America" cannot change that truth.

The glare from the shining city of condominiums and corporate towers cannot blind us to the reality that we are now in fact a "Tale of Two Cities," one prospering, the other suffering.

We may want to deny it, we may choose to ignore it, we may resent those who remind us of it, but it's still the truth.

Look around. Look past the country clubs and the islands of wealth to the 9 million people who've sunk into poverty in the past five years.

One out of every four American children is now being raised in poverty; for blacks, it's one out of every two.

There are more homeless than at any time since the Great Depression.

Hunger, real hunger, has reappeared in our midst.

While the grandchildren of immigrants rise to new success, drive Mercedes-Benzes, and build walls of shrubbery around their communities, more and more people sleep on heating grates in the streets of our cities.

And consider the philosophy that we as a people are being asked to accept.

The only way we can prosper, it's said, is to rape the land, to level the forests, to allow the pollution of the water and the air.

The way to help people pull themselves out of poverty, we're told, is to leave them to their own devices. Let those young mothers and their children hack their way through.

Let their suffering be their inspiration. Eventually, it will drive them to greater self-help . . . and then success.

We should surrender, we're told, the aspirations and expectations that for half a century motivated and infused America—the hope that we could create a society where millions didn't have to go hungry or cold, didn't have to go without an education or the chance to work, or even a roof over their heads, that we could do it without bankrupting ourselves, without destroying the ambition of the already-strong or confiscating the wealth of the already-rich.

Now we're told this was all idealistic and weak. We can't afford compassion anymore. We have to be hard, even macho.

We have to electrocute more convicts. We have to support governments that torture their own people. We have to buy bigger weapons and deny impoverished nations the help they need.

We have to settle for less than we once believed we were capable of.

Seven percent unemployment—the symbol of failure five years ago—is now the signal of recovery.

Consider as well the idea embodied in the current proposal for tax reform. It epitomizes this new world of shrunken aspiration and diminished confidence, especially insofar as it would double-tax the most troubled of our states.

It suggests to the American people that the only way we can make our tax law better—fairer and more efficient—is to sacrifice some of our people in the interests of the rest. To punish some regions so that others may thrive. It's a great game of winners and losers, in which a blind evenhandedness is confused with equity. It says that in order to reduce the rates for some people at the bottom of the economic ladder it's also necessary to give special advantage to the oil companies, to cut in half the tax rate for the richest people in the country and punish all the states and communities that have borne the burdens of the immigrants and the poor.

We have to be content if 10 or 20 or 50 percent of the people are able to make it, because that's all the opportunity we're capable of.

We are being asked to consent to a retreat from the sense of the common good, from caring about each other, from the central thread of Western culture and American history—from intelligent compassion.

In this new dispensation, convenience replaces compassion, self-interest takes precedence before family or community, the satisfaction of individual ambition precludes consideration of mercy or justice for our neighbor.

And, I'm afraid, it's a philosophy that's succeeding.

More money for missiles, for bombs, for megatonnage. Less to feed babies, less for people in wheelchairs, less for those trapped on the margins of our society—women without work, children without dreams.

More help for the wealthiest, more poor than ever, and a tax reform that punishes the middle class, the great mass of Americans who are denied real affluence and struggling to avoid poverty.

And the temptation for those of us who are already comfortable to accept—even to profess—this philosophy is great.

The temptation is always there for the rich to see the poor as the victims of their own lack of ambition. For the strong to hoard their strength. For the golden circle of success to close in upon itself.

It's easier for those of us who've made it to wave the flag and invoke all the symbols and poetry of patriotism than it is to insist our patriotism be translated into the prose of government, into programs that buy some opportunity for a child in Roxbury.

And if we could accept these shriveled expectations, if we could resign ourselves to them because they were ordained by a fate—if we could believe the arms race is divinely predestined, if we were truly convinced there was nothing we could do about apartheid, if we could look into the eyes of a homeless woman in a doorway of New York and explain to her that her suffering is required by immutable economic laws—then our consciences might be free.

Our responsibilities to each other and to the universe might then end at our own doorsteps.

But they don't.

We *know* they don't.

We *know* that as much as we might blame fate or God or luck, the fault "is not in our stars, but in ourselves."

Harvard has taught you that.

It has taught you that our greatness was never an accident of history. That it arose from the certainty that together we can diminish the suffering and injustice in the world. From the understanding that if the misery and exploitation around us grow, it's not because God ordained it, but because we've failed each other.

Harvard graduates, this magnificent country of ours—and this world of which it's part—will only become unfit for human life because we choose to let it become so.

Because we grow tired of caring for each other.

Because we substitute excuses for aspirations.

Because we ignore our power as a people to do more than pile missile on top of missile.

Because we retreat from the goal of *real* excellence.

I don't believe that's our destiny.

Looking around this yard, I believe our potential for greatness— as individuals and as a nation—far outweighs our problems. I believe your proven capacity for excellence can flood this country with success, with a whole new wave of achievements, with a rising tide of hope, making even the barren places bloom.

As you go, Harvard, so will go students all over America.

So, in the words of a great American, go for it!

All of you.

Go for, and with, each other.

Go against oppression and despair and indifference and lowered aspirations.

Go with the certainty that your one life can make a difference and that together you can share and shape this country and this world.

Go for it, Harvard!

And go for it now!

ABRAHAM LINCOLN AND

OUR "UNFINISHED WORK"

FEBRUARY 12, 1986

ABRAHAM LINCOLN ASSOCIATION BANQUET

HOLIDAY INN EAST, SPRINGFIELD, ILLINOIS

What a great gift Lincoln is! In this speech I use him to inspire us and to remind us that we are still in the process of perfecting the Union, still a "Tale of Two Cities," still struggling to complete America "the unfinished work." Lincoln serves, too, as a strong witness against the Reagan assault on government as a pernicious force. Lincoln's own view was a balanced one using government to do things which he believed the private sector was not doing adequately, such as making "land improvements." Today that would mean investing in our infrastructure.

Something else was at work in the 1980s that was troublesome and could benefit from Lincoln's soaring intellect and penetrating rhetoric. There was a harshness growing, a loss of civility. Lincoln, who stretched his sinewy arms around his young nation and kept it from division and fragmentation with his strength and compassion, is still a powerful voice against the destructive force of racial, ethnic, and religious discrimination. I had in mind especially some new unpleasantness involving Italian-Americans that had been in the news just before the time of this address, and I talked about it specifically in the speech.

It is for us, the living, rather, to be dedicated here to the unfinished work . . . that this nation, under God, shall have a new birth of freedom—and that government of the people, by the people, for the people, shall not perish from the earth.
        —*Gettysburg Address (Everett Copy)*
                November 19, 1863

It is an intimidating thing to stand here tonight to talk about the greatest intellect, the greatest leader, perhaps the greatest soul, America has ever produced.

To follow such legendary orators as William Jennings Bryan and Adlai Stevenson.

Only a struggling student myself, to face as imposing an audience as the Lincoln scholars: Tough-minded. Demanding. Harsh critics. Highly intelligent.

And to face so many Republicans: Tough-minded. Demanding, harsh critics.

And I certainly wasn't encouraged after I learned that when another New York governor, Franklin D. Roosevelt, announced his intention to come here to speak on Lincoln, a local political stalwart threatened him with an injunction.

To be honest with you, I feel a little like the Illinois man from one Lincoln story. When he was confronted by a local citizens' committee with the prospect of being tarred and feathered and run out of town on a rail, he announced, "If it weren't for the honor of the thing, I'd just as soon it happened to someone else."

I should tell you one more thing before I go on with my remarks. It would be foolish to deny that there has been some speculation surrounding this event about ambitions for the presidency. Let me be candid. I don't know anyone who wouldn't regard it as the highest possible political privilege to be president. And governors are, perhaps, better prepared than most to be president.

Governors like Teddy Roosevelt and FDR and even governors from places like Georgia and California. Particularly governors of great industrial states with good records. That's because governors do more than make speeches. They have to make budgets and run things—and that's what presidents do.

So, the truth is, despite what might be said about planning to run again for governor, the speculation about the presidency is plausible.

I wouldn't be a bit surprised—if the election goes well this year for him—if early next year you heard a declaration of interest from a reelected governor of a large state—Jim Thompson of Illinois.

Good Luck, Jim!

But seriously, this is an event beyond the scope of partisan politics.

When Lincoln gave his one and only speech in my capital, Albany, New York, he told the Democratic governor, "You have invited and received me without distinction of party."

Let me second that sentiment, and thank you for inviting and receiving me in the same spirit.

To be here in Springfield, instead of at the memorial in Washington, to celebrate this "high holy day" of Lincoln remembrance gives us a special advantage.

In Washington, Lincoln towers far above us, presiding magisterially, in a marble temple.

His stony composure, the hugeness of him there, gives him and his whole life a grandeur that places him so far above and beyond us that it's difficult to remember the reality of him.

We have lifted Lincoln to the very pinnacle of our national memory. Enlarged him to gargantuan proportions in white stone recreations.

We have chiseled his face on the side of a mountain, making him appear as a voice in the heavens.

There is a danger when we enshrine our heroes, when we lift them onto pedestals and lay wreaths at their feet. We can, by the very process of elevating them, strain the sense of connection between them and the palpable, fleshy, sometimes mean concerns of our own lives.

I have come to remember Lincoln as he was. The flesh-and-blood man. Haunted by mortality in his waking and his dreaming life. The boy who had been uprooted from one frontier to another, across Kentucky and Indiana and Illinois, by a father restless with his own dreams.

To remember some of Lincoln's own words—which, taken altogether, are the best words America has ever produced.

To remember the words that he spoke ten days after his lyrical, wrenching farewell to Springfield on his way to his inauguration as our sixteenth president.

"Back in my childhood," he said then, "the earliest days of my being able to read, I got hold of a small book . . . Weems's *Life of Washington.*

"I remember all the accounts there given of the battlefields and struggles for the liberties of the country and the great hardships of that time fixed themselves on . . . my memory.

"I recollect thinking then, boy even though I was, that there must have been something *more* than *common* that those men struggled for.

"I am exceedingly anxious that the thing which they struggled for; that something even more than national independence; that something that held out a promise to all the people of the world for all time to come; . . . shall be perpetuated in accordance with the original idea for which the struggle was made . . ."

Here was Lincoln, just before his inauguration, reminding us of the source of his strength and eventual greatness. His compelling need to understand the meaning of things and to commit to a course that was directed by reason, supported by principle, designed to achieve the greatest good. He was a man of ideas, grand and soaring ones. And he was cursed by the realization that they were achievable ideas as well, so that he could not escape the obligation of pursuing them, despite the peril and the pain that pursuit would inevitably bring.

Even as a boy he grasped the great idea that would sustain him—and provoke him—for the rest of his days. The idea that took hold of his heart and his mind. The idea that he tells us about again and again throughout his life. It became the thread of purpose that tied the boy to the man to the legend—the great idea, the dream, the achievable dream, of equality, of opportunity . . . for all.

"The original idea for which the struggle was made . . ." The proposition that all men are created equal. That they are endowed by their Creator with certain unalienable rights. That among these are life, liberty, and the pursuit of happiness.

Even by Lincoln's time, for many the words had been heard often enough so that they became commonplace, part of the intellectual and historical landscape, losing their dimension, their significance, their profoundness.

But not for Lincoln.

He pondered them. Troubled over their significance. Wrestled with their possibilities.

"We did not learn quickly or easily that all men are created equal," one Lincoln scholar has observed.

No. We did not learn those words quickly or easily. We are still struggling with them in fact.

As Lincoln did. For a whole lifetime. From the time he read Weems's little book, until the day he was martyred, he thought and planned and prayed to make the words of the Declaration a way of life.

Equality and opportunity, for *all*. But truly, for *all*.

Lincoln came to believe that the great promise of the founding fathers was one that had only begun to be realized with the founding fathers themselves. He understood that from the beginning it was a promise that would have to be fulfilled in degrees. Its embrace would have to be widened over the years, step by step, sometimes painfully, until finally it included everyone.

That was his dream. That was his vision. That was his mission.

With it, he defined, for himself and for us, the soul of our unique experiment in government: the belief that the promise of the Declaration of Independence—the promise of equality and opportunity—cannot be considered kept until it includes everyone.

For him, that was the unifying principle of our democracy. Without it, we had no nation worth fighting for. With it, we had no limit to the good we might achieve.

He spent the rest of his life trying to give the principle meaning. He consumed himself doing it.

He reaffirmed Jefferson's preference for the human interest and the human right. "The principles of Jefferson," he said, "are the definitions and axioms of free society."

But Lincoln extended those instincts to new expressions of equality.

Always, he searched for ways to bring within the embrace of the new freedom, the new opportunity, *all* who had become Americans.

Deeply, reverently, grateful for the opportunity afforded *him*, he was pained by the idea that it should be denied others. Or limited.

He believed that the human right was more than the right to exist, to live free from oppression.

He believed it included the right to achieve, to thrive. So he reached out for the "penniless beginner."

He thought it the American promise that every "poor man" should be given his chance.

He saw what others would or could not see: the immensity of the fundamental ideas of freedom and self-determination that made his young nation such a radically new adventure in government.

But he was not intimidated by that immensity. He was willing to *use* the ideas as well as to admire them. To mold them so as to apply them to new circumstances. To wield them as instruments of justice and not just echoes of it.

Some said government should do no more than protect its people from insurrection and foreign invasion and spend the rest of its time dispassionately observing the way its people played out the cards that fate had dealt them.

He scorned that view. He called it a "do nothing" abdication of responsibility.

"The legitimate object of government," he said, "is to do for the people what needs to be done, but which they cannot, by individual effort, do at all, or do so well, for themselves. There are many such things . . ." he said.

So he offered the "poor" *more* than feedom and the encouragement of his own good example: He offered them government. Government that would work aggressively to help them find the chance they might not have found alone. He did it by fighting for bridges, railroad construction, and other such projects that others decried as excessive government.

He gave help for education, help for agriculture, land for the rural family struggling for a start.

And always at the heart of his struggle and his yearning was the passion to make room for the outsider, the insistence upon a commitment to respect the idea of equality by fighting for inclusion.

Early in his career, he spoke out for women's suffrage.

His contempt for the "do-nothings" was equaled by his disdain for the "Know-Nothings."

America beckoned foreigners, but many Americans—organized around the crude selfishness of the nativist movement—rejected them. The nativists sought to create two classes of people, the old-stock Americans and the intruders from other places, keeping the intruders forever strangers in a strange land.

Lincoln shamed them with his understanding and his strength. "I am not a Know-Nothing," he said. "How could I be? How can anyone who abhors the oppression of Negroes be in favor of degrading classes of white people? . . . As a nation we began by declaring 'all men are created equal.'

"We now practically read it: 'All men are created equal except Negroes.' When the Know-Nothings get control, it will read 'All men are created equal except Negroes, and Catholics and Foreigners.' "

Then he added: "When it comes to this I shall prefer emigrating to some country where they make no pretense of loving liberty—to Russia for instance, where despotism can be taken pure, and without the base alloy of hypocrisy."

Had Lincoln not existed, or had he been less than he was and the battle to keep the nation together had been lost, it would have meant the end of the American experiment. Secession would have bred secession, reducing us into smaller and smaller fragments until finally we were just the broken pieces of the dream.

Lincoln saved us from that.

But winning the great war for unity did not preserve us from the need to fight further battles in the struggle to balance our diversity with our harmony, to keep the pieces of the mosaic intact, even while making room for new pieces.

That work is today, as it was in 1863, still an unfinished work . . . still a cause that requires "a full measure of devotion."

For more than 100 years, the fight to include has continued:

- In the struggle to free working people from the oppression of a ruthless economic system that saw women and children worked to death and men born to poverty live in poverty and die in poverty, in spite of working all the time.

• In the continuing fight for civil rights, making Lincoln's promise real.

• In the effort to keep the farmer alive.

• In the ongoing resistance to preserve religious freedom from the arrogance of the Know-Nothing and the zealotry of those who would make their religion the state's religion.

• In the crusade to make women equal, legally and practically.

Many battles have been won. The embrace of our unity has been gradually but inexorably expanded.

But Lincoln's work is not yet done.

A century after Lincoln preached his answer of equality and mutual respect, some discrimination—of class or race or sex or ethnicity—as a bar to full participation in America still remains.

Unpleasant reminders of less enlightened times linger. Sometimes they are heard in whispers. At other times they are loud enough to capture the attention of the American people.

I have had my own encounter with this question, and I have spoken of it.

Like millions of others, I am privileged to be a first-generation American. My mother and father came to this country more than sixty years ago with nothing but their hopes. Without education, skills, or wealth.

Through the opportunity given them here to lift themselves through hard work, they were able to raise a family. My mother has lived to see her youngest child become chief executive of one of the greatest states in the greatest nation in the only world we know.

Like millions of other children of immigrants, I know the strength that immigrants can bring. I know the richness of a society that allows us a whole new culture without requiring us to surrender the one our parents were born to. I know the miraculous power of this place that helps people rise up from poverty to security, and even affluence, in the course of a single lifetime. With generations of other children of the immigrants, I know about equality and opportunity and unity in a special way.

And I know how, from time to time, all this beauty can be challenged by the misguided children of the Know-Nothings, by the shortsighted and the unkind, by contempt that masks itself as humor, by all the casual or conscious bigotry that must keep the American people vigilant.

We heard such voices again recently saying things like: "Italians are not politically popular."

"Catholics will have a problem."

"He has an *ethnic* problem."

An ethnic problem.

We hear the word again. "Wop."

"We oftentimes refer to people of Italian descent as 'Wops,'" said one public figure, unabashedly.

Now, given the unbroken string of opportunity and good fortune provided me by this great country, I might simply have ignored these references. I could easily have let the words pass as inconsequential, especially remembering Lincoln, himself the object of scorn and ridicule. But the words took on significance because they were heard far beyond my home or my block or even my state. Because they were heard by others who remembered times of their own when words stung and menaced *them* and *their* people.

And because they raised a question about our system of fundamental American values that Lincoln helped construct and died for. Is it true? Are there really so many who have never heard Lincoln's voice, or the sweet sound of reason and fairness? So many who do not understand the beauty and power of this place, that they could make of the tint of your skin or the sex you were born to or the vowels of your name an impediment to progress in this, the land of opportunity?

I believed the answer would be clear. So I asked for it by disputing the voices of division. By saying, "It is not so. It is the voice of ignorance, and I challenge you to show me otherwise."

In no time at all the answer has come back from the American people. Everyone saying the same things:

"Of course it's wrong to judge a person by the place where his forebears came from. Of course that would violate all that we stand for, fairness and common sense. It shouldn't *even* have been brought up. It shouldn't *even* have been a cause for discussion."

I agree. It should not have been. But it was. And the discussion is now concluded, with the answer I was sure of and the answer I am proud of as an American. The answer Lincoln would have given: "You will rise or fall on your merits as a person and the quality of your work. All else is distraction."

Lincoln believed, with every fiber of his being, that this place, America, could offer a dream to all mankind, different than any other in the annals of history.

More generous, more compassionate, more inclusive.

No one knew better than Lincoln our sturdiness, the ability of most of us to make it on our own given the chance. But at the same time, no one knew better the idea of family, the idea that unless we helped one another, there were some who would never make it.

One person climbs the ladder of personal ambition, reaches his dream, and then turns . . . and pulls the ladder up.

Another reaches the place he has sought, turns, and reaches down for the person behind him.

With Lincoln, it was that process of turning and reaching down, that commitment to keep lifting people up the ladder, which defined the American character, stamping us forever with a mission that reached even beyond our borders to embrace the world.

Lincoln's belief in America, in the American people, was broader, deeper, more daring than any other person's of his age—and, perhaps, ours, too.

And *this* is the near-unbelievable greatness of the man—that with that belief, he not only led us; he *created* us.

His personal mythology became our national mythology.

It is as if Homer not only chronicled the siege of Troy, but conducted the siege as well.

As if Shakespeare set his play writing aside to lead the English against the Armada.

Because Lincoln embodied his age in his actions and in his words.

Words, even and measured, hurrying across three decades, calling us to our destiny.

Words he prayed, and troubled over—more than a million words in his speeches and writings.

Words that chronicled the search for his own identity as he searched for a nation's identity.

Words that were, by turns, as chilling as the night sky and as assuring as home.

Words his reason sharpened into steel, and his heart softened into an embrace.

Words filled with all the longings of his soul and of his century.

Words wrung from his private struggle, spun to capture the struggle of a nation.

Words out of his own pain to heal that struggle.

Words of retribution, but never of revenge.

Words that judged, but never condemned.

Words that pleaded, cajoled for the one belief—that the promise *must* be kept, that the dream *must* endure and grow, until it embraces everyone.

Words ringing down into the present.

All the hope and the pain of that epic caught, somehow, by his cadences: The tearing away, the binding together, the leaving behind, the reaching beyond.

As individuals, as a people, we are still reaching up, for a better job, a better education, a better society, even for the stars, just as Lincoln did.

But because of Lincoln, we do it in a way that is unique to this world.

What other people on earth have ever claimed a quality of character that resided not in a way of speaking, dressing, dancing, praying, but in an idea?

What other people on earth have ever refused to set the definitions of their identity by anything other than that idea?

No, we have not learned quickly or easily that the dream of America endures only so long as we keep faith with the struggle to include. But Lincoln, through his words and his works, has etched that message forever into our consciousness.

Lincoln showed us, for all time, what unites us.

He taught us that we cannot rest until the promise of equality and opportunity embraces every region, every race, every religion, every nationality . . . and every class. Until it includes, "the penniless beginner" and the "poor man seeking his chance."

In his time, Lincoln saw that as long as one in every seven Americans was enslaved, our identity as a people was hostage to that enslavement.

He faced that injustice. He fought it. He gave his life to see it righted.

Time and again since then, we have had to face challenges that threatened to divide us.

And time and again, we have conquered them.

We reached out—hesitantly at times, sometimes only after great struggle—but always we reached out, to include impoverished immigrants, the farmer and the factory worker, women, the disabled.

To all those whose only assets were their great expectations, America found ways to meet those expectations, and to create new ones.

Generations of hardworking people moved into the middle class and beyond.

We created a society as open and free as any on earth. And we did it Lincoln's way—by founding that society on a belief in the boundless enterprise of the American people.

Always, we have extended the promise. Moving toward the light, toward our declared purpose as a people: "to form a more perfect Union," to overcome all that divides us, because we believe the ancient wisdom that Lincoln believed—"a house divided against itself cannot stand."

Step by step, our embrace grows wider.

The old bigotries seem to be dying. The old stereotypes and hatreds that denied so many their full share of an America they helped build have gradually given way to acceptance, fairness, and civility.

But still, great challenges remain.

Suddenly, ominously, a new one has emerged.

In Lincoln's time, one of every seven Americans was a slave.

Today, for all our affluence and might, despite what every day is described as our continuing economic recovery, nearly one in every seven Americans lives in poverty, not in chains—because Lincoln saved us from that—but trapped in a cycle of despair that is its own enslavement.

Today, while so many of us do so well, one of every two minority children is born poor, many of them to be oppressed for a lifetime by inadequate education and the suffocating influence of broken families and social disorientation.

Our identity as a people is hostage to the grim facts of more than 33 million Americans for whom equality and opportunity is not yet an attainable reality, but only an illusion.

Some people look at these statistics and the suffering people behind them, and deny them, pretending instead we are all one great "shining city on a hill."

Lincoln told us for a lifetime—and for all time to come—that there can be no shining city when one in seven of us is denied the promise of the Declaration.

He tells us today that we are justly proud of all that we have accomplished, but that for all our progress, for all our achievement, for all that so properly makes us proud, we have no right to rest, content.

Nor justification for turning from the effort, out of fear or lack of confidence.

We have met greater challenges with fewer resources. We have faced greater perils with fewer friends. It would be a desecration of our belief and an act of ingratitude for the good fortune we have had to end the struggle for inclusion because it is over for some of us.

So, this evening, we come to pay you our respects, Mr. Lincoln. Not just by recalling your words and revering your memory, which we do humbly and with great pleasure.

This evening, we offer you more, Mr. President. We offer you what you have asked for, a continuing commitment to live your truth, to go forward painful step by painful step, enlarging the greatness of this nation with patient confidence in the ultimate justice of the people.

Because—as you have told us, Mr. President—there is no better or equal hope in the world.

Thank you.

This address allowed me to discuss subjects that concerned me long before I became a politician: whether and to what extent the precise language of the Constitution should be molded to accommodate new realities and to what extent the matter of the selection of a Supreme Court justice is different from selecting a president or member of Congress. My answer to the latter question places me in a distinct minority. I believe the selection process has been improperly used most of the time over the last 200 years. None of the Supreme Court justices who were on the stage as I spoke told me they disagreed, and I like to believe that at least some of them thought I was not altogether wrong.

Let me welcome you to the Big Apple and the Empire State. We're honored to have you with us.

You'll find as you move around the city that we're still celebrating the glorious one-hundredth birthday of the Lady in the Harbor.

It's been an exciting time. A joyous explosion of good feeling.

It's been a time for thinking about ourselves, too.

Remembering how millions of people, deprived opportunity elsewhere, came here and found the chance to earn security, comfort, dignity, even affluence and great power. Not by inheritance, but by the miracle of this amazing place America.

Of course we rejoice! The significance of this place and of this experiment is so vast, so profound, that it compels our exultation even as it challenges our understanding.

"Too big for words." That's how an eighty-eight-year-old immigrant described it. He and his young wife had passed through Ellis Island in 1921 with nothing but hope and good health. Since then he had built a large and flourishing family.

Now he was standing on the deck of a ship in the middle of the harbor. Nearby was the aircraft carrier bearing the president, surrounded by thousands of boats, with flags and bunting and horns blaring. Next to him stood his godson, the governor of the state of New York, himself a first-generation American. Together they watched the glorious spectacle of the nation's 210th Fourth of July.

"Too big for words," he said. "You have to feel it in your heart. God, it's a miracle!"

A miracle indeed. Difficult to explain. Difficult to understand fully.

But one thing seems clear. Much of the reason for the unique strength of this place is our system of law. It has made the hope for opportunity and equality tangible, and converted distant dreams into everyday realities for millions of us.

A hundred years before the towering symbol of liberty was raised in our harbor, geniuses had written the fundamental law that would justify that symbol, the Constitution of the United States.

It is, as you know so well, one of the most extraordinary legal instruments ever produced.

Nothing is more responsible for our success, nothing better describes our uniqueness . . . nothing deserves more our reverence and our protection.

Much of the Constitution is deliberately and unavoidably ambiguous—*written in its time for all time, its genius is that it can be stretched to fit changing realities without tearing.*

Its history—and especially the Supreme Court's application of its language to ever-changing circumstances—has been marked by controversy.

But it has worked. Order has been preserved and the nation has grown stronger for 200 years.

And all the time the only real power available to the Court to enforce its rulings has been, and remains, the trust of the American people and their insistence on the rule of law.

It is not too much to call this another miracle.

You lawyers are the acolytes of the law.

Without you, there would be no law. Without your intelligence and hard work and integrity, the law—and the land—would be less than they are.

You have come here to New York both to celebrate the miracle and to assure its continuance.

We are grateful. And wish you well in your work.

I'm particularly interested in your deliberations from two separate personal perspectives.

First, as a former law secretary to a judge of New York's highest court, a practicing lawyer and adjunct professor of law for more than a decade.

I have enjoyed public service. But I have always *loved* being a lawyer. I confess to you I have missed my close association with the practice of law. I hope to return to it, but as Augustine said about his desire to achieve chastity, "Not quite yet."

I'm interested also as a public official who works every day seeking not just to execute and enforce the laws, but to develop new ones.

If I may then, I'd like to share with you some observations about the Constitution, its interpretation, and the selection of those who interpret it for the nation.

•   •   •

The whole question of interpretation began shortly after the Constitution was adopted and has continued since then, sometimes raging, sometimes simmering, but never disappearing. It flares up on occasions when a decision by the Court proves to be controversial.

Dred Scott, Brown v. the Board of Education, Engel v. Vitale, Roe v. Wade all offended some considerable numbers of our people. Each raised again the question whether the Court was arrogating to itself too much power, whether the high priests were writing their own Ten Commandments or just interpreting the word of the lawgiver.

That perennial argument, over whether and to what extent the precise language of the Constitution should be molded to accommodate new realities, is again the focus of national debate.

In that debate, the two sides seem frequently driven to unreasonable extremes. For example, it seems absurd to believe *literally* in the notion of "original intent," that the reach of our fundamental law should be limited to only the specific realities known to the founding fathers two centuries ago. It seems obvious that interpretation is necessary in order to keep the Constitution a workable document.

But the case isn't as easy as that, because it's outrageous to believe, *on the other hand*, that the Constitution empowers the Supreme Court to design *its own* social policy without having to find justification in the Constitution.

As usual, the truth lies somewhere between Scylla and Charybdis, and finding the safe route can be difficult.

It would be a relief if we could find our way by breaking down all the nuances and complex propositions into two contending polar positions neatly labeled: "Conservatives against liberals." Or perhaps "the unruly activists against the reliable original intenters." Think of all the long articles we wouldn't have to read, all the analysis we could skip, all the complexity we could avoid . . . if only these pat phrases, slogans, and labels accurately represented the issues.

•   •   •

But the evidence that things are not that simple is everywhere.

For example, how would you label the Court led by Chief Justice Burger? It has been popular to describe it as a "conservative" Court as distinguished from the "liberal" Warren Court. And "conservative" of course implies *"strict construction"*—those labels are a matched pair. And "liberal" then equals "activist" or, dare we say it, "loose construction."

But the Burger Court, many contend now, has been more activist than the Warren Court.

We could go on and on with illustrations. The slogans and labels simply fail to capture the truth.

That's particularly evident in the matter of judicial selection.

In recent days our newspapers and television screens have been chronicling the Senate confirmation process at work. Commentators, analysts, and reporters have been quick to take sides. To most of them, it seems clear that it's all a matter of the red shirts against the blue shirts.

A page in one of New York's major newspapers summed it up in one dramatic, side-by-side confrontation of two columnists, one notoriously "conservative," the other even more notoriously "liberal."

The conservative said it was wonderful that the Republican nominees would probably be confirmed because they would be "populist" judges who would agree with the people on what the laws should be with respect to abortion, crime, and sex.

The president, incidentally, made a similar statement to the Knights of Columbus last week.

The liberal said it was terrible because the nominees were less than sympathetic on civil rights, human rights, and the death penalty.

The debate reads as though the matter of selecting and confirming justices to the Supreme Court is no different from electing a president or a senator and judging them by their positions on the current political issues.

What is, I think, most distressing is that I haven't read any columns that say we're liable to get the wrong answers here, because we're asking the wrong questions.

Let's look more closely: One hundred and one men and one woman have been appointed to the Supreme Court in the past 200 years. For the last 150 years, the question of the appropriate criteria of selection has been a vital and elusive one.

One of the more provocative questions raised by the process over the years is what role ideology, social philosophy, or political philosophy should play.

It's a question again before the nation today.

Most of the nominees of the current administration have been from the same party and are distinctly branded as leaning hard to the right in their political outlook. That's not a coincidence. It is not unusual for a president to try to bend the Court to fit his own ideological, social, or political beliefs. Or even to try to assure favorable decisions on issues he regards to be specially important to the nation. Presidents Lincoln, Jackson, Franklin Roosevelt all come quickly to mind.

Indeed, I would guess most observers expect that to be the case, and many approve.

The present effort, however, is a particularly emphatic one. The 1984 Republican convention urged that judicial candidates should give evidence of fealty on key social issues. Today, it is implicitly conceded by the president's people that he would like a Court that would change the law to reflect his political views, and he believes he's getting one.

The abortion case is a good example. No one doubts the president wants *Roe v. Wade* overruled and considers that in selecting candidates. And no one doubts that the president is being urged— by promoters of the so-called "judicial philosophy of original intention"—to try to create a Court that would overrule important parts of the last 100 years of progress, the century of the Lady Liberty.

No one suggests the president is exceeding his *legal* right in making whatever selections he wants.

But at the very least it must be said that this raises some interesting questions for lawyers, and everyone else who lives here, about the best way to handle the matter of judicial selection.

•   •   •

Of course, the temptation to appoint judges that will carry out a president's political agenda in the Supreme Court must be a powerful one, as indicated by the frequency with which presidents have succumbed.

But, conceding it is legal, that it has been done before, and that the nation has survived the experience, I respectfully submit to you that this is not the only *practical* way to select judges . . . and it is *certainly* not the best way.

An insistence on selecting those, and only those, who are philosophically or politically in lockstep with the president at the very least reduces the chance of finding the best judicial talent available. It excludes those who may exhibit far superior judicial talent but happen to belong to the wrong party or philosophical school.

One example, among many, makes the point: Consider that if President Hoover had persisted in demanding someone who agreed with his so-called conservative philosophy, Benjamin Nathan Cardozo would never have made it to the Supreme Court. The truth is that because he was a so-called "liberal," he nearly didn't. Only because Cardozo's judicial merit was so well known and the voices of his supporters so insistent did he make it past the impediment of "ideology."

To me, the problem with Mr. Daniel Manion's appointment, confirmed by the slimmest margin, is just the opposite. With all due respect to the judge, there was good reason to believe he was nominated because of his ideology rather than because he was the most judicially competent candidate available for the United States Court of Appeals for the Seventh Circuit.

The use of ideology as a norm raises an issue even more fundamental than that of finding the best judicial talent available. To use ideology or political or social philosophy as a standard of selection is, I think, to confuse the basic nature of the judiciary.

As lawyers, we know that judges are different from politicians, or at least should be. Politicians, whether executive or legislative, make statutes or rules or decisions *prospectively*, using their own best judgment. They need not find a mandate in the Constitution as long as they find no prohibition there.

Judges are different. They are not left unfettered to consider their own values, judgments, and views of what is best for the community. They are required to find reasons for their judgments rooted in the law, be it the Constitution, a statute, or the common law. *The reasons must dictate the result and not vice versa.*

Moreover, judges are supposed to approach each case with an open mind as to how the law applies to the *particular* facts and circumstances placed before them in a *particular record*. The unlimited range of reasoning and information available to persuade the executive and legislator is, by the exquisite design of our law, denied to the judge.

And the Supreme Court is additionally constricted by the requirement that it deal with a case or controversy brought before it; it cannot give advisory opinions.

Now, of course, in applying the Constitution to a world of ever-changing realities, a general sense of good public policy—perhaps even what Holmes called intuition—may come into play.

But it's one thing to recognize that social vision may affect the justice's interpretation of the Constitution in a specific controversy, on a specific record, at a specific time in the future. It is quite another to use the selection of a judge to attempt to *assure* a result in advance. Everyone would agree that it is patently wrong to commit a judge *explicitly* to a conclusion before he or she has read the record.

It seems to me just as wrong to commit the judge implicitly by saying, or suggesting, his or her predictable vision was a reason for selection. That way produces a judge guided by an inappropriate precommitment to a fixed decision or one perceived as disillusioning the expectation that accompanied the judge's selection.

That's the difficulty created by recent public predictions from the current administration that their judicial nominees would change the law on abortion, pornography, crime, and other issues.

The best way to pick a judge is by picking someone who's good at doing what a judge is supposed to do, not at what a president, a governor or legislator is supposed to do.

If this country wanted its Supreme Court to reflect the immediate social or political wishes of the nation's people it would provide for the election of the Court. And if the founding fathers had wanted it that way, they could have said so . . . or at least hinted at it. They did just the opposite: they designed a system that tried to immunize the Court from the changing moods and passions of the people, leaving it to tend the Constitution as free as possible from external pressure.

They believed our freedom, liberty, and good order were best preserved by a judiciary independent of the other branches of government.

It comes down to this: under our system, cases should be decided in the courthouse. They should not be decided in the Oval Office or the Senate chamber. This is a matter of profoundly important substance. Whether it's Franklin Roosevelt or Ronald Reagan, liberals or conservatives, the president and the Senate should not be trying to fix the judicial deal.

It wasn't meant to be that way and it's not good for the country in the long run. The exquisite balance of powers that has kept this ship of state afloat and moving forward depends upon an independent Supreme Court. When the executive—or the Senate—attempts to weaken that independence by forcing the judicial branch to do the political work of the other two branches, they threaten that balance. When the intrusion becomes obvious and substantial, it can become a grave danger because it can dilute the people's confidence in the Court. And, ultimately, the people's confidence is both the Court's shield and its sword.

I suggest that a better way to choose judges is to prescind from ideology, party, so-called political philosophy, and use instead what for lack of a more meritorious label we call the "merit" criteria. I think the American Bar Association criteria, the criteria in the Constitution and statutes of the state of New York, and the writings of the founding fathers all wisely leave out ideology, philosophy, and party. Instead, irreproachable integrity, experience, wisdom, knowledge of the law, judicial temperament, collegiality where appropriate, and ability to communicate orally and in writing are fit criteria, and all we need.

That's the way we have been doing it in New York for the last few years.

Until 1978, the seven judges of our highest court were elected. Now they are appointed by the governor from a list provided by a nominating commission. By law the commission considers the following: character, temperament, professional aptitude, and experience. Nowhere is it stated or implied that party, philosophy, or ideology is relevant.

We have chosen an approach that strengthens the law and facilitates the nomination of the best candidates by depoliticizing the process. *We believe that when you read a good opinion, you shouldn't be able to tell whether it was written by a Republican or a Democrat.*

I have selected six judges in three and a half years, five of them already sitting judges. All were confirmed unanimously by the state senate, which is dominated by the opposite party.

I did not measure my nominees for their political or philosophical compatibility with my views. Without referring to the party of any nominee, I studied their opinions to see whether they were scholarly, thoughtful, and well articulated, not to see whether I liked their results. Half of my selections, as it turned out, were Republican, *including the chief judge,* and half Democrat. They have not always agreed with my actions. They have quickly developed a reputation for judicial excellence and *independence* that makes them the strong balancing part of the governmental trinity they were designed to be.

Of course, there are differences between the Supreme Court of the United States and the highest courts of the various states, including our own. But they are sufficiently similar to be worth comparing, and I believe our way works better than the federal way.

The application of these principles of merit selection and judicial independence to the nominations recently—and currently—before the Senate are fairly apparent.

Whether Mr. Daniel Manion was competent in terms of experience, wisdom, knowledge, and capacity to communicate was a proper question for the president and the Senate.

Character is always a relevant subject. So the investigation into whether Justice Rehnquist has told the truth about events in his past, whether he ever approved of bigotry or violated the canons of ethics, cannot be called extraneous. *But surely, a clear and compelling case would have to be made against him to justify an assault on the integrity of a man who has served as an associate justice for fifteen years.*

Whether any of the candidates' views of the Constitution's applicability are so aberrant as to suggest judicial incompetence, or so ideologically hidebound as to suggest a lack of judicial temperament, would be appropriate inquiries.

Whether any of the candidates would seek to overrule *Roe v. Wade, Miranda, Engel v. Vitale,* or any other specific precedent, are *not* appropriate questions for the president or the Senate.

And whether Judge Scalia is a registered conservative, liberal, or progressive pragmatist, or thinks like any one of them when he's thinking politically, should be irrelevant.

If Judge Scalia is what he appears to be—bright, knowledgeable, extremely articulate, a man of irreproachable integrity, firm in opinion but not closed-minded, with a deep respect for the Constitution—he should be confirmed. I do not agree with all the decisions Judge Scalia has made. But as long as he is not so ideologically mesmerized that his decisions on important social issues appear to be precast, the fact that some may disagree with conclusions reasonably arrived at in past cases should not be relevant.

The Senate had the right to complain nearly fifty years ago when Roosevelt tried packing the Court with people he thought would do his political bidding. And the Senate has the right to complain *today* if it believes the president is trying to commandeer the Court by packing it with political sympathizers.

But the Senate should not insist that the president reflect its own philosophical outlook either. Neither the president nor the Senate should apply an ideological litmus test to judicial nominees.

The way past Scylla and Charybdis is by pointing the tiller toward judicial competence, not political compatibility.

•   •   •

Many will label as naive this suggestion that we can improve the way we are selecting our federal judges and justices. Many will claim it's impractical to think that a president or the Senate can be persuaded to put judicial talent before their desire to project their political philosophy into the courts.

I think *that* conclusion actually contradicts our history . . . a history we all have reason to be proud of.

Our success as a nation has indeed been "too big for words." But it would be a mistake to believe we have already become as strong as we can be.

Part of the wonder of this nation built on a dream is that, for all our success, there is still so much we can do, still so much of the dream to be fulfilled.

The law has been our strength. Our sturdy foundation. But it can be stronger, sturdier, and support even greater progress. And it must. A nation's journey is no different than a person's. If we do not go forward, we go backward. If we are to grow, we must be ready to change. No nation knows that better than we do: our history has taught us.

For two centuries, despite our occasional failures, and even a Civil War, we have moved forward.

And in large measure it has been America's lawyers who have encouraged, protected, and insisted on this progress. In thousands of cases, in thousands of courtrooms, by their advocacy through important voices like the American Bar Association, year after year throughout our history, it has been the lawyers who have developed and strengthened the law that preserves our democratic faith.

It was the lawyers' passion for predictable and equitable standards that taught our ancestors to make the political system subject to the legal system, so as to assure, as nearly as possible, that politics would be required to serve the ends of justice, and not the other way around.

This morning, I respectfully submit to you that, concerning the selection of the justices who will serve as guardians of our cherished lady of the law, we lawyers have both a challenge, and an

opportunity, to make still further progress . . . *if* we choose to.
I commend the subject to your attention.

I am proud that you have chosen this state for your annual meeting;
I am flattered that you asked me to speak. I am grateful for all you
have meant, and continue to mean, to this great nation.
Thank you.

A BRIEF ON THE FREEDOM OF THE PRESS

NOVEMBER 25, 1986

NEW YORK PRESS CLUB, NEW YORK, NEW YORK

Democracy would not be safe without freedom of the press. This speech by a politician who has felt the press's sting—more than once—underscores that obvious first principle of our republic, while reminding the press that its vast power to inform, instruct, and uplift is accompanied by the concomitant power to distort, mislead, and demean. It was better received by the public at large, who heard it, than the press who were in attendance, many of whom dismissed it because it wasn't "news."

President Marcia Kramer, members of the New York Press Club, thank you for this invitation to speak on an extraordinarily significant subject: "the freedom of the press, its importance to this nation and what we must do to keep it strong."

I've called my remarks "A Brief on the Freedom of the Press."

I've spoken on this subject frequently in the last few years. It's never been easy. The subject is complex, in part arcane, and—I think, unfortunately—more controversial than it should be.

It also involves some sensitive and fragile relationships—between the press and the public at large, between the press and public officials, and among members of the print and electronic press community itself.

My discussions—of the press, with the press—have occasionally produced unexpected reactions. That happened a couple of weeks ago, around election time.

A friend of mine in the press called me a few days ago to talk about the effect of my own attempts at constructive criticism. He said, "Mario, I know what you had in mind, but I don't think it came out the way you wanted it to. Instead, you reminded me of the errant knight in the old story."

I know the old story. It's one of my favorites. It goes something like this: It's about the knight who left the castle to go riding out to do battle to gain one further element of distinction in the king's eyes, another plume for his helmet. He was gone for two years. One day the watch looked out and saw the knight returning across the plain, reeling in the saddle, his armor battered, bloody, beaten—a caricature of what he'd once been.

They let down the drawbridge. The horse clattered across the moat, into the courtyard. The knight fell out of the saddle, at the feet of his king, and the king looked down and said, "Sir Knight, what has happened to you!"

And the knight said, "Sire, I have been out attacking, razing, and pillaging your enemies on the north side of the mountain."

And the king said, "But I *have* no enemies on the north side of the mountain." To which the knight responded plaintively, "You do *now*, Oh Sire!"

Matilda hasn't made it any easier for me.

As I left Albany to come down here tonight, she gave me some last-minute advice. She said, "I know it's a difficult subject and a tough group. But don't be intimidated. And don't try to be charming, witty, or intellectual. Just be yourself."

I'll try.

The more I learn about government and especially about this democracy, the more deeply convinced I become that one of our greatest strengths as a people is our right to full and free expression.

No people have benefited more from the gift of free speech and a free press. Never before in history has the gift been so generously given, nor so fully used. From the very launching of our nation, these freedoms were regarded as essential protections against official repression.

When the geniuses who designed this wonderful ship of state came to draw the blueprints, they remembered Britain and other lands which had discouraged criticism of government and public officials, declaring it defamatory and seditious. The founding fathers considered that to be one of the worst parts of British tyranny. They were convinced that much of the struggle for American freedom would be the struggle over a free press.

So they were careful to provide that the right of free expression, through a free press, would be preserved in their new nation, especially insofar as the press dealt with government and public officials. They declared that right of free expression in the First Amendment to the Constitution. And wrote it in the simplest, least ambiguous language they could fashion.

Listen to its clarity, its sureness: "Congress shall make no law respecting an establishment of religion, or prohibiting the free exercise thereof, or abridging the freedom of speech or of the press. . . ."

Having provided for the right of free speech for the whole citizenry, they went further and provided *separately* for "freedom of . . . the press." As broadly as possible. Not tentatively. Not embroidered with nuances. Not shrouded and bound up in conditions. But plainly, purely.

Remember the context. The founding fathers knew precisely what they were dealing with. They had a press. And the press of their time was not only guilty of bad taste and inaccuracy; it was partisan, reckless, sometimes vicious. Indeed, the founding fathers were themselves often at the point end of the press sword.

In view of that experience, they might have written amendments that never mentioned freedom of the press. Or they might have tried to protect against an imperfect press like the one they dealt with, with conditions, qualifications, requirements, penalties.

But they didn't.

They knew the dangers. They knew that broad freedoms would be inevitably accompanied by some abuse and even harm to innocent people.

Knowing all the odds, they chose to gamble on liberty.

•   •   •

And the gamble has made us all rich.

Overall, the press has been a force for good—educating our people, guarding our freedom, watching our government, challenging it, goading it, revealing it, forcing it into the open.

Teapot Dome, the Pentagon Papers, Watergate, even the recent revelations of corruption in New York City, these are all examples of disclosures that might never have occurred were it not for our free press.

The press's insistence on forcing the White House to begin to tell the truth about the Iranian transaction is the most recent dramatic reminder of how the press works incessantly to assure our liberty by guaranteeing our awareness.

Less dramatically, the work of revelation by the press goes on day after day at all levels of government, all over the nation.

Surely, the preservation of this extraordinary strength is worth our eternal vigilance.

That's why I believe it's appropriate to consider the matter of freedom of the press now, at this moment.

It appears to me—and to others as well—that we are approaching a time when shifts in our law may seriously dilute the protection of the press and thereby weaken the fabric of this society.

Let me elaborate on what I mean by a shift in the law. Remember that our Constitution is not self-executing: it must be interpreted and applied by the Supreme Court. In effect, no matter how plain the language of the great document may appear to the rest of us, the Constitution will say what the Supreme Court says it says. The dimensions of the right to a free press are therefore in the care and at the mercy of the Supreme Court.

In recent decades, the Supreme Court has dealt often with the First Amendment and most of the time has expanded its reach, culminating in the landmark protection for the press in the case of *New York Times v. Sullivan* in 1964.

Sullivan said that notwithstanding the press was inaccurate, even negligent, and the inaccuracy substantially damaged a public figure, there would be no liability on the part of the press. Only if the press were guilty of actual malice—that is, a deliberate falsification, or conduct that evinced a reckless disregard—could there be a recovery.

The protection obviously was designed to free the press from the chilling, maybe paralyzing, effect of huge damage awards as a consequence of inaccuracy in trying to report the truth. Some believed this was too much protection: they called it a license to defame, an invitation to dangerous, harmful carelessness. But some, I among them, thought it was good and necessary policy, good and necessary law: that the gamble our founders took was still a good one. I continue to believe that.

We should remember something else about how our system works: Supreme Court law is not static or permanent. It changes.

Last year Justice White, who joined the majority in *Sullivan*, announced that he had become convinced that the Court struck "an improvident balance" in 1964. He urged that a better approach would be to return to much less protective common-law standards of liability.

And in a case this year, Justice Rehnquist indicated that he, too, would like to revisit *Sullivan* with an eye to the possibility of overruling it.

A number of lower court decisions are, if anything, even less encouraging.

All of us know about the *Westmoreland* and *Sharon* cases, in which two distinguished federal trial judges denied the requests for summary judgment made by the media defendants. In my view we should be even more interested in the *Tavoulareas v. Washington Post* case, not just for what it suggests about malice and liability, but for what it implies with respect to hard investigative journalism.

The opinion of the majority of the three-judge panel that upheld the jury's award of more than 2 million dollars in damages is indeed ominous. It showed a willingness—more, an enthusiasm—for detailed scrutiny of the reportorial and editorial process. And it implied, as I read it, that a reputation for hard investigative journalism should be scored against the defendant as some evidence of a penchant for maliciousness.

• • •

That's like saying if I catch you playing the game hard, I'm going to assume you're playing it dirty.

Chilling, indeed.

And still another harbinger: Justice Antonin Scalia, whose vote in the *Tavoulareas* case would have made the *Washington Post* liable, is now a member of the highest court and has been added to those already unhappy with *Sullivan*. He is a concededly excellent judge, a man of charm and persuasiveness. But he does not share the reluctance of the majority in *Sullivan* to threaten the press with vulnerability to libel judgments.

Ask Rowland Evans and Bob Novak. In *Ollman v. Evans*, a Circuit Court of Appeals decision in 1984, Judge Scalia argued strongly for a *relaxation* of the protection of reporters and urged the court to leave the protection of the press to legislatures.

Conservatives generally seem to sense this is a good time to strike. Some have recently proposed making simple "negligence" the standard for responsibility for injurious inaccuracy. That's good news for public figures who may become plaintiffs and more bad news for reporters and the media generally.

What would it do to a small newspaper, magazine, or station to be subjected to a multimillion-dollar verdict because a jury discovered its reporter didn't make what the jury considered to be a reasonable search, perhaps in the library, perhaps through the clips, perhaps seeking out witnesses, perhaps checking their stories, checking out their references, going to experts?

There is considerable other evidence to suggest that the courts are moving gradually, but consistently, away from *Sullivan* and toward less protection for the press.

Floyd Abrams, noted attorney and expert on the First Amendment, says the *Sullivan* principles are now under "sustained attack." Numerous legal analyses are available describing the signs of what another well-known attorney and champion of the First Amendment, Victor Kovner, has called "the move to modify *Sullivan*," which he warned would be a "true tragedy."

One more point about the Supreme Court: Putting aside its somewhat esoteric legal jurisdiction, the truth is that the Court is a living institution. Its nine members are subject to the same influences and instructed by the same public events that affect and instruct you and me.

Their decisions to some extent reflect changing circumstances in the world around them, or changing ideas about what is reasonable or wise. That means that when trying to predict a change in First Amendment rulings, the quality of the press as perceived by the public is a relevant factor.

In the *Federalist Papers*, Alexander Hamilton asks: "What is the liberty of the press? . . . Its security, whatever fine declarations may be inserted in any constitution respecting it, must altogether depend on public opinion and on the general spirit of the people and the government."

That's still true.

A press regarded by the public as careless or reckless invites the attention of the Supreme Court and tempts it to perform corrective judicial surgery. That's what Mr. Dooley meant when he said, "Th' Supreme Coort follows th' iliction returns."

That raises the questions: What is the public perception of the press today? Is it regarded as less than perfect? And if so, how specifically?

It might be worth noting here that in earlier times many of our leading public officials were among the press's harshest critics.

Today the press is apt to refer to a public official who criticizes the media as "Nixonian." Well, if presidential labels are appropriate, the media might just as fairly call its critics "Washingtonian," "Jeffersonian," "Wilsonian," "Rooseveltian," or "Kennedyesque."

For example, George Washington called the press "infamous scribblers."

Jefferson wrote: "Even the least informed of the people have learnt that nothing in a newspaper is to be believed."

Theodore Roosevelt added action to his vitriol: he had Joseph Pulitzer and his *New York World* indicted for criminal libel after the newspaper charged corruption in connection with the digging of the Panama Canal.

William Howard Taft found one paper so bad as to be "intolerable." He told his assistant not to show him the *New York Times*: "I don't think reading the *Times* will do me any good and would only be provocative in me of . . . anger and contemptuous feeling."

Woodrow Wilson lost his conciliatory disposition in dealing with the press. He said, "The real trouble is that the newspapers get the real facts but do not find them to their taste and do not use them as given them, and in some of the newspaper offices, news is deliberately invented."

How about FDR? He invented a dunce-cap club to which he would banish reporters whose questions annoyed him.

And of course President Kennedy tore up all the White House subscriptions to the *Herald Tribune* because he didn't think its coverage of him was fair.

Frankly, I think all those guys were a bit thin-skinned.

Obviously, governors are a good deal more forbearing than presidents have been.

But the truth is that criticism of the press by its natural targets, by public officials, governors, presidents, however illustrious, is not necessarily good evidence of the press's imperfection. Indeed, it can be argued that it is the best evidence of the press's effectiveness.

The press's job is to find the whole truth, especially that part of it which is forgotten, ignored, deliberately concealed, or distorted by public officials. The better the press does its job, the more likely future generations will be reading colorful condemnations of reporters and commentators by today's politicians.

And the more likely that the historical record will be truthful and accurate.

I think I understand this as a public official myself. Although I believe I have been treated very well by the press overall, from time to time

I have had occasion to make my own criticisms of some members of the press and their coverage in particular cases.

Frankly, the response has revealed that politicians aren't the only ones who are sensitive. I'm sure that despite that response, I will continue to express occasional criticisms of the media, as I'm certain you will of me. I hope we will both profit from such exchanges.

But of much more concern to the press than criticism from me and other public officials should be the criticism that comes from candid, thoughtful members of the press itself. Recently, it has been harsh indeed. What's worse, the public at large appears to agree.

Harper's Magazine observed that when the *Westmoreland* case hit the headlines, a "flood" of commentary from the press ensued. Editorial writers noted that the press was "widely maligned, criticized, abused, and, worst of all, 'distrusted.' " They pointed to numerous polls and "the public's conspicuous failure to be outraged when reporters were barred from Grenada."

Harper's continued: "Though Americans ritually intone their devotion to the 'freedom of the press,' they delight in repeating another prized national dictum: 'Don't believe what you read in the papers.' "

The press itself attributes much of this public disfavor to its own curable defects. Thus "pack journalism" is a frequently heard complaint: the press's dependence on one another, forging a uniform point of view so as to avoid embarrassing differences . . . the automatic acceptance of what other reporters have written, as though every statement previously made by any reporter is indisputable . . . and the clannish locking of arms against critics from outside.

Hodding Carter says: ". . . we are very, very good at pitching and very, very bad at catching . . . The press appears to be paranoid when facing criticism itself."

Of course there are times when a reporter's only reasonable access to important information requires that he or she assure the source of anonymity. The right to use that prerogative seems essential to effective reporting.

But another complaint frequently heard has to do with the press's *excessive* and unfairly exploitative use of unnamed, so-called confidential sources without checking their credentials, their motivation, or their reliability . . . sometimes even concealing them. Like quoting a political opponent against a public official anonymously, without identifying that significant characteristic of the source.

The habit of using unnamed sources on the naive, or cynical, assumption that because something was said at all it was true, seriously weakens the credibility of many stories and many reporters. The practice was forcefully condemned at the 1985 meeting of the American Society of Newspaper Editors in the keynote address by Richard D. Smyser, the president of the Society.

The editor of one of our national news magazines—Rick Smith of *Newsweek*—summarized the current criticism of the press, in seeking to inspire a graduating class of his alma mater to help the media help itself.

He said: "We [journalists] had proven ourselves to be the tenacious watchdogs of American society. But who was watching *us?*

"The searchlight has uncovered *our* abuses. Many Americans now express serious doubts about the techniques used to gather and report the news. Unidentified sources, ambush interviews, trial by allegation . . . instant analysis, impersonation are all questionable, yet increasingly commonplace, ways to 'get the story.'

"As a result, the press has acquired a reputation for being sneaky, devious and even untrustworthy.

"How has the press responded?

"Too often we have run for cover. We have hidden from our critics. And worst of all, we have hidden behind the First Amendment."

Tom Wicker adds a larger and more substantive complaint. He feels the media generally is too prone to promote what it believes is easiest for people to accept and in the process fails to cover significant issues adequately.

Obviously, the criticism that is set out here could be offset with generous accolades from sources equally credible. That is not the point. No one is more eager than I to proclaim how successfully the press has done its job over the last couple of hundred years, or how much better government might do its job.

But we must recognize the fact that right now this nation is debating—in the place where we make the rules, the Court—whether or not to limit the freedom of the press *despite* its good record of 200 years.

The possibility of limitation is a real one. I believe it requires that we admit the media's confessions of imperfection and what appears to be a disconcertingly serious loss of public favor that could encourage restrictions of First Amendment rights.

What specifically should we do?

The first thing we must do is sound the alert: to make it clear that we *are* facing a real threat of restriction of the constitutional freedom of the press. That's not easy. The drift of the Supreme Court doesn't get reported in the morning headlines. It's an elusive subject to which we must *direct* attention. Then, we must hope—and we can't be sure it will work—that the reaction will affect, for the better, both the press and the courts.

State government has a role.

In New York we have already created a strong tradition of governmental support for freedom of both speech and press. We have worked to give the press and the public the fullest possible opportunity to know and report on the workings of our state government.

Freedom of information laws, open meeting laws, whistle-blower laws, unique disclosure requirements, shield laws, and maximum accessibility for the benefit of the press on a day-to-day basis have been hallmarks of our administrations since 1975, and will continue to be as long as I am governor.

We can do more in New York. We can enlarge open meeting laws, adopt effective penalties for violation of the freedom of the information law, put cameras in the courtroom, and adopt new disclosure laws for public officials. We can push for an expanded use of our cable television outlet "New York Span," making it more like the extremely effective C-Span national cable that has been a dramatically useful addition to the nation's media.

•   •   •

But in the end, I think the best answer to the threat to the First Amendment is going to be found, as Fred Friendly, former president of CBS News, put it, "not in the courtrooms but in the newsrooms of America."

And so . . . what can the press do?

I believe it's basically a matter of improving the quality of what is both the best media the nation has ever known and a media still perceptibly far from the excellence it is capable of. But don't take it from me.

Tom Wicker made the point by saying that the most effective way to avoid incurring the wrath of the judicial gods is to work harder to guarantee thoughtful, informed, complete, and accurate reporting of the news. The *New York Times* put it this way in a January 1985 editorial:

> To deserve the extraordinary protections of American law . . . all of journalism needs a stronger tradition of mutual and self-correction. The more influential the medium, the greater the duty to offer a place for rebuttal, complaint, correction and re-examination. Beating the arrogance rap is even more important than escaping the rap for libel.

The notion of self-criticism is now being pursued by some well-known newspapers like the *Boston Globe, Hartford Courant, Newark Star-Ledger, Washington Post, New York Times,* and, most notably, the *Wall Street Journal.* All are undertaking various efforts at self-correction. It's an idea worth encouraging further.

As is the possibility that print, television, and radio organizations might want to make explicit and public the standards they expect of the press. There is, as Fred Friendly reminds us, a difference between the right to do and the right thing to do. Perhaps that difference should be spelled out. My former profession, the practice of law, does so. The medical profession does. We're fighting to institutionalize stronger and clearer standards of ethical behavior for politicians and public officials.

Why couldn't journalists at least state theirs? Because of the special place held by freedom of the press, it would have to be done without legislation or even private imposition. It could be done by just articulating and recommending the standards. By itself, that could help.

And let me offer you what I believe is an opportunity for all the media to make a contribution to the forming of public policy in this nation: Cover the public issues more thoroughly. Cover campaigns even more extensively. Cover state and local government more deeply. Not just press events created by candidates or public officials.

There is near-unanimity that the recently concluded campaigns, federal and state, were among the most unproductively negative in our history. Many believe this is attributable largely to the fact that so much of today's campaigning for major office must be done through extravagantly expensive twenty-eight-second TV and radio commercials, which practically mandate simplistics and labels . . . that in turn invite negativism.

This development is encouraged, I think, by the fact that our people are not well enough educated by the media in the details of the substantive issues that are central to our government, and that are presumably the most intelligent subjects for discussion in any campaign.

Is it really economically impossible for network television to voluntarily devote a half hour every night, while most people are still awake, to the discussion, maybe even at some length, of important public issues, a kind of prime-time "Nightline"? Couldn't all the networks voluntarily agree to the same half-hour slot to make the only competition one concerning *which* public issues the viewers are most interested in?

Is there no alternative to the habit of newspapers refusing to discuss issues in campaigns for statewide office or even national office or to give full treatment to the campaign until just a few weeks before Election Day, on the theory that people aren't interested until then? Can't the media focus on important issues even if the candidates or officials don't?

Isn't it possible you could make people *more* interested?

Let me make clear, too, what I am not suggesting.

I do *not* suggest that the government *impose* additional requirements on electronic media in the name of the public interest. As a matter of fact, I have made the point a number of times before that I believe the interpretation of the constitutional right of free press should be changed in one particular: it should move toward the conclusion that the electronic press deserves the same kind of freedom that is enjoyed by the print press.

There are, of course, differences, but the functions are basically the same: Like print, the electronic press informs, educates, advocates, and entertains. And it becomes increasingly apparent that its function is as vital as the print media to the welfare of the nation.

I daresay if there had been a a six o'clock news in the eighteenth century, the word in the First Amendment might have been "media" instead of "press."

Let me conclude:

The press is about finding the truth and telling it to the people.

In pursuit of that, I am making a case for the broadest possible freedom of the press.

But that great gift comes with great responsibility.

The press—print *and* electronic—has the power to inform, but that implies the power to distort.

You have the power to instruct, but that implies the power to mislead.

You have the power to uplift, but that implies the power to demean.

You can lead our society toward a more mature and discriminating understanding of the process by which we choose our leaders, make our rules, and construct our values.

Or you can encourage people to despise our systems and avoid participating in them.

You can teach our children a taste for violence, encourage a fascination with perversity and inflicted pain.

Or you can show them a beauty they have not known.

You can work wonders—on a page, on a screen.

You can make us all wiser, fuller, surer, sweeter than we are.

• • •

Or you can do less. And worse.

And one of the miracles of this democracy is that you are free to make all the choices.

The heart of my message tonight is that we must *work* . . . to keep it that way, to keep the miracle alive.

Thank you for asking me to speak.

·

PART II

———

1987 — 1989

·

This second inaugural provided me with a chance to describe accomplishments instead of just making promises. It was a pivotal time in my administration, for it gave me an opportunity to assess the first term while setting an agenda for the second. The speech also pointed out the potential we had not yet realized in our great state. What it failed to anticipate was the lurking recession that would strike the nation and New York in the last months of my second term, although the contradiction between America, the land of miracles, and the actual state of the country in 1987 is discussed. Looking back, I'm not sure whether that was inadvertence or a reluctance to mar this opportunity to be optimistic with dire predictions of impending hardship.

I feel many things at this moment. Most of all I feel gratitude:

Gratitude to Matilda, our parents, our children, our family.

Gratitude to all of you who supported us and encouraged us. Especially in the early years, when my obvious limitations and imperfections seemed to make the chance for success in public life so remote.

Gratitude to the hardworking men and women on my staff and in my cabinet, in all the state agencies and in the legislature, who, working together in the past four years, created a record of achievement that helped earn us an extraordinary election victory.

I am grateful to a kind Providence that bestows blessings with a generosity far beyond anything we could earn. And in a very special way, I feel gratitude to the Empire State, and to this amazing place of miracles, called America.

"Miracle" is, I believe, not too grand a word for the magnificent idea of democracy and its blueprint, the United States Constitution, whose two-hundredth birthday we celebrate this year. We began with thirteen diverse and often quarrelsome colonies, native peoples with their own separate and powerful cultures, and a vast land, much of it wilderness. And from these things we created a country that now reaches from ocean to great ocean and beyond, the freest and most powerful nation in the world.

For two hundred years this nation has met challenge after challenge.

For two hundred years it has grown and prospered, realizing more and more of the daring promises of the Declaration of Independence, the promises embodied by our Statue of Liberty. Opening, ever wider, the circle of opportunity. First to the colonists, then to the pioneers, then to immigrants from every part of the earth.

No, "miracle" is not too grand a word for America's success in providing sustenance and opportunity for the people of ten generations, many of whom, were it not for this place, would have lived whole lives without hope.

My administration has been built on that belief . . . that the miracle is not over.

Built on the belief that New York is *still* a place of hope and opportunity for those willing to join the unique American experiment in democracy.

I talked about that belief four years ago when I stood on this platform for the first time.

I talked about progressive pragmatism and the idea of family. About the dangers of social Darwinism. About Rabbi Hillel and Pope John the Twenty-third and Momma and Poppa and Ellis Island.

I said then all of the things that were in my mind and in my heart.

Some approved of the words but said that four years of actual governance would show them to be unrealistic. But now, four years later, having applied those ideas to the task of serving this wonderful state of nearly 18 million people, I believe it all, *even more assuredly and more passionately* than I did then.

For nearly 1,500 days we struggled to make our inaugural rhetoric everyday reality. And now we can look back and see how our beliefs have worked to improve the lives of our people in tangible ways.

In 1983, we promised jobs. Now over 900,000 more New Yorkers are at work.

In 1983, we reminded people that part of what makes the "miracle" work is our reverence for the rule of law, which gives us the order and stability that in some parts of the world are imposed with tanks and bayonets and secret police.

And since then, we have restored and strengthened every part of our criminal justice system.

In 1983, we committed ourselves in a special way to the middle class and the working people of this state . . . those struggling to pay their taxes, meet their mortgage or their rent payments, and educate their children.

We kept that commitment.

We enacted the largest tax cut in our history and removed from the rolls altogether 500,000 New Yorkers who work and are still poor.

We provided thousands of hardworking families—not poor enough to be on welfare, nor rich enough to be worry-free—an opportunity they would not have had without this government's help: the chance to own their own homes.

We made massive new investments in the public schools that have given opportunities to our children for nearly 200 years.

And *still* we balanced our budgets more rigorously than ever before.

In the process, we did not forget the most vulnerable of us.

I said four years ago that a society as blessed as ours should be able to find room for all at the table, shelter for the homeless, care for the elderly and infirm, and hope for the destitute.

And those words became laws.

We adopted strong nutrition programs and the most ambitious programs for the homeless and for people suffering with AIDS in the United States. We helped relieve the burdens of families caring for their retarded children. We increased shelter allowances. And we gave new opportunities for work to New Yorkers on welfare.

This list of accomplishments is no personal boast: these were not *my* achievements.

They were produced by a government led by Democrats and Republicans. By upstaters and downstaters. By men and women from every part of the state, people of every creed and color, representing all of us.

We proved, together, that the New York idea works: That government can have both a heart and a head, both common sense and compassion. That we can balance our books without ignoring the reasonable needs of the struggling middle class and poor.

Most of all, by our performance, we have made one point, over and over. We have shown that we are at our very best as a people when we recognize a single basic truth:

That we are, all of us, connected one to another. That "no man is an island . . ." No woman. No neighborhood. No village. No state. No nation . . . either.

That we touch one another. That we need one another. And so we should work together and hope together for the good of all of us.

That's the essence of the New York idea.

I think it's right to recall our achievements, if only to *remind* ourselves what we are capable of if we work together.

And we *need* to be reminded. Because it would be wrong to let the rejoicing obscure the fact that we still have much to do.

We have more people at work than ever before in this state, but still too many are denied the chance to earn their own bread.

There are single parents desperate for the day care that will allow them to work in order to provide for their families.

There are families—and individuals—who live in dread of a hospital bill that will deny them the little security they have earned with years of toil.

There are families anguished by their inability to take care of aging loved ones not able to care for themselves.

And there appear to be more homeless than ever, despite all our efforts.

There are thousands of children having children. Thousands more ravished by drugs. Some so desperate . . . that they take their own lives.

Faced with these hard facts, we have a number of choices.

Those of us who are comfortable can choose to pretend that the problems don't exist.

We can look around at the unemployed steelworkers and the other thousands denied the chance to work, at the hard-pressed middle class, at the homeless huddled in doorways, at children barely in their teens who turn to drugs or parenthood as an antidote to despair.

We can see more and more elderly living in fear of destitution and abandonment; we can hear the eloquent cries of America's religious leaders, including the Catholic bishops, on behalf of our voiceless poor. . . .

. . . And we can dismiss it *all*, on the assumption that *the price of comfort for most of us is that government must forget the rest of us.*

Or we can say, as we are being urged to by some on the national scene, that we have stretched our minds and our wills and our resources as far as they will go. That, for all government has tried to do over the last several decades, we have only been "losing ground."

That we now have to settle for less than we once believed we were capable of. Less than was done by our forebears who lifted an entire generation out of poverty, defeated fascism, and built this country into the strongest nation in the world.

We have another choice!

We can aim higher.

We can try to do more with this wonderful opportunity.

We can dare to be bolder.

And wiser.

We can recall that since Franklin Roosevelt lifted himself from his wheelchair to lift this nation from its knees, until just a few years ago, America found the strength and the intelligence to help millions of people rise from poverty to the middle class and beyond. Your grandparents, your parents . . . and mine.

And in a more modest way we can be encouraged by our own last four years, all of us working together to produce a record of balanced budgets without forgetting that the first purpose of government in New York is to improve the conditions of people's lives.

Ladies and gentlemen, I do not believe that our future is beyond our control.

I do not believe that this great state, or this great land, has been exhausted in the process of helping earlier generations. Or that we must now resign ourselves to a future of lower expectations.

I do not believe that the "miracle" is over and that the circle of opportunity has closed.

Make no mistake about it; the path I would suggest is a hard one. It would be easier to surrender to lower expectations or give in to the temptation of reckless expenditure . . . as others have.

Making the miracle work requires our greatest skill and courage. It requires that we continue the economic resurgence that provides our state with the wealth we need to prepare for our future and cope with the present.

To do that we must contain our expenditures and the taxes that support those expenditures.

We will have to have the intelligence to continue to avoid the kind of foolish *mis*management of revenue sources and profligate spending that has left the federal government with a punishing 200 billion dollar budget deficit and debtor status in the world of international trade.

Here in New York *we will have to have the will to say no to some of the things we may want, so that we can say yes to the things we really need.*

And all the time, we must keep in mind that nicely balanced

budgets, which ignore the need to educate our children or to care for our mentally ill, or keep strong our criminal justice system, would be the emblem of failure and hypocrisy.

A hard challenge indeed . . . doing it all, with balance and fairness.

We will not do it perfectly. There will be failures and disappointments along the way. But in the four years that ended yesterday, we proved that, working together, over time, we can meet that challenge. That should be a matter of immense satisfaction . . . and great encouragement.

It is to me.

I am not afraid of the days ahead.

I believe that we are strong enough and wise enough to reach higher ground than ever before, and I believe that we will.

I see our economy growing, spurred by lower taxes and our state's vast capacity for high technology. Improved by fiber-optic thruways linking our computers and communications systems and businesses. Our growth assisted by opportunity zones, new forms of collaboration between management and labor, new forms of worker participation, and new sources of investment from billions of dollars of pension fund monies.

I see more jobs: good jobs for all who are able to work. I see less need for welfare.

I see a future where our children and young people get a better start in life than anywhere on this planet.

I see our air and water cleaner and safer, our natural beauty preserved—with the help of our bond issue and Superfund.

I see a new emphasis on the basic values that over the years made sweet and strong the soul of the American people at their very best. Values like: Honesty. Courage. Responsibility. Dignity. A concern for one another. Yes. A sense of family.

I see leaders—of all political persuasions—who have the wisdom and courage to compromise when compromise is in order, and the strength to stand up when principle demands it.

I see a new era of accountability ushering in a new era of opportunity.

I see a future with *all* the government we need but *only* the government we need.

I saw it four years ago. And today, I see it even more clearly.

Together you and I, and all of us in New York, have the ability to make the Constitution's third century and Lady Liberty's second our greatest ever, with a better, freer, more prosperous, more just society.

That vision is as real to me as the sight of Liberty Island and our magnificent Lady Liberty.

And that sight has been real to me for half a century.

I remember it from my childhood in South Jamaica, in Queens. I remember having visited the statue and I remember later, on hot afternoons after supper, my friends and I would go up to the rooftops of the tenements and apartments where we lived on 150th Street.

We would stand on the tar roof, still hot from the summer sun, lean against the low walls, and look west toward the horizon and the faraway towers of Manhattan.

And if we turned our eyes a little toward the great harbor, we could imagine Lady Liberty holding up her lamp, like an evening star.

New York State. A place of miracles. The Lady Liberty . . . beckoning us to opportunity. Together, New York and the Lady allowed us to dream all that might be.

Even now, if I try, I can remember. I can see the torch . . . the star . . . in the distance. I can feel the aching to belong. I can see my father, again, weary from the long day's labor, his arms folded, his shirt stained with sweat, watching us as we looked out to where the Lady stood. His tired, hopeful eyes telling us, "Go on, make your wish." Offering his silent prayer for his children.

I can bring it all back. And then I make my own silent plea.

"Lift your lamp, Lady.

"Lift it for those you've always welcomed.

"For the lonely and the friendless.

"For all the members of the human family the world so often finds it convenient to ignore, to despise or persecute.

"And for our brothers and sisters in this country. For the farm families and factory workers fighting to hold on to their farms and their jobs and their dignity.

"For the parents struggling to give their children more than *they* had. More education, more opportunity, more hope.

"For the children. The children especially. The children everywhere who are lost and confused, adrift without values, without guidance. . . . Lift your lamp, Lady.

"For the millions among us who are without work or enough to eat or even a roof overhead.

"And lift your lamp, as well, for the fortunate among us. For the well fed, for the well educated, for the satisfied.

"Don't let us forget who we are and where we came from and what your promise has pledged us to.

"Remind us always, as you lift your lamp beside the golden door.

"Make us remember the beauty . . . the wonder of this place of miracles made for sharing.

"Write it in our hearts, Lady."

No, ladies and gentlemen, the miracle is not over.
Thank you!

Five years before Vice President Dan Quayle tried to introduce the question of traditional values into the 1992 campaign by referring to the television character Murphy Brown as evidence of dissipation, my administration was focusing on the question of values as a vital one in New York. I haven't stopped.

Since this talk, in 1987, on values, I have given many others, including a portion of my 1993 State of the State Address that is included in this volume. There I described the New York proposition, a philosophy built on basic values: the chance to provide oneself with a good living through work; the freedom to think, believe, speak and act; the citizen's responsibility to earn his or her own way; and the absolute necessity of people in a diverse society like ours to understand our interconnectedness and interdependence.

The format of this morning's program puts me in an unenviable position.

Although the Constitution is a subject I study and talk about with relish, and although the gift of literacy that I was given by P.S. 50 in South Jamaica, Queens, is one I regard with immense gratitude, you've already heard those topics treated by Chief Judge Wachtler, Louise Matteoni, and the other distinguished panel members—people much better equipped than I to discuss them.

Instead, then, of trying to expand on what the panelists have already said so well, let me suggest another direction in which their words on the Constitution and on literacy may lead us.

It's a direction into territory that's already been explored and charted but is, nevertheless, somewhat perilous—with few sure footholds or reliable signposts and much disputed land.

It's the whole question of teaching values in public schools.

When, finally, we use our gift of freedom to make ourselves all as literate as we should be, when we are all able to read and understand the Constitution—and the Declaration of Independence and the *Federalist Papers* and all the documents that order us and describe us as a people—what ultimate ideas will we find in them? What values, norms, and codes of conduct will they teach us?

Should we then, having found them, try to teach any of these values to children in our public schools?

If so, which?

Or should we avoid even trying to teach any at all, for fear that we may encourage the teaching of religions, or specific orthodoxies, that will threaten our most precious gift of all . . . our freedom.

Difficult questions. Exactly the kind we politicians like to avoid.

But I believe they are so important it would be wrong to neglect them.

Le me add quickly that the very idea that anyone my age should purport to talk about values—let alone teach them to our children—is a personally difficult one.

How can anyone of my generation, the generation largely in control of things in recent years, talk about values and try to teach lessons that we seemed to have learned so imperfectly ourselves?

How could *we*—who have so often done the wrong thing to one another—tell students that it is *their* duty to use all that they have been given to make a better world? We who did so much to pollute and poison the environment? We who allowed drugs to become so widely available that they are now one of the most menacing threats to the future of this generation? Isn't it hypocritical?

Mark Twain made the same point . . . a little more gently: "To be good and virtuous," he said, "is a noble thing, but to *teach* others to be good and virtuous is nobler still—and much, much easier."

That's good. Because if, as I fear, we have little right to hold ourselves out as examples, still I believe we have an obligation to try, at least, to teach the values on which our nation was founded.

We know that despite our personal failures, when this nation *has* remembered and acted upon those basic values we have made progress and thrived as a people.

Despite Howard Beach, Queens, and Forsyth County, Georgia, the civil rights of all citizens are more respected today than they were two decades ago.

Despite some of the failures in our schools, education *is* more widely available today than ever in our history.

Despite lingering discrimination, women are closer today than ever before to occupying the place they deserve in our society.

These are all embodiments of strong basic values on which this nation is built.

I believe we must point that out to our youth. And I believe they would welcome that instruction. They need it.

Today's children are confronted with more complexity, more distractions, more psychological pressures, more temptations than we were.

Every night prime-time television assails them with mindless sitcoms and soap operas that present ostentatious materialism and unrelenting self-gratification as the only goals worth pursuing, confronts them with "action" shows in which vigilantism is portrayed as the answer to crime and macho heroes who live by a code of violence are glorified, with videos that demean women and make a mockery of gentleness.

There's another syndrome involving children today—one my generation hardly knew—that is even more menacing . . . and can be deadly: drugs.

The statistics on the self-inflicted madness of drug abuse are frightening—hospital emergency rooms crowded; treatment centers overwhelmed; more and more victims, many of them adolescents and even preadolescents; a rising death toll.

And the drug epidemic is only one aspect of a broader *syndrome of self-destructive activity* involving our youth: the steady rise in alcoholism and other forms of reckless abuse of their own minds and bodies . . . even teenage suicide.

Add to these a disgraceful school drop-out rate and the confusing wave of adolescent pregnancy, and we're left with profoundly disturbing, fundamental questions: Have we cared enough about what happens to our children? What is it that we believe in, that we value? What *are* we teaching them? Are we sure enough about our own values to convince youngsters to live *for* something, to believe in themselves, in the significance of their own lives? To believe in believing?

If so, how do we go about doing it? How do we stop the madness?

And there are more questions. . . .

What do we do about AIDS? If, in fact, it is now threatening a wider and wider part of our population, do individuals have the right to engage in personal expressions of intimacy that threaten themselves with perhaps deadly illness . . . and threaten those beyond them? Is it time to surrender privacy in the name of public safety?

Can a surrogate mother "own" the child she carries from an implanted seed by agreement with a man and woman who understand that she was merely hosting *their* fetus?

Is the governor from a western state right to raise a question as to whether we are trying too hard to keep people alive for too long because society can't afford the costs?

How do we decide if life is worth living in a society where the technology needed to make it happen is available only to the superrich?

What should be the test for opening Shoreham: Economic necessity? A new chance for economic growth? The threat to health and life? How much of a threat? How important is one life? Who should decide?

By what rules?

By what *values?*

These are powerful questions that can hit one with great force.

It happened to me not long ago, in a New York City schoolyard. I was there to talk to a couple of hundred ninth- and tenth-graders about the dangers and madness of using crack.

I spoke about the beauty of life, the opportunities in their future, and the threat to all their hopes and dreams that drugs posed.

After I'd finished, I asked them if what I'd said made sense to them.

Most of them nodded. One didn't. A boy, maybe fifteen, with a chipped front tooth, who looked at me with his head half-cocked to the side, his face impassive but his skepticism showing through quite clearly.

"Didn't you agree with me?" I asked. "That your life is too precious to give away to drugs?"

"I'm not sure," he answered. "The stuff you said sounded good, but I don't really know. I'm not sure what my life is for, why we're here. I really don't understand it."

I was stunned by his answer. By its simplicity. By its staggering profundity.

I was at a loss.

I told him he was awfully bright to be thinking about those kinds of questions, and that a lot of what life was about was looking for answers to those questions.

And that if he did that with his whole mind and his heart, he'd never be sorry, and he'd discover all sorts of wonderful things as he searched. But that if he started looking for answers in three-minute drug highs, all he'd ever do was cripple his searching and all he'd ever be was sorry.

I don't think I reached him.

And I didn't leave those questions behind when I left the school-yard. They have followed me ever since that afternoon. And they've followed me here this morning. . . . That boy's need to be told and to somehow understand that his life—and everyone's—is good. And precious. And full of purpose. That he has value.

And that we have values.

So, setting aside the personal tentativeness I have about speaking of values, let me tell you what I think.

Ideally, the primary and best source for instruction in values is the family.

There are other sources.

Churches and synagogues, youth organizations, and community groups, all of these can project a strong sense of values as well.

But it's clear that today we need more.

And I believe it's clear we need to turn to our public schools.

Of course, schools cannot, alone, counter the messages and pressures that bombard children. It's too much to ask teachers to do single combat with all of those influences.

But if schools can't be expected to do it all, they have proven in the past to be one of the best ways we have for exposing youth to the ideals and traditions—intellectual, ethical, moral—that form our common heritage.

Actually, asking whether schools should teach values may be the wrong question. The truth probably is that they do it, *inevitably*, whether formally or informally, deliberately or inadvertently.

Even when schools try to be totally silent on the question of ethics, of morals, their silence is *not* a neutral lesson. Silence teaches!

Silence teaches that the choice between good and evil is not important, the difference between right and wrong not significant, the difference between being a good or a bad citizen inconsequential.

That's a very real kind of instruction.

Given that, it seems to me that at the very least, schools should work to make young people aware that *some* standards of virtue and decency do exist.

I believe that can be done without teaching a specific religion or philosophy or instilling someone else's orthodoxy.

Not easily, but nonetheless, it can be done appropriately and effectively.

We can begin with the recognition that whether formally taught or not, at the core of every society is a set of moral values, a code of behavior, a credo. That has been so throughout history.

Even here in our uniquely free society where diversity of belief is protected and cherished, there is a rough—but clear—national understanding of what is right and wrong, what is allowed and what is forbidden, what we are entitled to and what we owe.

We can find much of that consensus in the original documents that defined us as a people. The Declaration of Independence and the Constitution reflect values at the core of American life . . . values implicit in the concept of ordered liberty, to which the founders of our nation mutually pledged their lives, their fortunes, their sacred honor . . . and our nation's future.

What were those values?

Here are some: An awareness of the profound ways in which we are all equal; reverence for the individual rights that issue from that equality, the rights of others as well as our own; a sense of the importance of working for a good greater than our individual goals, a common good; a respect for our system of laws, which so majestically balances individual rights and that common good; and, finally, a love for this place, America, that has dared to try to be true to these revolutionary insights and principles.

Now, these are real, tangible, specific values. And we can teach them to our young specifically. We can show them that:

equality,

individual rights,

the common good (or *community,* what I prefer to call "family"),

the rule of law, and

love of country

aren't just pat phrases to be wheeled out and paraded on national holidays. They are some of the realities on which our national life was founded. On which we have flourished. And on which America's future will be built.

As we study these values—and explicate them—it becomes clear that for all the genius and daring of their ideas and actions, America's founders did not invent these basic principles.

In drafting this magnificent new chapter in the history of government, they drew from a deep well of wisdom and history, from philosophical, cultural, and religious traditions that stretched back thousands of years . . . traditions that yielded other values on which our own great civic values are based. Traditions that were supposed to shape us and guide us in our coming together as a nation.

They include: a sense of personal worth, the importance of each individual person, the protection of one's self and others from all forms of degradation or abuse.

We can call these values *dignity* and *integrity.*

There are others. Real and specific values. Like:

compassion,

service, and

love of knowledge.

These values are not just sweet abstractions. Nice generalities. They are not inert ethical entities, but dynamic ways of understanding human nature and purpose—ways that men and women have struggled for centuries to define and develop.

As are the companion values of *responsibility* and *accountability*—the limitations on freedom created by the rights of others—and *the need for discipline and order*.

These are things that have been taught in places for centuries. They have guided much of the progress in this civilization. They can be formally taught again.

When the great thinkers of the Greek city-states first made explicit the dignity inherent in our nature as human beings, their insights were as startling and unsettling to the Mediterranean world of their day as gene-splicing is to ours.

Integrity isn't something that an ancient philosopher simply stumbled over on his way to work one day. It is the fruit of a tradition of learning that produced the Book of Exodus and the Psalms. It is an idea that Virgil and Cicero, Aquinas and Thomas Jefferson grappled with . . . refining and expanding it.

The development of the idea that we should love our neighbors as ourselves—the golden rule used by the great philosophers to teach compassion and service—has been as crucial to the course of human history as the splitting of the atom.

And basic to all these achievements has been a respect for knowledge—at best a *love* of knowledge—a sense of wonder and excitement for the human enterprise. A sense of delight that comes from understanding what you didn't understand before, from stripping away some of life's mystery, unraveling some of the reasons for things.

If there is anything that is the mark of a successful school—and of a successful society and civilization—it is the presence of that electric sense of wonder on which all our knowledge has been built.

Not all these values are written explicitly into our laws.

But they are part of the consensus—sometimes spoken, sometimes unspoken—that underlies our nation's conscience. They all continue to play a crucial role in how we live, how we conceive of ourselves and of others, what we cherish, and even how we construct our hopes and ambitions.

To recollect these things and to recall our history is a helpful reaffirmation of the existence of the essential understanding of values in this nation.

And to do it explicitly by making a list of shared values is an exercise I recommend to teachers and school boards and community groups.

But simply making a list is not enough. If we're serious about it, if we really believe that a life lived according to our code of values is a more fulfilled, more fully human life, then we must find concrete ways to teach values in our schools.

The obvious experts on that are those among us who are teachers and education professionals.

In many instances they have been doing it, and doing it well, for years. Our own Regents have included values components in the curricula they have already produced. What we need to do *now* is elaborate and expand their experience and the efforts of the other professionals.

Our educators remind us that a school should be a place where students have a pervasive exposure to the best we're capable of; where they learn self-esteem because they're treated as individuals with their own special dignity; where they begin to see that a community works best when each individual—their peers and those in authority—respects the rights of others, and that their actions have an effect on the community.

A school should be a place where students learn, as well, the necessity of discipline. Where they come to appreciate more fully that success—in the classroom, in the gym, or on the athletic field—requires self-control, practice, some measure of denying oneself immediate gratification . . . training that gradually corrects weaknesses and perfects strengths.

How can we accomplish all of this?

To a nonprofessional like myself, some broad ideas occur. We know that the curriculum—especially in areas like history, science, and literature—can be an effective instrument for transmitting values.

History can teach students that no man, no woman is an island . . . no people, no country either.

It can teach them to see events as connected, to realize that the world is ever-changing and evolving, but that the best—and the worst—of human instincts are constant.

Students can be taught that our own nation's history—and our state's—is more than a jumble of dates and events.

It's a continuous story built on outrageous dreams in millions of men and women, early settlers and wave after wave of those who came later, many in steerage or in chains, and who fought and struggled to make the dream they believed in come true for their children and those who would come after them. A real life struggle in which men and women gave all their talents—and sometimes their lives—to uphold freedom and equality. To eradicate racism and discrimination. To preserve the Union and the rule of law. To expand opportunity. And throughout this entire history, properly taught, it will be clear that this progress was largely guided and propelled by the values I speak of today.

So teaching history *well* is a good way to teach values.

And we can derive powerful instruction from biography and autobiography—in all their forms. Children need heroes. We all do. We can all benefit from reading Carl Sandburg's life of Lincoln or Dumas Malone's life of Jefferson. *A Man for All Seasons*, the dramatization of Thomas More's life; the diary of Anne Frank; the monumental achievements of Eleanor Roosevelt or of Martin Luther King, Jr.—all these, and many others, can teach us about integrity and courage and steadfastness. We can learn from people admired for their willingness to devote their lives to serving others.

If our teachers will point it out, literature can teach children that they're not the first ones in the world to experience fear or disappointment, failure or sorrow. It can teach them the great nobility we are capable of, at our best.

And it can show them, especially as they develop intellectually, how difficult it sometimes is to resolve the conflicts among values.

How patriotism doesn't always require us to march lockstep to the same drummer.

How integrity can mean standing alone.

Beyond the curriculum, schools should offer students opportunities to apply the values we say we share. Real opportunities to serve the community and its people—younger students and older residents, the sick, the homebound, anyone in need of the help students can provide, if given the chance. There are all sorts of community organizations that will provide them the opportunity. We should get them involved.

It is a common experience of people who volunteer their services that they get out of the experience more than they put in. For adolescents, particularly, one benefit may be a new sense of self-esteem . . . a new understanding of the idea of community.

Others are more competent than I to suggest all the specific ways to teach values. My point is that we need to be clearer about what we believe and what we value. We must overcome any reluctance to teach our values from every public pulpit, especially in our public schools.

Not just talk about them, but teach them.

And that work will involve everyone—the Board of Regents, school boards, teachers, administrators, parents, public officials, all the people of this state.

Where it's not being done it should be. Where it's being done we should continue to do it . . . and do it better.

If we do all these things—if we identify our basic values and teach them throughout the curriculum of our public schools—will it answer all the hard questions?

Will it make a difference? Where it counts, in the lives of our children?

Would it have made a difference to the boy in the schoolyard? Will it convince some youngsters that they are too good, too valuable—that they have too much to contribute to our society—to throw it all away by using drugs?

Will it keep some from committing suicide?

Will we see a decline in the drop-out rate, in teenage pregnancy? Will there be diminished violence and vandalism in the schools?

No one can say for sure.

Perhaps our efforts won't make a difference.

But I believe that, unless we try, we are conceding—in full view of our children—that there are forces whose evil power and sweep are too great to be met by instruction in values or by a summons to dignity and self-respect.

I don't believe such a concession to hopelessness is one any of us wants to make.

It would be an abdication of our responsibility as parents, as teachers, as public officials.

We must value responsibility more than that.

•　　　•　　　•

And, we know, our responsibility cannot end with mere exhortation. Hard as it is to teach values, we know there are other basic needs which, if not met, make instruction too difficult.

We have to invest more intelligently and more generously in our schools and our teachers.

We must remember that a child who comes to school malnourished will not learn well.

That lessons in self-love can be too hard to teach to a child who is abused at home.

That lessons in civility will ring hollow to students who wage a daily struggle merely to survive the violence of the streets.

That without the prospect of a job or of the chance to go to college if they choose, students won't be sufficiently motivated to succeed.

In the end, the best lesson in values is the example we give as individuals and as a society. What we do to give this generation of students, all of them, the same opportunities that most of us were given, the same chance to be everything they can be.

For me as a child, that work began at home, with my parents. With Momma and Poppa and church and rules, and discipline learned from the hard end of a broom.

But for me and probably most of you—and millions like us—it was continued and reaffirmed, fleshed out and fortified in public school.

I believe we need that help from our public schools today more than ever.

It may be the most important thing our schools can do.

I believe that as we teach literacy, we must teach the values that have made us a special people in the 200 years since we were joined together by the miracle of our Constitution.

Thank you for having me.

This address was more than a tribute to the courageous and valiant Israelis. The presidential primaries of 1988 produced a new outbreak of racial and religious alienation and hostility. I felt it was important to call on the members of the Jewish community to summon the memory of their long history of working constructively to overcome such divisions. The Jewish community did remember, as they always do, and worked hard to keep the peace. Eventually this moment of high tension passed and is now only a vague memory for most New Yorkers. I included the speech because the subject matter seems, regrettably, to be always a timely one. We must all continue to remember.

We are here today, as Americans, to pay tribute to Israel—our sister democracy in the Middle East—and to commemorate her forty years of existence.

Anniversaries are meant to be pleasant, reminiscent, full of joy and congratulation.

This celebration is all of that.

The state of Israel—economically afflicted, forced to bear a monstrous burden of arms, her very existence challenged by every nation save one in her region of the world—stands today after forty years, as a living testimony to the tenacious determination of a people to conduct their government as a true democracy.

Israel is, like our own country, a miracle of a place.

An immigrant nation where after two millennia of persecution Jews can live openly, proudly, securely . . . as Jews.

An immigrant nation where the survivors of the Holocaust can see their children and grandchildren protect and enrich and continue the truths they suffered for.

Where the Jews of Syria and Russia and Iraq—persecuted Jews—have freedom.

Where the Tribe of Dan—the Jews of Ethiopia—are reunited to the source of their faith, their hunger ended.

The miracle of Israel is, indeed, something to celebrate.

But we are here for another purpose as well.

It is not just pleasant to be here; it is necessary to be.

For the past four months, there has been a growing sentiment—even among some Jews—that it is not easy to be a friend of Israel, that Israel is in danger of losing her soul, of becoming a modern-day Sparta, an occupier and oppressor, willing—even eager, some say—to crush brutally a "children's crusade" among Palestinians.

The truth is that it's never been easy to be a friend of Israel. Her enemies have seen to that. But it's always been, and remains, if not easy, right for us as Americans. Right because there is a mutuality of interest between us and Israel; a mutuality of heritage embodied in the common foundations of Israel and America, two nations joined together by the same underlying principles, the same belief in the dignity of the individual, and in the responsibility of representative government to balance order with justice.

We have understood from the beginning that our obligation to the Israelis is based not on the shifting sands of geopolitical strategy, nor on a need to make shallow propaganda, but on the hard rock of moral obligation, on the sameness of values held in common.

Our obligation to Israel is built on a mutual belief in the same ultimate truths which have kept us together as peoples for the last forty years—and always should.

In a world where these beliefs are rare, the close relationship of Israel and America is a moral and philosophic imperative for both nations.

That it is right should be enough to gain support for the cause of Israel. But ever since Adam and Eve conspired to bite the apple, most people need something more than moral imperatives: they need pragmatic reasons.

153

And so there is a second perspective, based on hard facts. Israel remains the only reliable friend and ally of the United States and the democratic nations of the West in a region of vital, inescapable concern to us, a region where medieval monarchies or religio-political dictatorships are the rule.

I don't mean to suggest that the present troubles in the West Bank and Gaza are inconsequential, no more than a temporary inconvenience. In many ways, the peril posed by the uprising in the West Bank and Gaza is as dangerous as the massive military assaults she turned back before.

In each of her four decades of existence, Israel has faced a new threat. In 1948, she came to life under the guns of the Arab armies. Again, in 1956, and in 1967, in 1973, and now, in 1988.

What Israel's enemies have never been able to accomplish directly, they hope now to achieve by indirection, by convincing Israel's friends and allies to accept, perhaps even seek to impose, a solution that would give Israel untenable, indefensible borders, and that would signal for her the beginning of the end.

It would be foolish to say that this campaign could not succeed.

Too many people, I'm afraid—embarrassed by the broadcast scenes of conflict, appalled by the sight of beatings and bloodshed, confused by the images of a friend reacting with force to what, on the TV screen, might appear slight provocation—too many are willing to see the conditions Israel's enemies propose as reasonable.

But there are larger truths than the fleeting scenes flashed for a moment on the TV screen. There are the truths of history and the dominant truth of the present.

The fact is that, since her founding, Israel has lost more than 16,000 of her sons and daughters in warfare with forces threatening annihilation, not only of the state of Israel, but of the Jews who make their lives there.

The truth is that, despite the enormous cost of remaining strong under siege, Israel has never shrunk from the self-imposed obligation she assumed for the health, welfare, and education of both Jews and those willing to live in peace with Jews.

No child, born less than perfect, is denied the opportunity to correct what nature denied him or her at birth.

No child is denied food or medical care.

No child is denied the education needed to allow full participation in society.

No Jewish child, no Muslim child, no Christian child.

The truth is that when Arab states and Palestinian Arab leaders have had the chance to resolve the Palestinian Arab question, they've not done it, preferring to make refugees of their fellow Arabs.

Israel, by contrast—a tiny nation, neither oil-rich nor revenue-abundant—has welcomed an equal if not greater number of refugees forced from Arab lands, people in flight from true danger who found in Israel sanctuary, new homes, a chance to rebuild their lives.

The truth is that Israel has been willing to trade land for peace, to negotiate with enemies who—at a minimum—recognized her right to exist and to have defensible borders.

Those are some of the truths of history, all of them verifiable facts.

The first responsibility of Israel's friends at this moment is to remember these facts.

As to what solution, if any, can be fashioned in this present circumstance, there must be no rush to judgment or to action. Israel must never be forced onto the Scylla of nervous allies or the Charybdis of political expediency.

No matter what opinions others offer, the most important debate about solutions is the democratic debate taking place within Israel itself.

It would be a desecration of our friendship and of our historical memories now to demand that Israel become a co-conspirator in her own suicide; that she acquiesce in the establishment of a state within the occupied territories under a leadership not only hostile to Israel, but officially dedicated to her annihilation; that she cede, as part of this deadly pact, control of all or part of what is in fact—and should be recognized as—her capital, Jerusalem.

If we shouldn't try—and we shouldn't, either unilaterally or through international conferences—to dictate terms to Israel's people or to her Knesset, we can't help but be affected by the debate.

Since 1948, when one of our great presidents, Harry Truman, committed the full prestige of the United States to the protection and survival of Israel and the Jews who chose to make their lives

155

there, Israel has been an important—and bipartisan—element of our foreign policy.

And this year, forty years later, is an appropriate time to consider how our own democracy, as well as Israel's, has fared.

At the moment, Americans and New Yorkers are being challenged once again—as we have been throughout our history—to make of our deliberate diversity a great strength rather than an occasion of divisiveness, suspicion, and schism.

Howard Beach; Forsyth County; charges of police recklessness against minorities; a new outbreak of anti-Semitism; a resurgent nativism in the form of an "English-only" movement; a growing, palpable disparity between the haves and the have-nots—all these have all come together . . . incensing some, frightening many, and troubling everyone.

The matter of race relations has riveted our attention in recent days. And another event has sharpened the focus.

Just a couple of weeks ago the world's media gathered here to describe and record an election. They trained their cameras and their attention especially on one candidate, a black man. His name is Jesse Jackson.

He has had an unprecedented success: far beyond anything predicted.

He has millions of zealous supporters—and opponents just as fierce in their opposition.

He is much more talented than most, but like the rest of us, he is imperfect.

But he is something else . . . something much larger than himself, something that goes far beyond his own personal abilities and limitations.

He is a great cry for empowerment by a people fighting for the right to be judged on their merits.

Not everyone sees it this way.

But the campaign in New York did what campaigns are supposed to do: gave the voters in a democracy an opportunity to judge the merits of each candidate. It was the voters, not the candidates themselves, and not the media, who delivered the verdict.

In the end, I believe, New York's voters acted evenhandedly, sending Mike Dukakis and Jesse Jackson out of New York on the high road, with the city of New York making Jesse Jackson its winner and the state overall choosing Dukakis.

It's in these exercises of democracy—not in violence or propaganda—that we find the best hope of reconciling our differences.

And again—as in the case of the present Israeli troubles—history can be instructive.

It would be wrong for any of us to allow our differences—or even the hurt and righteous anger we've all felt at times, all of us, Jew and Gentile, white and black—because of racial or ethnic slurs . . . it would be wrong, and a terrible waste, to allow that to rob us of the memory of what we are at our best.

The memory of how much we have accomplished working together, in coalitions of people whose own individual and different histories of oppression, persecution, exclusion, and even attempted extinction, taught them to value freedom and each other.

Perhaps no group in this city is better equipped than blacks—through their own history—to understand the biblical account of the Jewish people's shedding of Pharaoh's chains.

Black Americans' pursuit of the vision of justice and equality in America has been no less epic than the journey of the people of the Exodus out of Egypt, as they followed the pillar of fire and pursued the promise and the dream of a new land and a better life.

Blacks, like Jews, have persevered through harsh times and hard times, through rejection and pain and hostility.

They have seen the worst in men, even here in this great miracle of a place called America, but never abandoned the dream.

The greatest black leader of our time even echoed the biblical language of the Jews: "I've seen the promised land. And I want you to know that we as a people will get to the promised land."

Like Moses, Martin Luther King, Jr., did not live to see his people's dream fulfilled. But he inspired a whole generation to keep on striving towards the dream.

During the 1960s, at a peak of the civil rights movement, it was Jews as much as any other group who joined blacks in the struggle to loose the chains of oppression.

Two young Jews from New York, Andrew Goodman and Michael Schwerner, joined a young Mississippi black, James Chaney, in trying to persuade blacks to register to vote. They died together, in a field in Mississippi—for freedom, for each other, for all of us.

Rabbi Israel Mowshowitz, a dear friend of mine who at the moment is ill and whom we remember with our prayers, marched with Martin Luther King, Jr., over and over, under all sorts of circumstances.

Over and over again through the years blacks and Jews, black organizations and Jewish organizations worked, and struggled, together, in pursuit of freedom and justice.

It would be easier not to admit there is a long distance yet to go.

It would be easier to ignore the fact that over these past forty years our society and our state have become even more diverse.

Hispanics, with a long and proud history of contribution to our country, have become a dynamic force in our state and particularly in this city. Seekers from all over the world—from India and Indochina, from East Africa, from every corner of the world—have enriched the American mosaic.

It would be easier, especially for those of us who are doing reasonably well—or even unreasonably well—to pretend that our comfort is everyone's comfort, our good fortune everyone's good fortune, to pretend that all is well.

But you know that would be a pretense.

You know that our recent history has represented a retreat not just from the civil rights advances of the past, but from much more.

You know the chains that shackle the teenager who is dropping out of school and turning in despair to drugs. The despair of the single mother who has lost any hope for her present—or for her children's future.

The desperation of men and women who are out of work or working at jobs that provide them with only a scant living and no real dignity.

The anguish of the illiterate, the homeless, of all those being told this nation can no longer afford them a chance to achieve their share in the American dream.

God knows there's work enough for all of us—black, white, Hispanic, Jew, and Gentile—to expand equality here at home, and to lead the world again by our example, to face down apartheid in South Africa, to insist on human rights in Latin America, in the Soviet Union, wherever people are exploited and oppressed.

And if any of us, Jew or Gentile, black or white, becomes discouraged by the struggle and begins to lose heart, if our will begins to falter or the dreams fade, if we need to remember how much can be accomplished even in a short lifetime, then we can look to the tiny state of Israel whose birth we celebrate tonight.

To how Israel has impressed the world with what it has been able to do despite wars and constant harassment.

And think how Israel might astonish us all with what it could accomplish in forty years of peace.

We can look to her legendary ability to make deserts bloom and wastelands bear fruit.

We can see in her the embodiment of the human will to endure and to transcend . . . to persevere against the forces that would crush human freedom and dignity . . . to bring hope, decency, equality where they never before existed . . . to create a society that preserves its traditions while mastering its future.

She is a living proof of what a people committed to freedom can achieve.

As such, we who cherish freedom so see her as an ally and a friend.

Today, together, we offer the state of Israel both a greeting and a prayer.

Shalom.

MEMORIAL SERVICE FOR SYRACUSE

UNIVERSITY STUDENTS

JANUARY 18, 1989

THE CARRIER DOME, SYRACUSE, NEW YORK

I can't recall anything more difficult than trying to talk to the families and friends of the victims of tragedies, like the Lockerbie plane disaster, discussed here, or the explosion of a school in East Coldenham, Orange County, which occurred in 1989. In both cases, young people were killed. It took me hours to draft these few lines. I stopped writing only because I became convinced I was not able to say what I felt any better, even though I knew these words fell far short of conveying my thoughts adequately. The families and friends of the children were grateful anyway, because there are moments like these when all people expect is the effort.

We are here—all of us—because we need to be. As the reports of the ugly tragedy in the skies over Lockerbie became clearer, the meaning of the news for families across our nation—for New York families and for the whole family of New York—became more and more terrible . . . more and more shocking.

It made everything we were doing at the time—wrapping presents, marking exams, preparing a speech, enjoying a party—seem instantly insignificant, perhaps even inappropriate.

And now, with immeasurable sorrow still heavy on the hearts of families and loved ones, with the Syracuse academic community still in mourning, with people all across this city and state and nation still shocked at the thought of this awful loss, we gather here, because so great a grief cannot be borne without being shared.

We gather because we need to, to share our grief, to try—however difficult it is—to reconcile to that grief.

Whatever we believe about the hereafter, this much we know: our most precious gift is life.

And whatever else we believe, death, like life, is a mystery beyond our comprehension. A mystery deepened when those taken from us are, like the students we remember today, so young and bright, so full of promise, so loved . . . and so loving.

Perhaps it is better not to pretend it can be explained, because that only increases the torment of those who seek vainly to understand it.

Perhaps it is as simple as the ancient story from the Talmud, about the rabbi whose two brilliant and beautiful sons were taken from him one Sabbath afternoon.

Because it was the Sabbath, his wife did not tell him of the tragedy.

After the Sabbath she said to him:

"A man came to see me before the Sabbath and left with me for safekeeping two precious diamonds. Now that the Sabbath has passed, he wants me to give them back to him. What should I do?"

The rabbi replied, "Of course you must return them to the one who gave them to you."

The rabbi's wife then explained, "The Lord gave us two precious diamonds, our two wonderful sons, and now he has taken them back to him."

Whereupon the rabbi paused and, as the tears came to his eyes, said, "The Lord gave and the Lord has taken away; blessed be the name of the Lord."

Today, even amid our grief, we remember the blessing these young men and women—these gems—were to everyone their lives touched.

Their parents and families and friends will always treasure the special and most personal memories of their short lifetimes. But all of us—even those of us who came to know them only in their deaths—can admire the ambition, the energy, the dreams that shone from them, and that led them to seek to be educated at a great university. And the love of life that led them beyond their campuses to broaden their experience and their horizons.

If, as all the wisest people of all the generations have taught, seeking is rewarded with knowledge, sacrifice with joy, love with love, then for all the brevity of their lives, they have reached a rich fulfillment.

May the memory of them continue to be a consolation for us.

May it inspire us to cherish more dearly our own precious gift of life.

Remembering them, may all of us in this state help dry one another's tears and help restore each other to the joy that is our best memory of them.

And may their young souls rest in peace.

For all the time I have been governor, the death penalty has been a subject of intense debate, and disagreement. I have studied the subject since I became a law student, known individuals sentenced to death, been in the death house, reviewed all the arguments and alleged proofs that are generally available, and I'm surer now than I've ever been that the death penalty not only is ineffective as a deterrent, but is probably more likely to encourage than to discourage violence.

I have vetoed bills that would impose the death penalty every year I have been governor and probably will again in the years ahead. My veto, however, is not certain to prevent it: with a two-thirds vote of the legislature New York can have any law it wants, despite the governor. So far, there has not been that much support for death in our legislature, although the vote has come close.

In truth, I believe it is not death the people want; it is an end to the violent crime in our society. The call for the return of capital punishment is another way of demanding that something more be done to stop the nearly incredible brutality of recent years. I acknowledge that crime is uglier and more debased than ever, but this speech gives all the reasons why I believe that responding to brutality with brutality will only make it worse.

Together, the legislature and the governor every year make thousands of judgments that are important.

But occasionally we are confronted with a question that has transcendent significance: one that describes in fundamental ways what we are as a people; one that projects to ourselves, and to the whole world, our most fundamental values; one, even, that helps configure our souls.

This is the right setting for such a discussion, here at the College of St. Rose, surrounded by excellent leaders like Bishop Hubbard and Bishop Ball and Rabbi Silverman and so many clergy. Right, not because it is a Christian or a Jewish setting, or even a religious setting. Right, because this is a place, and these are people, who believe in reason, enlightenment, and the uplifting of the human condition.

The question that confronts us is whether this state should choose to kill human beings by electrocution, as punishment for commission of the crime of murder.

I have spoken my own opposition to the death penalty for more than thirty years. For all that time I have studied it, I have watched it, I have debated it, hundreds of times.

I have heard all the arguments, analyzed all the evidence I could find, measured public opinion when it was opposed, when it was indifferent, when it was passionately in favor. And always before, I have concluded the death penalty is wrong. That it lowers us all, that it is a surrender to the worst that is in us, that it uses a power—the official power to kill by execution—which has never elevated a society, never brought back a life, never inspired anything but hate.

In recent years I have had the obligation to cast my vote on bills passed by the legislature to bring back the death penalty. And I have voted against it each time. On each occasion that I did, the legislature might have passed the bill despite my disapproval by obtaining a two-thirds vote. So far they have chosen not to.

Now the death penalty bill is before me again, and there can be another chance for the legislature of this state to speak on this subject in the name of the people they represent.

Because of the awesome significance of the matter, and the imminence of the decision, I sought a chance to speak directly to the public so that I could add my voice to and underscore the cogency of the arguments made by the bishop, the assemblypeople, and so many of you. And made already so cogently, so forcefully, so eloquently.

I thank Dr. Vacarro, the College of St. Rose, and the Coalition for providing me this opportunity.

Clearly, there is a new public willingness to return to the official brutality of the past, by restoring the death penalty. And it is just as clear what has provoked this new willingness.

Life in parts of this state, and nation, has become more ugly and violent than at any time I can recall.

Many, like myself, who have spent more than fifty years in this state, are appalled at the new madness created by drugs. And frustrated by what appears to be the ineffectuality of the federal, state, and local governments to deal with this new crisis.

Savage murders of young, bright, and committed law enforcement people, and other citizens, enrage us all.

Our passions are inflamed by each new terrible headline, each new report of atrocity.

We know the people have a right to demand a civilized level of law and peace. They have a right to expect it.

And when it appears to them that crime is rampant, and the criminal seems immune from apprehension and adequate punishment, and that nothing else is working, then no one should be surprised if the people demand the ultimate penalty.

It has happened before. It will no doubt happen again.

To a great extent it is a cry, a terrible cry of anger, a cry of anguish born of frustration and fear in the people.

I know that.

I understand it.

I have been with the victims, too. I have felt the anger myself, more than once.

Like too many other citizens of this state, I know what it is to be violated—and even to have one's closest family violated, in the most despicable ways.

I tremble at the thought of how I might react to someone who took the life of my son.

Anger, surely . . . terrible anger. I would not be good enough to suppress it.

Would I demand revenge? Perhaps even that.

I know that despite all my beliefs, I might be driven by my impulses.

So how could I not understand a society of people like me, at times like this, wanting to let out a great cry for retribution, for vindication . . . even for revenge, like the cry we hear from them now.

I understand it.

But I know something else.

I know this society should strive for something better than what we are in our worst moments.

When police officers are killed, violence escalates, and lawlessness seems to flourish with impunity, it isn't easy for people to hold back their anger, to stop and think, to allow reason to operate.

But that, it seems to me, is the only rational course for a people constantly seeking to achieve greater measures of humanity and dignity for our civilization.

And so, for a few moments, we should try to reason our way to a solution.

We need to respond more effectively to the new violence. We know that. But there is absolutely no good reason to believe that returning to death as a punishment will be any better an answer now than it was at all the times in the past when we had it, used it, regretted it, and discarded it.

There are dozens of studies that demonstrate there is simply no persuasive evidence that official state killing can do anything to make any police officer, or other citizen, safer.

There is, in fact, considerable evidence to the contrary. Consider just this: For the decade before 1977, we had the death penalty in New York State. In that period eighty police officers were slain. For the decade after, without the death penalty . . . fifty-four were killed.

The argument for deterrence is further weakened by realization of how rarely and unpredictably it is applied.

For hundreds of years we have known that the effectiveness of the law is determined not by its harshness, but by its sureness.

And the death penalty has always been terribly unsure.

The experts of the New York State Bar Association's Criminal Justice Section, and the Association of the Bar of the City of New York, have come out strongly against the death penalty after hundreds of years of cumulative lawyers' experience and study.

One of the points the state section made is that the death penalty must be regarded as ineffective as a deterrent if for no other reason than because its use is so uncertain. Execution has occurred in only about five-hundredths of one percent of all the homicides committed in America over the past decade.

And then, despite Ted Bundy, it seems to threaten white drug dealers, white rapists, white killers, white barbarians a lot less than others.

Think of this: of the last eighteen people executed in this state, thirteen were black and one Hispanic. And that seems an extraordinary improbability for a system that was operating with any kind of objective sureness.

And there's more.

Some of the most notorious recent killings, like the gunning down of the DEA agent, Everett Hatcher, and the killing by Lemuel Smith, occurred in the face of existing death penalty statutes.

And psychiatrists will tell you that there is reason to believe that some madmen, like Ted Bundy, may even be tempted to murder because of a perverse desire to challenge the electric chair.

For years and years, the arguments have raged over whether the death penalty is a deterrent. That used to be, frankly, the only argument when I first began debating it.

But the truth is now that because the proponents have never been able to make the case for deterrence convincingly, they have moved to a different argument. It is phrased in many ways, but in the end it all comes down to the same impulse.

It was heard in the debates in recent weeks on the floor of the senate and assembly, which I listened to and read with great care. Things like this: "Whatever the studies show, the people of my area believe that the taking of life justifies the forfeiting of life." Or: "Our people have the right to insist on a penalty that matches the horror of the crime."

Or even this: "An eye for an eye, a tooth for a tooth."

"An eye for an eye, a tooth for a tooth."

Where would it end? "You kill my son; I kill yours." "You rape my daughter; I rape yours." "You mutilate my body; I mutilate yours."

And we will pursue this course, despite the lack of reason to believe it will protect us—even if it is clear, almost with certainty, that occasionally the victim of our official barbarism will be innocent.

Think of it: At least twenty-three people are believed to have been wrongfully executed in the United States since the turn of this century. Twenty-three innocent people officially killed. But it is not called murder.

And tragically, New York State—our great state, the Empire

State—holds the record for the greatest number of innocents put to death over the years. We lead all the states in the nation with eight wrongful executions since 1905.

Here are the names of the victims of the state of New York's killings: Charles Becker. Frank Cirofici. Thomas Bambrick. Stephen Grzechowiak. Max Rybarczyk. Everett Appelgate. George Chew Wing. Charles Sberna.

These are real names. These are real people. Like Mario Cuomo or Ralph Marino. Like Mel Miller or Fred Ohrenstein. Like Clarence Rappelyea or Joe Serrano or Al Vann.

Or your son. Or your father, or your mother. Real people who were killed, innocently.

The proponents of the death penalty in this state assume that the criminal justice system will not make a mistake.

They seem to be unconcerned about the overly ambitious prosecutor, the sloppy detective, the incompetent defense counsel, the witness with an ax to grind, or the judge who keeps courthouse conviction box scores. But that, ladies and gentlemen, is the human factor, and it's the deepest, most profound flaw in their argument.

In this country, a defendant is convicted on proof beyond a reasonable doubt—not proof to an absolute certainty. There's no such thing as absolute certainty in our law.

The proponents of the death penalty, despite this, say we should pretend it cannot happen.

They do not discuss the infamous case of Isadore Zimmerman, who got so far as to have his head shaved and his trouser leg slit on the day of his scheduled execution in 1939, before Governor Herbert Lehman commuted his sentence to life imprisonment.

And then, twenty-four hours later, Zimmerman was released from prison, after it was determined that the prosecutor knew all the time that he was innocent and had suppressed evidence. Zimmerman died a free man just a few years ago.

They do not discuss William "Red" Gergel, age sixty-two, released in Queens just this year after spending 535 days in jail for a triple murder he did not commit. It was a case of mistaken identity.

They do not discuss a young man named Bobby McLaughlin of Marine Park, Brooklyn. Bobby McLaughlin was convicted of the robbery and murder of another young man in 1980. This was a one-witness identification case—the most frightening kind. In July of 1986, Bobby McLaughlin was released after serving six years for a murder he did not commit. Wrongly convicted by intention or mistake—take your pick of the facts—right here in the great state of New York.

It all started when a detective picked up one wrong photograph. One wrong photograph, one mistake, one date with the electric chair. It could have been one more tragically lost life. It didn't happen. But it took an almost superhuman effort by his foster father and some aggressive members of the media to keep the case from falling between the cracks of the justice system.

Bobby McLaughlin had this to say after he was released: "If there was a death penalty in this state, I would now be ashes in an urn on my mother's mantel."

Yes, it can happen. And it will again, if we allow it to.

And what would we tell the wife, what would the governor tell the wife then, or the husband, or the children, or the parents of the innocent victim that we had burned to death in our official rage? What would you say to them?

"We had to do it"?

Then we would be asked, "But *why* did you have to do it? If you were not sure it would deter anyone else, *why* did you have to do it?" And what would we answer? "Because we were angry. Because the people demanded an eye for an eye . . . even if it were to prove an innocent eye"?

What would we tell them? Should we tell them that we had to kill, because we had as a society come to believe that the only way to reach the most despicable among us was to lie down in the muck and mire that spawned them?

I hear all around me that the situation has so deteriorated that we need to send a message, to the criminals and to the people alike, that we as a government know how bad things are and will do something about it.

I agree.

Of course we must make clear that we intend to fight the terrible epidemic of drugs and violence. But the death penalty is no more effective a way to fight them than the angry cries that inspire it.

We need to continue to do the things that will control crime by making the apprehension and punishment of criminals more likely.

We've made a good beginning. Since 1983, we have increased funding for local law enforcement alone by 65 percent.

We've added 500 more state troopers to the force. We've opened 13,000 new prison beds, and we will be adding room for another 4,000 by 1990. We've tripled the number of drug felons sentenced to state prison, and increased dramatically our rehabilitation efforts.

We should be doing more.

The legislature should be giving me the forfeiture bills I've asked for. I hope they will. Those bills will allow us to take the wealth away from the drug dealers and put it to use fighting them and rehabilitating people who are addicted to drugs.

They should give me the judges I've asked for, the troopers, the money for courts and prisons and rehabilitation programs.

And one other thing.

The legislature should finally vote for a real, tough, effective punishment for deliberate murder.

And there is one. Better, much better than the death penalty. One that juries will not be reluctant to give.

One that is so menacing to a potential killer, it could actually deter.

One that does not require us to be infallible in order to avoid taking innocent life.

One that does not require us to stoop to the level of the killers.

One that is even—for those who insist on measuring this question in dollars—millions of dollars less expensive than the death penalty, millions . . . true life imprisonment, with no possibility of parole . . . none, under any circumstances.

If you committed a murder at twenty and you live to be eighty-one, you'll live sixty-one years behind bars. You'll go in alive and come out only when you die. Now that's a tough penalty.

Ask the people who know how tough this penalty would be. The people who know Attica or Auburn. Ask the people who know how hard such places are.

They will tell you that to most inmates, the thought of living a whole lifetime behind bars, only to die in your cell, is worse than the quick, final termination of the electric chair.

Anecdotal evidence is, of course, limited in its usefulness, but it can give you an insight.

Just recently, in an article in the *New York Times Magazine*, a young man on Death Row named Heath Wilkins was asked whether people underestimated the deterrent power of life without parole. "Absolutely," Wilkins responded. "Death isn't a scary thing to someone who's hurting inside so bad that they're hurting other people. People like that are looking for death as a way out."

For the six years I have offered it to the legislature, I have heard no substantial arguments in opposition to the proposal for life imprisonment without parole. I've heard none.

If it fails once again this year to achieve its preferred choice—the electric chair—I hope the legislature will put aside any temptation simply to preserve a political issue and, instead, finally give the people of this state what I believe is a smarter, saner, more effective answer . . . by adopting real life imprisonment, without parole.

Finally, while we are fighting the criminals in the street with the relentless enforcement of firm laws and with swift, sure punishment, we must at the same time continue to do all the things we know dull the instinct for crime.

Education, housing, healthcare, good jobs, and the opportunity to achieve them.

All the old-fashioned effort to deal with root causes that has never lost its relevance, even when it lost its popularity.

That, in the end, I think personally, may be the best antidote of all against the kind of terrible crime we are now experiencing. Certainly it offers us more hope than does the politics of death.

Now, ladies and gentlemen, brothers and sisters, there will be few questions more difficult for us than the one we now face.

And few opportunities as good as this to prove our commitment as a people to resisting the triumph of darkness, and to moving our society constantly toward the light.

For a politician, like the people from the Assembly who have joined us today, and myself, rejecting what appears to be a politically popular view can be troublesome.

But I—as they do—make the same decision I have before. In my case, I make the same decision now that I have for more than thirty years. This time I believe on the basis of even more evidence, and with a firmer conviction than before.

And I do it with a profound respect for the people who have

raised their voices . . . and occasionally even their fists . . . asking for the death penalty.

I have not as governor ignored those voices. I have listened intently to them. But after the sincerest effort, I have not been able to bring myself to agree with them.

I continue to believe, with all my mind and heart, that the death penalty would not help us, it would debase us; that it would not protect us, it would make us weaker.

I continue to believe, more passionately now than ever, that this society desperately needs this great state's leadership.

We, the people of New York, ought now, in this hour of fright, to show the way. We should refuse to allow this time to be marked forever in the pages of our history as the time that we were driven back to one of the vestiges of our primitive condition, because we were not strong enough, because we were not intelligent enough, because we were not civilized enough to find a better answer to violence . . . than violence.

Today I will veto the death penalty bill sent to me by the legislature and return it with my proposal for life imprisonment without parole, with the hope and the prayer that this time the legislature will once again choose the light, over the darkness.

The union movement is not as popular now as it used to be. I believe it's because the country has forgotten how vital the unions' influence was to this nation's development as a place of decency and power. Moreover, the country fails to appreciate how important organized labor will be to our future competitiveness. This speech tries to remind us that, for more than a hundred years in this country, there existed strong government, powerful business, influential religious groups, philanthropists—and nevertheless women and children were abused by employers, and men were forced to work for a lifetime and still died poor.

It was the union movement, and not the other great institutions, that protected the powerless from exploitation. I made the point that the Republican administration's neglect went far beyond the concerns of union members. Its supply-side policies diminished support for virtually every category of disadvantaged citizens. Three years later a group of auto workers told me at the 1992 Democratic convention, "This time, they'll listen, Governor!" They were right.

It's a special privilege to be asked to address this convention . . . to talk to this union that holds a preeminent position in one of the world's most powerful labor movements.

Anyone who understands this nation's history should feel that way.

Since I began my political career in 1974, the UAW has supported me, suffered with me, stood by me more than once . . . in good times and bad.

And believe me, it was rough for a while.

In 1982, when I first ran for governor against Ed Koch, who was then the second most popular politician in the country, and Lew

Lehrman, the conservative Republican who was the second richest, it was so bad that early on in the campaign a friend held a fundraiser for me at his home . . . and no one showed up.

With the help of union members, things began to change.

My platform consisted of just three words: "Jobs and Justice."

It was a summing up of what I and other people later called the politics of inclusion.

And I remember that, at the time, the nation at large was hearing another message, from a genial and convincing president. A message that said, as I interpreted it, that we should leave it to the rich to take care of the rest of us.

Many were lulled into accepting that message, willing to forget the lessons of history.

But eventually, what we—you, other representatives of the union movement, and I—had to say together, and what we believed in deeply, prevailed in New York. It would have been better for this country if it had prevailed everywhere in this nation.

That simple platform—Jobs and Justice—is as relevant today, probably *more* relevant, than it was then.

All the things we said then, seven years ago, we should be saying now, even louder: that this country should be able to provide everyone who can work an opportunity to earn his or her own way with dignity and a chance to rise up on his or her own merits, a chance to share, fairly, in the immense abundance of this place of miracles.

No one understands that simple, but profound, principle better than you, the brothers and sisters of the United Auto Workers.

Your union was *born* to that understanding.

Out of the depths of the Great Depression, inspired at first by a handful of courageous men and women, growing from a scattering of small unions, gradually pulling together tens of thousands of working people of every color, culture, and creed . . . the United Auto Workers grew.

Once formed, *nothing* stopped you! Not scabs. Not hired thugs with lead pipes. Not battles within labor's family. Nor American political struggles, or powerful anti-union presidents, or difficult economic times.

From the very first sit-down strikes at Kelsey-Hayes and Flint, to the battle of the overpass at the Rouge plant, the United Auto Workers proved—perhaps more than any other union before or since—that as long as they stay together, as long as they put small differences behind them and lock arms pushing for common purposes, the working people in America *can* take control of their own lives, with their own hearts and their own hands . . . and can establish dignity and justice on the job, in cities, towns, and villages all across America.

Through all of it, the UAW has remained the embodiment of intelligent, progressive, and courageous labor policy. A movement that has protected, encouraged, and brought prosperity to millions of men, women, and their families who, left unorganized, would have continued to know only bleak, exhausted nights and grim, gray dawns.

We should remind the nation, again and again, that it was less than a lifetime ago that American men, women—and children— could work every day of their life, live a whole life, and die . . . in poverty.

We should remind America that less than a lifetime ago owners could take from those who labored everything they could, and give back as little as possible.

That children and women could be treated like beasts of burden, and hundreds of people would be allowed to die in terrible accidents.

Despite a powerful government that could win world wars. Despite wealthy owners. Despite churches, foundations . . . and even prayer.

We should remind the nation that the answer to those prayers was the union movement . . . without which nothing would have changed.

The nation should be made to remember that the union movement was the voice of *decency*, proclaiming that the people who were building this nation—people who worked the cutting tables and the jackhammers, who poured the steel, torqued the bolts, and installed the drive shafts, who served in commerce and delivered government services—should *not* be abused or debased.

The union movement was the voice of *justice*, demanding that working people be dealt with as human beings, with dignity. That they be paid a decent wage, be protected against accidents, be provided for in their old age . . . because they had earned it.

It's clear that America is a more decent, fairer place today because—and only because—the union movement fought to make it that way.

Now there is a new challenge. Today, in industrial America, there is a whole new world of competition from abroad, a tough new global economy that we don't dominate, and that we will have to fight to do well in.

Who would have dreamed it possible just twenty years ago that an American car today would be permitted to have a coil made in Japan, a transmission made in Mexico, and a fuel injection system made in Germany?

This new world requires new tactics and new approaches by labor, by management, and by our government.

It's clear we cannot sustain ourselves by service industries alone.

And it's clear that we can't let the industrial, the manufacturing, part of our economy be pounded and damaged by *unfair* competition from foreign countries.

In order to maintain the standard of living which Americans have earned with 200 years of struggle, American workers must be allowed to make things . . . to manufacture and produce goods.

You can't eat a leveraged buyout. You can't drive a junk bond. Flipping burgers doesn't put a permanent roof over a worker's head.

We need to keep our industrial base, strengthen it, and expand it.

The Japanese know that. The Germans know that. The newly industrialized countries are learning it fast.

It would be foolish of us to forget it.

To keep our manufacturing strength, and to increase it, this nation has to demand that our foreign trading partners play fair.

We must demand simple fairness. That can start with vigorous enforcement of our new trade bill.

Then, with the assurance of an honest playing field, we have to strengthen our own team.

This nation has always been at its best when all our different parts work together. We must do it more, and better. Business with labor. Labor with government. Government with business and labor. In partnership. All of us working together to strengthen our economy, and by doing so strengthening our strategic, global position as well.

And in order to be effective, the partnership must operate according to a few basic rules.

First of all, it must be a partnership in which management is committed to longer-term growth, *not* quarter-to-quarter returns alone. Owners and management must make a firm commitment to three-year and five-year strategies to increase market share.

Second, it must be a partnership in which everyone shares the same goals: reasonable wages, good working conditions, high productivity, and high profits.

The partners must recognize that we can't succeed as a nation by insisting that the way to compete and increase profits is simply to reduce wages. That's wrong.

We said we believe in fair trade, but it is not fair to try to make our businesses competitive by matching shamefully low wages in other parts of the world. We shouldn't try to compete by turning back the progress we have fought for and earned over four generations. It is not fair to reduce the living conditions of millions of American workers and their families in order to compete with standards we declared were indecent 100 years ago.

Instead of reducing wages, we need to raise them. A pretty good place to start initially is with a decent minimum-wage bill.

Unfortunately, the president has taken care of that—for now.

The national minimum wage has not been increased since 1981. It's past time to begin moving toward the day when no one who works full-time—day in and day out—at minimum wage has to support a family with an income that falls below the poverty level.

We should encourage the Democratic leadership in Congress to continue to lead the effort to bring our minimum wage to a higher—and fairer—level.

Then—to earn the good wages—the UAW knows that we need the best-trained, best-educated work force possible.

Progressive unions can do a lot in that area. Your Human Resource Center in Michigan has served as a model for labor unions throughout the nation. It offers some of the most innovative retraining, tuition assistance, and dislocated-worker programs available today to America's labor force. We're pleased and proud that based upon its success, you've opened a regional Human Resources Center in Buffalo, New York.

And your workplace literacy programs have been magnificent, providing the gift of reading to thousands of workers, many of them in New York State. We're grateful to you for that as well.

Yes, the UAW knows what must be done and is doing more than its part.

But the principal role here is *not* the union movement's; it's government's. Lincoln explained it.

To deal with this country's economic challenges, we need strong, positive, enlightened government. A federal government that puts education before missiles. A government that puts the savings of America's families ahead of the board of directors of a corrupt savings and loan.

A government that will find ways to discourage leveraged buy-outs, takeovers, and threats that are nothing more than a concession to individual and corporate greed. And encourage corporate activity that produces growth, jobs, and long-term profits.

A government that will correct the mistakes of its recent past and begin to invest in the human resources and programs we need to make progress in this new, more dynamic world.

The last eight years have left us with the biggest national government debt and recurring budget deficits *ever known* to our civilization.

The unions didn't create that problem, and the unions can't solve it. It is a *government* deficit, and it will have to be solved by *government* action.

That means some hard decisions need to be made—and so far, we're *not* making them. There has been no real action on our deficit, notwithstanding two new huge expenses have been added to our budget—the cost of dealing with the savings-and-loan scandals and the cost of cleaning away nuclear wastes from federal repositories.

The federal government can't kite checks. The piper—and the creditors—must be paid!

If the Congress doesn't want to raise the revenues, they have to cut military expenditures. If it's too hard to cut expenditures, they have to raise revenues. If they do neither, it will be like taking their hands off the ship's wheel in the center of a storm.

I think we need a firmer grip on that wheel.

We need to make the hard and smart decisions necessary to give us the wherewithal to do the things we need to do. It will take more than words.

We need to have government help improve education; offer more job training; and improve production methods as well as research and development. That takes more than speeches. It takes revenues.

We need a federal government willing to tackle the incredible damage done by drugs and drug addiction in this country. It is damaging today's work force, and threatening to cripple the work force of the twenty-first century. It is destroying a large part of a generation of children. It is frightening and weakening the entire nation. It will take more than sermons; it will take billions in resources.

Despite that, total federal spending on criminal justice amounts to less than 1 percent of the entire 1989 federal budget.

The states have been left to do battle with a scourge that the federal government refuses to face. In New York, we spend hundreds of millions of our own state money to battle drugs, with little help from the feds—money that would be better spent on enormous social needs. And most of this crime is federal responsibility. The cocaine and heroin are not from Los Angeles or New York City. They get here from overseas because of the failure of the federal government to keep them out.

But that doesn't seem to bother this administration much. They're perfectly content with letting the states bear the horrible burden of fighting drugs.

Let me describe the president's attitude about the drug problem to you this way: A radical government from Canada invades New York state. Mr. Bush declares this an outrage, and demands that it end immediately.

"But will you send us troops to help, Mr. President?" the governor of New York asks. "Or money to pay for our own troops?"

"Oh no, we can't afford that," says the president. "Let New York handle that. Let them use the state militia and volunteers."

179

That's how the Bush administration wants to fight the drug war. . . . They'll fight as long as they don't have to purchase the equipment, muster the troops, or face the angry, bloody fire on the front line!

That's abdication of a clear responsibility.

And the abdication of responsibility by the federal government continues in other critical areas as well. We need a federal government willing to deal with serious social problems like poverty, housing, fair treatment for the elderly, and good jobs.

We need resources for day care, child care, education, housing, infrastructure building and rebuilding. So far, we have been offered an excellent imitation of Democratic poetry, and little else.

And we need federal help in another critical area. The United States and South Africa are the only two industrialized nations that still *don't* have universal health care.

Universal health care *must* be a national goal. When so many others already do, certainly the wealthiest nation in the world can provide this basic right to all our citizens.

We need a government that cares for workers, that cares when factories close.

Last year, Congress passed the nation's first plant-closing legislation in the nation's history. . . . This year, we must fight to make certain that the new administration funds these efforts at an adequate level. Our workers deserve nothing less.

We need strong overseas markets to sell *our* products in, with our products purchased by workers who are fairly paid in their own countries . . . workers who are members of vigorous and free labor unions. We should teach the world what we taught this country about decency and fairness to workers. We need a rising standard of living worldwide—and to accomplish *that*, we need to relieve debt burdens that crush developing economies. Government will have to help to do that, working to relieve staggering Third World debt.

And we need a federal government dealing more effectively with our environmental problems. No economy or government, democratic or totalitarian, will survive a superheated coffin caused by global warming.

The fact is that we need a government that is a positive, active, and progressive force—like the union movement. Labor is showing government how it should be done. Labor is on the move. And the UAW is in the lead.

The innovative labor-management programs of the UAW—like Harrison Radiator in Lockport, New York, and Chrysler's new process gear in Syracuse—are models for the country.

We in the state of New York are proud of the Tarrytown agreement. Prouder because our state government helped make it a reality.

With state assistance to provide cheaper electricity and to clean up factory pollution, and through the establishment of joint labor-management committees, we were able to help GM cut production costs, improve efficiency—and at the same time save 5,000 UAW jobs that were on the brink of being lost.

Partnerships like that reflect a high level of mutual commitment by the UAW to the principle that workers should be involved in the decision-making process.

And the innovations continue.

Corporations are now learning that partnership—working *with* unions to meet the changing needs of workers—means productivity and profit.

You're showing industrial America the path to greater competitiveness in the new global economy. As are our brothers and sisters in other progressive unions.

But not *all employers* understand that we are all in this together—labor and management, government and the private sector.

That's what Eastern Airlines is all about.

Your voices have been strong there. All of labor's have been. Some of us in government have spoken as well. I have, more than once, on the picket line and elsewhere.

Here's what I said to the Eastern Airlines strikers in New York City. I told them that they were not fighting for themselves alone. That the whole country was watching them . . . and Eastern's management . . . and Washington . . . because the Eastern situation casts a shadow over management and labor relations in America.

And I told them that if this is a test case, then it's a good one for our side.

Because the union's position is fair and reasonable. They have bargained in good faith, made immense concessions, and proved that they can raise productivity. They have lived within and by the law.

"And in return," I said, "you have been met by a management that does not care about fairness, or good faith, or workers.

"Instead, it is a management that is apparently set on a course of cannibalizing companies, ripping off their assets to put cash into places where it can be raked off by people who do not believe in sharing, and who don't know how to build a long-range success."

I told U.S. transportation secretary Sam Skinner to ask the president to call on Frank Lorenzo and management to take a step forward.

I told him that every time we ask the machinists to make a concession, every time we ask the pilots or flight attendants to abandon an issue that is important to them, we need to ask the same thing of management.

That's fair, isn't it?

The president disagreed.

"This isn't a one-sided strike," I said. "This is a refusal by workers to surrender to an inflexible management that refuses to accept mediation, arbitration, or bargaining in fairness, hoping that today's politics will be sufficiently hard on the workers—so that they will be crushed in the end.

"We can't let that happen! That's why we have to speak out on Eastern and every other time and place where the union movement and the fairness and intelligence it represents are threatened."

That's what I said to Eastern—and to Americans all over this country, whether union or not, over and over again.

I will continue to, because it is an essential message. America must be reminded that we cannot allow ourselves to be moved back toward the darkness of sweatshops, toward the cruelty of the conveyor belt that stopped for nothing but the owner . . . or death.

Rather, we must move constantly forward, toward the light.

New York knows that.

For us in New York, and you good people of the UAW, the dignity of work, its ability to ennoble and empower people, are not just sweet abstractions, something we read about in a book.

The chance to work, to earn a decent wage, to have some stake in the American dream are parts of our personal histories. It's why my people—and many of yours—came to this country.

Thanks in large part to the union movement, and to the UAW, millions of those people found a country ready to make real their dreams. I think it's important we remind America of that, if we want to keep the dream alive.

We, in New York, will be there to help . . . wearing the union label, using union products, sharing the union spirit and ideals, moving forward—toward a better life for workers, and for the better world they help to build.

God bless you all.

Thank you for having me!

I chose to include this speech because it makes two simple points that continue to elude many Americans—the drug problem begins with a federal failure, which the federal government has still not adequately corrected, and, in the end, the real solution to the problem is not an army of police, but a society that can learn to reduce its demand for drugs. I think most people have come to understand that latter proposition, but too many politicians are still reluctant to make a real commitment to it: they think "law and order" sells better to voters. And maybe it does. Surely the federal government has been more willing to spend wealth on police action, stealth, and even a war on Panama than it has on educational programs and treatment centers.

There is something else in this speech, something almost emotional. It is a plaintive recitation of the loss of fundamental values in our society that has left many of us morally empty. Some have chosen to fill the vacuum with drugs. This emptiness and our response to it is a profound problem and will require a profound solution. That's worth saying again and again until Washington listens . . . and hears.

For more than a half-century, the FBI National Academy has been helping local law enforcement agencies stay on the cutting edge of their profession, helping them to adapt their strategies to meet the ever-changing challenges that present themselves. There is no way to measure the enormous difference this good work has made, but it is clear from your reputation, from constant reports, and from the attendance at your sessions that the Academy has been a great success.

When he addressed the graduates of the thirteenth session of the Academy in 1940, New York's Mayor Fiorello La Guardia forecast that "the National Academy would develop into a West Point for police officers."

La Guardia was right in his prediction. And you are right to be proud of now being a part of the Academy's tradition.

For myself, I am grateful to the FBI. Not only for the Academy, but for all its excellent cooperation with the state. It's good to come to a place like Lake Placid. Especially good, I think, that the spouses and families are part of the meeting.

A career in law enforcement puts unique demands on the families of officers. They sacrifice a lot and risk a lot, and I know it can take its toll. So it's good to have time together in this serene and beautiful setting.

I know you have spent a good deal of the time reflecting on where we are and where we are going in law enforcement. And I'm sure that most of you have concluded—as I have—that, for our society, there's one reality today so menacing and destructive that it overshadows every other concern and has undermined much of the progress we had made in reducing the level of violent crime.

It is, of course, the proliferation in drug trafficking, drug addiction, and drug-related crime, much of it traceable to crack. The situation is so bad that it is no exaggeration to call it warfare. Millions of lives have been lost, destroyed, crippled. A generation of children threatened.

As a result, the nation's people are angry, demanding a return to death as a cure for their anger and confusion—saying, in effect, that they believe the criminal justice system is just not working. So deep is the anger that now our Supreme Court tells us we are allowed officially to kill children and the mentally retarded as a punishment for their crimes.

It is a war indeed—one in which we are losing a lot of important battles.

In New York, we've engaged the enemy in the field.

It has been an immensely demanding struggle.

In my seven years as governor, we have nearly doubled the state's criminal justice expenditures—to almost 2 billion dollars annually.

During this time, appropriations for state criminal justice agencies have risen 116 percent, and state assistance for local agencies has increased by 79 percent.

We raised our state police troop strength to 4,000—the highest level in the division's history. Today, over 300 state police investigators are assigned full-time to drug investigations and every troop fields a narcotics investigation unit.

Over the past six fiscal years, almost 124 million dollars in direct state aid has gone to local law enforcement and prosecution agencies statewide to add police, prosecutors, and support staff and to purchase equipment.

We created the statewide Anti-Drug Enforcement Task Force, chaired by the director of criminal justice and representatives of state, federal, and local law enforcement.

To disrupt drug distribution networks, we developed our regional drug enforcement task forces—another cooperative effort with state, federal, county, and municipal agencies working together.

To back up all of these law enforcement and prosecution efforts, we undertook the largest expansion of prison space in the state's history—by the end of next year we will have built more than 27,000 additional beds, nearly doubling the number of cells we had when I became governor.

And once drug offenders are in the criminal justice system, they are not merely warehoused. At every level of the system—incarceration, parole, or probation—we provide, and in most cases require, appropriate substance abuse and alcohol treatment and rehabilitation programs. We've just added 2,100 beds in our prison system for addicted prisoners.

Much of what we've done at the state level we did with your help. You joined in developing many of our proposals, and we had your support every step of the way. Without that support, without the convincing and authoritative voice of the FBI and other efforts of the law enforcement community, we would not have been able to move our political process to give us the extraordinary resources we've invested.

We have received returns on that investment.

Our criminal justice agencies have performed at record levels in the War against Drugs. The statistics we compiled last November proved that. Narcotics arrests had doubled. Indictments and prosecutions had tripled. Three times as many drug offenders were being sentenced to state prison.

Those were tremendous results—a tribute to all of you, to state and local criminal justice agencies working together with your colleagues in the FBI, the DEA, and other federal enforcement agencies.

We've done a lot in New York. More than most states. And it took an awful amount of personal sacrifice by law enforcement officers and their families.

Recently we've been trying in a number of ways to express our gratitude and acknowledge the debt we owe to them. The care for our police and survivors (COPS) agenda we proposed, and the legislature recently passed, is part of that effort, as is the funding for soft body armor and better, more advanced equipment.

The COPS bill changed the law so that the pension benefits for the spouses of slain police officers will now continue for life, even if a spouse remarries. It also establishes scholarships for the children of police officers killed in the line of duty. And in a number of other ways attempts—inadequately, we recognize—to repay the debt we owe these officers and their families.

But, despite all the money, all the time, all the people we devoted to our War on Drugs . . . despite the unprecedented numbers of arrests, convictions and sentencings, despite huge expansion of our prison capacity, despite tough new drug laws, despite the creation of regional drug enforcement task forces, Tactical Narcotics Teams (TNTs), state police special narcotics units . . . despite all of these efforts, drug trafficking, drug addiction, and drug-related crime continued to proliferate!

The drugs keep coming, by plane, by truck, in satchels—tons of it. More and more is available to children on our streets; more and more of our people are hooked . . . and lost. Now, in addition to everything else, the use of needles is spreading our newest plague—AIDS—the disease that kills.

For all we have done, it's obvious we will need to do a lot more.

I want to talk to you about that.

The state will continue to do its part. Candidly, I don't think any reasonable observer could doubt that.

But now it's time for Washington to offer more help. The truth is this is more Washington's problem than it is ours.

We don't grow coca leaves in the Bronx or opium poppies in Buffalo.

And Noriega does not live in Binghamton.

Our drug crime is in large part a matter of international commerce or its result. Drugs make it to New York only because the federal government fails to keep them out.

Eighty percent of the crime we prosecute—and pay for—the federal government has jurisdiction to prosecute as well. They simply ignore it, unless it is a big score. Most of our arrests could be federal, with prosecutions by U.S. attorneys in federal courts producing prisoners for federal prisons.

The president has suggested he understands this by calling for a small expansion in federal enforcement capacity. But his present plan will not be nearly enough. For example, there is no expansion of the DEA. At present there are fifty-two DEA agents assigned to the New York City Drug Enforcement Task Force. On the state level, we've doubled our commitment to the task force, adding sixty state police. We don't think it's unreasonable to ask the federal government to double its commitment of DEA agents.

And there are other things the federal government should be doing.

Only the federal government can raise the issue of drugs in our relations with other nations.

Only the federal government can control the movement of drugs, dangerous firearms, including assault weapons, drug paraphernalia, and precursor chemicals in international and interstate commerce. We should use our military more aggressively in that regard.

And only the federal government has the resources that are needed by the states to fight the overpowering forces we face on our own land.

The 1988 federal drug bill authorized 2.7 billion dollars in new federal spending. That would have been a pretty good start. But then less than one-fifth of that amount—500 million dollars—was appropriated. That was nearly insignificant nationwide.

Last year, New York spent over 420 million dollars on its war against drugs, with two-thirds of the money going for law enforcement and the remainder allocated for treatment and prevention programs. This figure does not include the tremendous costs to local police and corrections. Nor does it include the nearly half-billion dollars devoted to health care costs directly or indirectly attributable to substance abuse.

The federal government's financial commitment was minuscule

in comparison and, in fact, represents a steep decline over previous years. The total amount of federal funds awarded to the state's eight criminal justice agencies and to our Substance Abuse Services Agency for 1989 is projected to be just 46 million dollars. Barely a tenth of the state's commitment.

At the highest levels of the federal government, there's much more to be done if its actions are to match the promises of its antidrug rhetoric. And the need is—as you know better than anyone—immediate and urgent.

Besides the things I've already suggested, there are other things the federal government should do. In response to William Bennett's invitation to the state to provide advice in preparing his drug strategy, I've written him with our suggestions. Here are some:

• Increase the nation's prison and drug treatment capacity by turning over surplus military bases for those purposes.

• Implement a drug intervention strategy that includes an expanded role for the National Guard.

• Restructure criminal forfeiture laws in order to speed up the filing and processing of actions, and to assure that treatment and prevention programs get a fair share of seized criminal assets.

• The Immigration and Naturalization Services must be revitalized. Illegal alien drug pushers and violent drug gangs are coming into this country in record numbers. The magnitude of the problem in New York State is enormous. Last year, over 51,000 aliens were arrested and processed by the New York City criminal justice system. Over 5,000 foreign-born inmates are now being held in state prison facilities. Federal reimbursement should be increased to approximate the cost of incarcerating aliens.

• Dangerous firearms, especially assault weapons, must be strictly controlled if not removed entirely from the stream of interstate commerce.

• Federal agencies that oversee the financial industries must be given the mandate and the authority to disrupt the interstate and international pattern of money laundering that makes it possible for drug racketeers to enjoy their profits.

Could the federal government act now even with its own budget problems? Well, first of all, the president admits we are at war. If we are, how could you not commit all the forces you need?

Beyond that, it is clear that the money is available.

Just look at the defense budget. Think of what is being spent on one of the largest—and most controversial—Pentagon programs: the Strategic Defense Initiative (SDI, "Star Wars"). . . .

Four-point-six billion dollars in fiscal year 1990 alone.

If redeployed for drug wars, that amount could pay for:

- the salaries of 148,000 additional police officers, or

- the construction of 57,500 new prison cells, or

- the annual operating costs of 313,000 inpatient drug treatment slots.

And if not all of the 4.6 billion dollars, why not part of it?

There's money available as well in nondefense budgets. For example, the federal government has already spent 800 million dollars on research for a plane—the so-called "Orient Express" aerospace plane—that could fly from the United States to Tokyo in two hours. The program is projected to cost a total of 3.5 billion dollars, with 254 million dollars in funding recommended in FY '90 dollars.

What a terrific plane that would be . . . if we could afford it. But I doubt anyone here thinks projects like that are more important than the War on Drugs.

We need this federal help desperately. And we need to continue our unprecedented law enforcement efforts at the state and local levels. But even then, it is clear that the most we can hope to do is to relieve some of the immediate threat.

You, the law enforcement community—the community closest to the problem of drug abuse and crime—know better than anyone that even the strongest law enforcement possible will not end all the violence, all the waste of human lives and potential.

As long as there is a demand, there will be a supply . . . and a supplier. If there is any hope long-term, it is in reducing the impulse to take drugs. We need to do everything we can do to convince our people, especially our young people, not to take drugs. We need to surround and saturate our young people with instruction to prevent them from ever starting, and if they are addicted we need treatment.

We have to recognize that at the base of the drug crime problem are the choices made by people. And this has a great deal to do with the values they have been taught by the society around them.

It seems clear that at the foundation of many of our problems as a society is a disorientation—a loss of commitment to fundamental values, like responsibility, accountability, a capacity for discipline.

Values like recognizing the dignity of each individual, a need for mutuality, a sense of community.

Today, there appear to be fewer stable families to give instruction and reinforcement.

There seems to be no impelling orthodoxy.

No powerful benevolent signal from an unquestionably virtuous government.

No, we are not sure of all the answers.

But we do know some things.

We know that you and I must begin by vigorously enforcing the law. That's our business and it's indispensable. We must teach one another responsibility, accountability, and a capacity for discipline . . . to the extent that we can, through the law and punishment.

But we know that will not be enough.

We must do more.

We must use our government aggressively to help youth to choose avenues to dignity instead of streets to despair, by giving them the wherewithal to succeed in life, and good reason for hope.

We can show them that we will do more than deliver sermons on brotherhood. We can live compassion, and demonstrate it by insisting on a government that will provide education, a chance to work, affordable housing, food for the hungry, care for the sick and the dying.

I believe we have already done more of these good things than most states. In addition, we have values components in our public school curricula. And we've used radio and TV spots and public appearances in the effort to reach our young people.

We have to do more of everything that works, more of everything that helps people—especially the young—avoid that first, bad choice that gets them involved with drugs.

We have to teach them values in our schools by words and pictures—and in our daily lives, by the hard and tangible work of a government teaching by example.

We have to surround them with a society that cares . . . and proves it.

We have to encourage stronger families.

And persuade more executives, sports figures, and artists to help us all by using their creativity and innovation to teach us pride, community, concern, and hope—instead of greed, lust, escapism, and violence.

The crime-drug crisis is real. We need to turn this problem around, with strong responses. But we need to get away from responses that sound tough but are not strong. Like executing children or mentally retarded people.

That's a sign of weakness, of frustration, or anger—not of strength.

And I think that it is inexcusable that because the legislature received letters from a gun lobby threatening to vote against them, they are afraid to answer the pleas of the state's police officers to take assault weapons out of the hands of killers. Or to do forfeiture. Or to give us the judges everyone—including the chief judge of the court of appeals—agrees we need.

We need better wisdom than that. And frankly . . . more courage . . . and strength.

In the months ahead we'll be calling on you, as we have in the past, to forge a thoughtful, intelligent, balanced approach to this complicated and desperate problem of drugs and drug-related crime.

You will do it brilliantly, as you always have. And for that I will be grateful.

But I want you to know that even after you have done all you can through law enforcement, I recognize the obligation to push our government to carry the struggle far beyond that, to the work of building a society strong enough in values and rich enough in opportunity to reduce the impulse that gives birth to crime.

We will continue to be there to help you to help us.

Thank you for all your good work . . . and for having me today.

PART III

—

1990 – 1994

The annual State of the State is the one speech each year that I look forward to with the greatest reluctance. It is essentially a listing of initiatives, attended by a long description of the state's current situation. It seldom has room for broad philosophical sweeps.

This typical recitation, which was my first formal speech of the new decade, contains most of the program directions and emphases that have characterized my administration: a strong commitment to economic growth as the source of opportunity and an equally strong commitment to help those who, through no fault of their own, are not able to benefit from even a flourishing economy.

The ideas expressed in this speech also reflected my administration's awareness of the critical urgency of creating realistic plans for our children and their children as we approach a new millenium. In fact, most of the speeches in the last section of this book reflect my concerns about the future.

Today we take the first steps into the last decade between us and the twenty-first century.

From here, we can see the outlines of a bright and exciting new time of progress—for our state, our nation, and the world beyond. You and I have been working together to prepare for this moment for seven years.

In 1983, the first time I had the privilege of addressing you, the state was still feeling aftershocks of our economic crisis in the seventies. We had to close a potential deficit of nearly 2 billion dollars.

We knew—despite that—that if we were to make ourselves ready for the challenges and opportunities ahead, we needed to further reduce our state income taxes and to put more people to work. We knew we would have to rebuild roads and bridges, cleanse and preserve our environment, revitalize our schools, reorganize our criminal justice system, and adapt our human services to new, rapidly changing realities.

The challenge was actually even greater.

Unexpectedly, a terrible new drug, crack, appeared on the streets and brought with it a surge of violent crime. Homelessness appeared across the nation on a scale unseen since the Great Depression. The lethal syndrome, AIDS, spread with frightening effect.

And just when we needed its help most, Washington withdrew resources that we required to deal with these problems. These were awesome challenges.

But we were not intimidated. Nor did we use the federal government's failure to help as an excuse. Instead, you and I went to work. We put aside the unimportant differences between us and developed a new, vibrant ethic of cooperation—a new sense of family.

A thousand times a year and more, you and I—Democrats and Republicans—came together to restore the strength of the Empire State, and to prepare us for the challenge of the nineties and the incalculable potential of a whole new millennium.

We must continue to look forward.

But I think it's important for us to recall how much we've already accomplished, so that we will be less daunted when we see how much is still to be done. Together, we produced the two largest tax cuts in our history and the lowest income tax rate in thirty years. New Yorkers have paid seven and a half billion dollars less in income taxes because of our cuts.

Now there are over 1 million more people at work than in 1983. Our last annual unemployment rate was lower than at any time since 1970, and 100,000 people have left the welfare rolls in the last two years alone.

Our economic development efforts have made our state economy one of the largest in the entire world. . . . Only seven nations have greater economies than New York State.

We knew we had to invest more in education. Together, we increased state aid for local schools by 83 percent. Today, New York awards more college tuition aid to middle-class and low-income families than any state in the nation. In fact, more than the next two states combined!

We are first again, with Liberty Scholarships, which others are now emulating. Never again in New York will a student who qualifies for college be denied an education because he or she is poor.

Our Excellence in Teaching program has dedicated more than 500 million dollars to help attract the best teachers possible. And we've provided nearly 150,000 new computers, so our children can succeed in the high-tech competition of the twenty-first century.

Our investments in our fight against alcohol and drug abuse and related crime are up 400 percent. We nearly doubled our prison cells. Brought our state police force to its greatest strength ever. And developed the largest drug and alcohol treatment system in the nation, serving 100,000 people a day.

For seven years, the care of our most vulnerable—and our disabled—has been our first concern. We invest more than any other state in the care of people with mental illness and developmental disabilities, more in affordable housing and help for the homeless. And more, per capita, than any state in the struggle against AIDS—although it is still not enough.

No New York State governor and legislature have understood better the importance of our agricultural and rural communities—nor done as much for them.

With the Milk Security Fund, agricultural research and development, fairer assessments of farmlands, millions invested in Cornell, the Seal of Quality program, revitalization of the wine and grape industries, and the creation of the Office of Rural Affairs.

We agreed we should lead in protecting the environment. Together we created the first controls on acid rain implemented in the nation, the first energy plan integrated with environmental needs, a huge environmental bond issue, aggressive recycling and landfill-control programs. Thousands of acres of our natural beauty acquired and preserved.

There's more. Governments are often judged by the bricks and mortar they leave behind. By that measure, you—and I—would do especially well. We created a dynamic period of construction—nearly 50 billion dollars worth of bricks and mortar.

On our roads and bridges from one end of the state to the other you can see today the results of the Rebuilding New York program. Combined with safer speed limits, the nation's first seat belt law, and the twenty-one-year-old purchase age, this construction work made our highways the safest in our history.

With the city of New York, we are completing the splendid Battery Park City, so successful that it will produce more than 900 million dollars in profit that we can use for affordable housing in other parts of the city.

We invested still billions more to modernize our airports and tunnels, our subway, bus, and commuter lines, the facilities of the state and city of New York universities, and to build and repair public housing and public schools.

Wherever the need was, we were there—rebuilding New York.

We made our investments boldly, but prudently as well. For the first time our budgets were balanced by generally accepted accounting principles. Balanced so soundly last year, despite the immense potential deficit, that the investment rating agencies improved our credit standing. That saved us 26 million dollars in our required borrowing.

This is not a good record for you to boast of. . . . It is a superior one. I am sure it will embellish your campaign literature this year—on both sides of the aisle—as you seek to tell your voters what you have done.

Why shouldn't it? This record proves what we can do together, despite serious challenges. And we should remember that, because there are again new difficult tests as we reach for the promise of the twenty-first century.

Washington now admits states have a cluster of extraordinary national problems like drugs and inadequate education. But Washington says it can't help with national resources because they must go to huge federal income-tax cuts that help a lot of people, mostly the richest: actually, this only shifts the burden onto the states and the real estate and sales taxes that hurt a lot of people, but the middle class and poor most of all.

That has hurt us. Now the weakness of the national economy is hurting us more. As a result, much of the Northeast, including New York, today faces large potential deficits. We will not have the revenues to satisfy all the demands upon us, or even our own desires.

For everything there is a season . . . and a time. This will be a time for renewed discipline in our spending.

That is so clear that I will ask you again this year—but with even more urgency—to pass a law that limits expenditures.

On the other hand, while it is a time for discipline, it is not a time to stop our progress. We agreed the prudent investments we made together were needed for our future. We must not risk losing their benefits now.

We must not reduce our state police, or cut back our commitment to affordable housing, or lose ground in the repair and maintenance of roads and bridges, or reduce the high level of support to education and human services achieved over seven years.

And we must not lose the benefit of the lowest income-tax rates in thirty years.

My proposals for this year are contained in detail in the printed message delivered to you this morning. Let me highlight a few important particulars.

The Anti-Drug-Abuse Council headed by the lieutenant governor has submitted an excellent, comprehensive report. In recent days it has taken on new relevance because a number of well-known people have advocated legalizing drugs.

Added to that, there have been news reports of federal administration sources saying that drug treatment is too expensive to be worth doing. This is a troubling development.

The legalizers—as I understand them—argue that we have done all we can to save our children and others from the ravages of drugs. We are told we can't win this war. We ought to surrender, save ourselves the cost of combating it, rely instead on the odds that addiction from legally sanctioned drugs will strike someone else's family . . . but not ours.

Let me say as clearly as I can: I reject this idea as the abandonment of a whole generation of children—and adults—now caught in addiction. And of generations to come as well. I would not do it to my children. We ought not let the state do it to our children.

Instead of surrendering, I will recommend strengthening every part of our drug effort—law enforcement, education, treatment, prevention. My agenda in 1990 will include an unprecedented ex-

pansion of our alcohol and drug treatment capacity: 15,000 new
residential treatment beds and outpatient treatment for 20,000 additional people. We will give special attention to pregnant women
and mothers with young children.

This year we should demand that every school develop a clearly
articulated policy for an alcohol- and drug-free environment for
students and staff. The schools that teach our children should be
alcohol- and drug-free.

And it is time to hold to account the so-called casual users.
Casual drug use is not victimless behavior. It contributes huge sums
of money to the illegal drug trade, and makes victims of us all.

We simply cannot afford to imprison every casual drug user—
nor should we. But stiff fines, community service, and loss of motor
vehicle driving privileges can help deter casual drug use. I recommend we use all of these and a full agenda of other measures to
combat drug and alcohol abuse and related crime.

One of the most important things we can do to build a world-
class future for New York is to assure access to effective health care
for all our people. Despite the immense resources we have committed, our health care system is hurting, and so are some of the people
it is meant to serve.

With that in mind, over the past several months I have conducted a series of colloquia with representatives of every part of the
system. There is a clear consensus of views.

We need new and better ways to deal with reimbursement rates,
to ease health personnel shortages, to regulate the system, and to
communicate with the men and women who make the system work.
One thing is particularly apparent: adequate primary care in the
community—prevention and early intervention—will reduce illness
and help limit the overwhelming expense of hospital care.

It's also clear that we must do more for the 2.5 million New
Yorkers who are among the 37 million Americans with no health
insurance of any kind.

This year—in the third year of the Decade of the Child—I
will propose a new program, a unique one, I believe. I call it New
York CHILD—for Children's Health Insurance for Life-long Development. It will help cover every uninsured child in this state from
birth through age seventeen, for primary and preventive care, and
catastrophic illness.

Other parts of our human service network need strengthening as well.

I hope you will agree that one group in particular, workers in the private and not-for-profit parts of our terribly burdened foster care system, deserves larger salaries, and we should help supplement those salaries.

And that we need—once again—to expand further the availability of prekindergarten and day care.

I will propose as well a neighborhood-based initiative to improve services for pregnant women, new parents, and at-risk children in our most disadvantaged communities.

It is absolutely essential we continue to make education a priority.

But let's be candid.

As I noted earlier, while the federal government was withdrawing from its obligation to education, this state increased its investments over the last seven years—substantially. Even if we didn't raise school aid a penny this year, we would still have increased it more than twice the rate of inflation since 1983. That's true of other areas as well . . . law enforcement, transportation, mental health, the environment.

These increases should be kept in mind when the cry goes up this year: "What have you done for me lately?" Maybe we should first ask, "What have we done with what we received already?"

The Salerno Commission Report on State and Local Schools has been well received. We should begin to implement its main recommendations. We can achieve greater fairness by accounting for regional differences in the cost of education, and by blending attendance and enrollment in the pupil counts that determine aid.

I propose we try a new performance-oriented approach to public education: providing clear goals and effective measurement of student achievement, evaluating schools by improvement in student performance . . . and not by technical compliance with the words of state mandates. I will offer a program to demonstrate how this can work.

As we journey toward the next millennium, we must continue to serve the needs of our most vulnerable people.

I will ask you for a new supplement to SSI for persons with AIDS who are in special adult-care facilities. We will expand prevention efforts for high-risk adolescents, women, and young children, increase help for incarcerated or paroled persons with AIDS, and expand support for the community organizations which serve as our front line of defense.

And we have a solid, new program this year, begun jointly by the state and HELP, Andrew Cuomo's not-for-profit corporation. It is the first public residential health-care facility for persons with AIDS in the country. It will provide sixty-six beds. We will replicate this cost-effective prototype to create hundreds of other beds.

We have a strong record of helping our growing elderly population. We should build on it with: expanded in-home services for the elderly, a more efficient prescription drug program, mandatory Medicare assignment . . . and more, including a new state veterans nursing home.

As part of our long-term plan to assist the homeless mentally ill, we'll work with New York City to develop additional beds, including new SRO and supported housing units. And we'll expand and improve services for people with disabilities.

One reason we accomplished so much is our better understanding of a basic truth: As a state we get most of our wealth from our own private economy. So, we must continue to strengthen our state economy—to develop the wealth we need to build, to teach, to house, to cure.

But there is a powerful new reality we must confront. We are locked in a global economic struggle—as dangerous to our future as the military competition of the cold war was.

As a nation, we are not doing well in this competition. Our competitors outproduce us. They outsell us. They take jobs and profits that used to be ours. We have become the world's largest debtor. We used to be the world's largest creditor. We now borrow billions of dollars from people who sell us things we used to sell to them. That national weakness hurts us in New York State.

At the same time, this new reality of global competition offers a golden new opportunity for trade, investments, jobs, wealth, and progress. While we wait for the federal government to adopt new economic policies for the 1990s that will help seize these opportunities, we must more aggressively help ourselves.

And we can. As the ninth largest economy in the world, we

can have considerable international influence. As a state, we have already begun to globalize our trade and investment.

Why shouldn't we be able to lead all the states in the Union in exports to Canada, the European Community, the African nations, Latin America, and the newly free peoples of Eastern Europe? And lead as well in obtaining from them—and the Asian nations as well—productive and beneficial investments here?

I have asked our director of economic development, Vincent Tese, to invigorate our promotion of exports—emphasizing high technology and agriculture—and to expand our current international partnership program. Our extensive "Global New York" agenda will be a centerpiece of our work in the months ahead.

To compete in the twenty-first century, we must adapt our world-class transportation system to speed the flow of goods.

For example, we will work with Washington and Ontario to reduce the growing congestion at our ports of entry that restricts access to the benefits of free trade with Canada. We will consider a major new crossing at the Niagara frontier—possibly a new bridge linking Buffalo and Canada!

I spoke earlier of all we accomplished in protecting our environment. It's time now for another solid down payment on a better and more beautiful future for the generations to follow us.

We all agree on the importance of these things: helping local governments deal with solid waste, preserving environmentally sensitive lands, maintaining our magnificent parks and historic treasures. To do all these things, I will ask your support for a twenty-first-century environmental bond issue of 1.9 billion dollars.

There is more, of course, that we must do together for our future—more than I can detail this afternoon. But let me mention a few more particulars.

Raising Workers' Compensation benefits and the minimum wage.

Extending—this month—the protections for Mitchell-Lama residents, or tens of thousands of people could lose their homes.

A strong law against bias-related violence. New ways to discourage investment in South Africa. A law banning assault weapons. And a law establishing life imprisonment without parole.

As freedom and democracy are enjoying a rebirth around the world, we should strengthen them here, at the source.

I will ask you to give New Yorkers an important extension of their right to participate in their government, with a limited initiative and referendum. It would require us to vote publicly—one way or the other—on proposals the citizens indicate by petition they believe to be particularly significant.

And we should go forward with election law, voting, and judicial reforms. This year we must finally provide the badly needed judges I have asked for—twice before.

My message contains other significant matters, including an attempt—beginning at page 42—at a broader discussion of the complex issue of abortion.

Honoring our individual political affiliations but honoring our responsibility to the whole state first—you and I have made good progress since 1983.

And now there is new hope for even greater progress. Now, finally, the cold war that cost us trillions of dollars of our wealth is over—smothered under the rubble of the walls that for forty-five years stood between freedom and the people of the Soviet Union and Eastern Europe.

In place of cold war, we have the chance of a lifetime . . . for peace, for building friendship, for growth, for goodness.

If we only understand this bright new chance fully and use it well, historians a hundred years from now will look back and write about the political miracle of the twentieth century.

Now, gradually, a significant part of our immense national budget can be freed for other purposes. Some of it to reduce the crippling federal deficit and debt. Some of it to deal with the urgent national concerns that have so burdened the states—the drug war declared by the president but so far lacking enough troops and equipment; the costs of education; affordable housing; deteriorated roads and bridges; child care.

Congress and the president will have to decide how to use the peace dividend, how to make happen this immense potential for all of us. But before they make their decisions, they should hear first from New York!

We should raise our voices, again, together, the way we did in the successful struggle we made against the denial of deductibility of state and local taxes in 1985 and '86. You and I—Republicans and Democrats—helped lead the nation then; we should do it again.

We should assemble all our political strength—Stan and Ralph and Mel, Rapp and Fred, Tom Whalen of Albany, Guy Molinari of Staten Island, Mary McPhillips of Orange County, David Dinkins and Andrew O'Rourke. Our Democratic attorney general, our Republican comptroller.

Let's go down to Washington together to see all of them there—Democrats and Republicans, Senators George Mitchell and Bob Dole, Congressmen Tom Foley and Bob Michel, and the White House.

Let them know we stand united in our determination to give our children and grandchildren the advantages needed to realize the full promise of the new millennium.

And what a magnificent promise it is!

Think of it. In two centuries, no matter how far we've come—and we've come far—we have not even begun to reach the full potential of all of our people. The work we've done together in seven years and the work I propose we do this year will bring us closer to realizing all the capacity inherent in the people of the Empire State.

Imagine what we could do if we realized it perfectly.

Think of it. If we could reaffirm the notion of family and reject—as we always have at our best—the proposition that we can exist and thrive as a house divided—or a world divided—fractionalized . . . by sex, or nationality, or race, or color, or religion. If we could rouse ourselves from indifference toward the growing gap between our wealthiest and most fortunate citizens and those who continue to struggle.

If we could wean ourselves from a national addiction that has made our country the prime market for the world's drug trade. If all those who wound up in treatment centers or prisons were, instead, working in laboratories or factories or offices, using their gifts productively, helping themselves, and the rest of us.

Imagine then, what we could do in this state . . . and in this nation.

Then, someday, not too long from now, another governor could stand here and tell his audience—no, tell her audience—that we, the generations that endured depression and global war and the decades-long threat of nuclear destruction, never lost hope and never stopped going forward.

That we took—always—as our continuing inspiration the words of a great New York poet, Walt Whitman, who beckoned us to come still further, by reminding us that ". . . the strongest and sweetest songs yet remain to be sung."

Let us sing them, together.

Thank you.

One of the most frustrating aspects of governance in this complicated age is the difficulty we have trying to communicate complex policy questions to the general public, without whose interest and support real change is impossible. This 1990 speech reflects such difficulties. It deals with Washington's so-called New Federalism that shifted more of the country's burdens to the states, while giving them a relatively smaller portion of the national resources.

That policy, so dominant in the 1980s and early 1990s, has produced huge increases in state and local taxes across the country, while the federal government boasted it had cut federal taxes. And still the states are not able to meet the growing burdens created by soaring health care costs, drugs, violence, homelessness, and AIDS. Few people talk about these problems, except at places like the Kennedy School. The result is that the general public is unaware of what's happening. Even a remarkably substantive presidential election in 1992 did not deal significantly with the matter.

Today, state and local governments face new challenges that have prompted scholars and students to ask some fundamental questions:

Is government working?

Can we, in 1990, say—as Lincoln did in the last century—that "the legitimate object of government is to do for the people what needs to be done, but which they cannot, by individual effort, do at all, or do so well, for themselves"?

If so, what role should the federal, state, and local governments have in that collective action? Are there options available? What has been tried? What has succeeded? What has failed?

As the governor of a large state who's been wrestling with these questions since 1983, I'd like to use this occasion to consider a few of them.

I should begin by noting that, while the challenges we face are new, obviously, the questions about government's role are not. No one in America knows better than this audience that the geniuses who founded our nation were searching for answers to these basic questions 200 years ago.

In 1781, thirteen disparate states—wanting not to be totally alone but concerned about sacrificing independence—had strung themselves together in loose confederation. But, the desire to be separate and independent overwhelmed the instinct for cooperation. Walls went up between the states, fragmenting them, denying them the strength that comes from unity.

So the founders made a new judgment . . . to *nationalize*, to try to form a more perfect Union whose basic understandings and principles would give the thirteen governments a common cause and a cohesive strength. They wrote a Constitution that created a new overarching government with greater central power, while reserving to the states significant rights and responsibilities.

It was a unique document describing a unique idea. It was written in broad strokes with room left for application to the unseeable, unknowable developments of an indefinite future. The original blueprint of our national unity would be tested—and shaped—by being stretched and configured on the Procrustean bed of reality.

It has been.

Through the early years of confusion . . . through years of growth by accession and conquest . . . through war and civil war . . . the *national* government it created has constantly moved America forward. Sometimes in fits and starts, but inexorably.

After a miraculous journey of only 200 years, the *United* States of America—through the power of coming together—have become the most powerful single nation on earth.

In this century, the strength of our national government rescued the entire nation from the depths of the Great Depression.

The *Social Security Act of 1935* created a covenant between generations to assure that senior citizens would live in dignity.

The *Marshall Plan* turned the devastation of World War II into a new age for democracy.

The *GI Bill of Rights* educated a generation of returning veterans.

The *National Defense Education Act* and the space program that followed put American footprints on the moon and made us first in technological advancement.

Positive national strength gave us *Medicaid, Medicare*, the *Civil Rights Act of 1964*, the *Voting Rights Act of 1965*, the *Clean Air* and *Clean Water* acts.

We could not have succeeded as we have, if we had not responded to *national* challenges with *national* solutions. Make no mistake: *The loosely tied raft of confederation would have broken up in the rough waters of our history.*

That familiar history is good to recall today when the whole nation faces a new series of challenges that raise disturbing questions about our future.

Even before the stunning invasion of Kuwait by Iraq, our national interest had been under siege . . . by the largest annual federal deficit and the greatest accumulated debt in our history; by lagging productivity growth, and stagnating wages; and by an astonishing plague of drugs and the violent crime it generates.

We have other national challenges.

Roads and bridges crumbling from coast to coast; acid rain pouring across state and national borders; AIDS; homeless families living out of automobiles; 12 million children going to sleep hungry; 23 million Americans who can't read a job application; 37 million Americans living in fear of getting sick because they have no health insurance to pay their bills.

These are not isolated, local vulnerabilities.

Surely, it would be a delusion to believe that if Florida or New York loses the drug battles raging in their states, Georgia or New Jersey can escape the consequences.

Or that if we fail to liberate children from poverty in Illinois or Arizona, Ohio or California will not suffer.

And surely it would be folly to believe—as long as the winds carry pollutants across our borders from the west and south—that New York or Massachusetts alone can stop the corrosive, killing effects of acid rain.

The nation can no more leave it to the individual states to fight these national problems than it can expect the states' valiant militias and National Guard units to fight and win a war in the Middle East without the federal army, navy, marines, air force . . . and Treasury.

Two hundred years of history have instructed us how to use national strength to deal with national challenges like these.

But in the last ten years, we seem to have forgotten—or ignored—those lessons.

About a decade ago, the federal government announced a different approach. It was called "the New Federalism." As the theory evolved, it called for the federal government to withdraw from previous commitments to help the states meet national needs.

The federal cutbacks over the decade were massive. Housing aid was cut 80 percent. Energy conservation, 67 percent. Job training, 65 percent. Revenue sharing, obliterated. Urban development grants, eliminated. Money for education, the environment, mass transit . . . all cut.

The states were told that we could fill these gaps and build a stronger nation, without the federal government using its hands . . . or its resources.

We would, instead, be delivered to the promised land by a magical force called "supply-side economics." Supply-side's magic started with huge income tax cuts, benefiting especially the richest Americans.

The theory was that because the wealthy had so much money already, they would not consume this new bonanza but would invest it in the private economy. The private economy would then get so strong it would create enough new revenues to balance the federal budget in three years despite these huge tax cuts and an accompanying huge military buildup.

There would be loaves and fishes enough for everyone.

So robust would the new economy be that, with the states gathering huge amounts of new revenues at *their* level, the federal government could rationalize cutting back federal support for domestic programs.

Well, supply-side proved to be more myth than magic.

Because the tax cuts didn't generate the revenues needed to pay our federal bills, today the nation borrows huge amounts from foreigners we used to sell to, to buy from them the things they used to buy from *us*—like cars, and steel, and electronics.

The effect of all this?

Supply-side has been such a palpable failure that even its most zealous high priests now shrink from acknowledging their worship at the altar of this false idol. In less than a decade we went from being the world's largest creditor nation to the world's largest debtor. The national debt—which has tripled to over 3 trillion dollars since 1980—is now a great albatross around the nation's neck, dragging it into a sea of red ink. It costs us nearly 200 *billion* dollars a year in *interest* alone, and seriously imperils the entire national economy.

There have been other effects.

Together, the New Federalism and supply-side have led to a massive, simultaneous, twin redistribution.

They have redistributed a large part of the burden of national problems away from the national government and onto the states, separately. And they have simultaneously produced a massive redistribution of the nation's *wealth*, away from the middle class and into the relatively small stratum of our wealthiest Americans.

The progressivity of our taxes—that is, their relationship to the amount of income and ability to pay—has been nearly destroyed.

At the federal level, the top income tax rate for the wealthiest Americans was cut from 70 percent down to 28 percent. At the same time, the Social Security tax, a blatantly *regressive* charge, increased for about 130 million American workers, and their employers. As the income tax went down, depriving the national treasury of revenues it needed, this payroll tax went up, dramatically, and was used to fill the hole.

This regressivity trickled down to the state and local level.

While Washington politicians chanted boastful slogans about their income tax cuts, state and local governors were forced to raise revenues to assume national burdens Washington once carried.

As a result, states and localities looked to the taxes they believed would least threaten their competitive position. That was sales and real estate taxes—taxes that also have *no* effective relationship to one's ability to pay. Nationally, sales and real estate taxes doubled in the 1980s.

In effect, the middle class and the working poor have been paying for the huge income tax cuts at the federal level. But the truth is that—at least until now—distracted by the increasingly harsh realities of day-to-day existence, few of the middle class and poor realized it.

Those of us whose business it is to observe these things do realize it, understand it, and resent it.

Now, to add further anxiety to already substantial injury, the federal government—desperate for ways to pay the bills resulting from fiscal miscalculation, and not willing to acknowledge its mistakes—is considering shifting still more of the obligation away from Washington and onto the states.

They are once again threatening states, as they did in 1985 and 1986, with the disallowance of deductibility of state and local income and property taxes. To put it more clearly, Washington wants to tax, at the federal level, taxes already paid by Americans to state and local governments, at the same time preserving the huge tax cuts for the wealthiest Americans and perhaps even adding a capital gains tax cut as a further sweetener.

The disallowance of deductibility would be a new double tax further punishing the separate states already bearing the load of federal abandonment. Today, thirty-seven states are in serious fiscal trouble, sixteen already in recession, many others on the edge, all being dragged down by the rapidly ebbing national tide.

This proposal would take still more resources from children, from police, from fire fighters, from hospital workers, from the people who perform the public services. And it would encourage more regressive taxation at the state and local level and widen regional economic disparities among the states.

The New Federalism offered up in 1980—and the supply-side miracle that was supposed to make it work—for a while fooled the nation into believing we could overcome national challenges without a unified national response. And left us off balance as we struggle to regain our footing for the global economic competition.

It happened because we forgot the lesson learned by our founding fathers 200 years ago.

Today, we have a "fend-for-yourself" federalism, which forces the states to try to go it alone. This creates a tension—between the needs of states to raise revenues for unmet problems and their need to create congenial tax policies to attract and hold increasingly mobile businesses. States are pitted against each other in the kind of destructive competition that we sought to move away from 200 years ago when we tore up the Articles of *Confederation.*

Ironically, this is occurring just as Europe moves toward *consolidation,* uniting, in order to make themselves *stronger.* In 1992, the European Economic Community will fuse itself into the largest economy—and the largest consumer market—in the world.

They, getting stronger by uniting; *we* growing weaker—by *fragmentation.*

And so, we are at a crossroads in our history.

We can allow a regressive federalism to push us back towards the idea of confederation, leaving our capacities unevenly distributed and weakened by the scattering among our several states. Or we can choose to forge a new *progressive federalism* to consolidate our strength and thereby increase it.

It seems clear to me that before we choose a path we need to remind ourselves of the truth that gave birth to this nation. We are *not* just a collection of individual communities.

At our *best,* especially when we are being tested, we are a *national community.* Today, as we struggle to rethink what form the future of federalism in America should take, we should apply a simple test: does it strengthen or weaken our national community?

The federalism that *best* suits our time is one that recognizes our *inter*dependence and acts on it. Not by *dividing power,* but rather by *sharing it.* By pooling efforts between local, state, and federal government—to forge a *progressive federalism* that directs our national strength toward achieving common national goals.

The rest of the world is not wrong.

Nor were we, 200 years ago.

A federalism for our times should return to the principles that made us strong. In place of the failed New Federalism, we should return to the recognition of *national* responsibility for *national* problems, *local* responsibility for *local* problems, and *shared* responsibility for *shared* problems.

State and local governments—those closest to the people— should continue to play a leading role in education; in maintaining their *local* infrastructure and their own amenities; and in designing, administering, and applying national programs to meet human needs, as efficiently and as effectively as possible.

Successful programs, already in place on the state and local level, can serve as national models to solve national problems. But, at the same time that we reaffirm the unique role state and local governments play, we must acknowledge that without national leadership and national resources, innovative state programs in housing and job training and drug treatment will address only a small part of our major national challenges.

We need a *progressive federalism* that recognizes our national problems will not be solved by sporadic successes in scattered states.

It has been established by no less a figure than the president himself that drugs—and the violence, destruction, and terrible expense they create—are a *national* problem . . . even public enemy number one!

How then can the White House declare war on drugs yet fail to give the states all the help they need to fight the battles raging in the streets of their cities?

Even President Eisenhower acknowledged that the roads and bridges and infrastructure that tie the states together are so vitally national in their implications that they should forever remain high on the list of federal concerns. But now the funds collected by Washington to help the states maintain and improve their highways are purloined by the federal government to conceal the true dimensions of its fiscal debacle.

We need to change that. The national government must decide to do the things that *only* the national government can do—like reducing the federal deficit to help reduce interest rates and jumpstart the national economy. Like negotiating with governments to open up foreign markets.

And where shared responsibility is needed, the federal government must lead, not abdicate its responsibility.

Only a *shared* national effort will end hunger in America and rescue 12 million children at risk.

Only a *shared* national effort can provide the necessary job training to prepare our work force and maintain our technological edge through renewed investments in research and development.

While some states have made valiant efforts to build new transitional and affordable housing, we won't end homelessness without a renewed federal role.

Only strong federal leadership will extricate the nation from its dependence on foreign oil. Some of the states—like my own—have extensive, carefully analyzed and constructed energy programs.

But a patchwork of state efforts will not be enough to secure our energy supply, or to protect our air, land, and water for future generations.

And if there is a need for further revenues to do all these things, then they should be gathered from those best able to afford them. For ten years those taxes have been essentially state and local and regressive. Now, to restore some balance, *new* taxes should be *federal* and *progressive*.

Conceding the truth of what we say here certainly does not make it easier to deal with what has been, until now, an intractable federal budget problem. But trying to make a budget that ignores our national challenges would be absurdly unrealistic.

Of course, it would be easier to balance the budget if Washington pretended the needs that are so obvious to every governor in America did not exist, but that would be like operating on the patient for ulcers and leaving a cancer in his stomach.

The threat will not go away because we find it difficult to deal with. And let's be honest with ourselves. The deficit is a hard problem, but we know that it is not the wallet Washington lacks; it is the will!

We know Washington can make difficult choices—and find the wealth—when it chooses to. It will find 500 billion dollars to bail out banks and bankers that stole the people's money.

Think about it: 5 billion dollars would allow us to reach nearly every child eligible for *Head Start.* And yet, we're told we don't have the resources. But when it comes to the S and L's, we are ready to commit 100 times that amount. How does that make sense? Are the savings and loans 100 times more important?

This is a challenging time. But it can be converted into the beginning of a whole new dynamic era, if it inspires a renewal of our commitment to a wisdom 200 years old.

We should begin by replacing the failed federalism of the past decade with a *progressive federalism*—a bolder, sounder pooling of the strength and wisdom of *all* the states to revitalize our full potential as a nation. And that potential is vast.

For all the wrong turns and meanderings our history has taken us on, we have always—in the end—moved toward the light. Something in us survives all the temporary distractions.

I think it is the power of the idea that lay at the core of the American story at its founding, and is resurrected throughout our history.

Because I am more comfortable with simple notions, I've called it "family."

But by whatever name it goes, it is something deep in our national psyche . . . something that rises to the surface in times of war or other national crisis . . . something we need now to tap into.

It is that hard-to-define feeling, that sense, that while we cherish our own individuality, *we are also part of something bigger than ourselves,* bigger than any individual . . . and yes, bigger than any state.

Perhaps it is to this idea that we should dedicate the Taubman Building. Perhaps with *it* as our inspiration, we can excite the imaginations and rouse the hopes of young and old alike. I hope so.

I hope the graduates of the Kennedy School, and the Harvard freshmen assembled here today—and all those who will help build America's future—will be exhilarated by the bright prospects still ahead of us.

I hope they will be believers and doers who will take what has been passed on to them and make it something better. Honoring us by their works, and by their desire to be more than we have been.

That, after all, has been the story of our history.

And it is a glorious story.

Despite our faults, in only 200 years we have become the greatest nation on earth. With one hand tied behind our back, without yet fully realizing the potential of women, of African-Americans, of a population disabled by social problems and failures.

Imagine how much stronger we could be if all our people were truly free to use the opportunity of this miraculous place.

Imagine how much more we could achieve if we could only remember—as we have when we had to in the past—that we are at our best *as a family,* coming together for common purposes.

Imagine how much more we could achieve, if only we could remember that we are at our best as a *nation.*

My ethnic roots have been an increasing source of pride to me over the years. I talked about ethnicity here in a speech that I rewrote in large part while sitting at the dais listening to a number of speakers—including Alan Alda, Dan Marino, and three or four other celebrities dazzling the audience. I did not get to the microphone until about 11 P.M. It was a last speaker's nightmare. Despite that, my call to my Italian-American brothers and sisters to lead America in a movement to assure that the kind of bigotry that has wounded us would not ricochet throughout society, wounding others in the process, was well received.

This room is filled with Italian-American men and women—and our friends—all having come together to celebrate our heritage. To show our respect, not just for each other, but for two lands—America, which claims our allegiance, our gratitude, our profound sense of indebtedness, and our love, and *Italy*, to which we are bound by the earlier ties of blood and remembrance.

It will be difficult to speak to you now. Not only because we are threatening to make the *annual* dinner a year long, but because what I could say has already been said—with as much and more eloquence and humor than I could muster.

Alan Alda even did it in three languages, although I thought his Italian had a bit of Fordham Jesuit Irish accent.

And Paola Fendi—in that truly magnificent Italian language—when she apologized for not talking to us in English. I thought it was like Caruso apologizing for singing because he couldn't whistle.

I'll have to settle for trying simply to recapitulate here at the end of the night, emphasizing a bit perhaps the Italians in our experience who never got the chance to wear tuxedos.

Tonight there is no problem recognizing in the four individuals the Foundation honors attributes and characteristics that have been Italy's legacy to the world for centuries, and that Italian-Americans have used to enrich the mosaic of our common life together here in America.

Paola Fendi—a contemporary trustee of Italy's great legacy to the world. A woman in the glittering tradition of Italian artists and sculptors, those with an eye for everything beautiful, graceful, and exquisite hidden in God's Creation, and a talent for bringing it forth with her touch for all to admire.

Dan Marino, a Caesar to his team—making the plan, sounding the signal, directing his troops. With strength and cunning and courage, pushing ahead through all the obstacles. Dan's sport is a metaphor of the power of generations of Roman and Italian leaders, and of the inspiring triumphs of the immigrants in America—won through struggle and sweat and muscles stretched to their limit.

Alan Alda—inheritor of the exuberant wit, and wisdom, of Dante and Boccaccio, holding up a mirror to life, making us laugh or weep at the joy and the folly and the sadness of the Divine Comedy as it is played out in modern American society.

And Alfred Checchi—his domain, private enterprise, travel and transportation and commerce, fields in which, as Ambassador Petrignani noted, and as any honest historian will admit, Italy taught the modern world much of what it knows.

Am I making too much of the qualities and attributes that these four outstanding individuals bring to their work?

I don't think so.

It's right to praise them. Right to project them!

In fact, I think that particularly *today* our world needs very badly to be *instructed* by what these four extraordinary leaders demonstrate in common, through their achievements.

An insistence on excellence, and a willingness to work for it. To hope and pray for change or divine favor, of course . . . but to understand that we have no control over that, only over how hard we try, what use we make of our talents.

They bring, too:

An approach to the world and to all of God's Creation that is passionate, creative, loving. That allows us to complement God's handiwork, to take *his* world—or *her* world—and re-create it.

And a spirit that refuses to be discouraged by hard circumstances, by the defensive line or corporate competitors, by Neilson ratings or drama and fashion critics.

All these qualities, I suggest to you, are as much characteristic of the Italian-American community as our physical resemblance or similar-sounding names, our common love of family, of fashion, of music and dance . . . and of intelligent joy.

It is all there—not bought, or stolen—there in the blood. Infused gradually until finally it is ineradicable.

From centuries of Italian culture, from the Italian Renaissance, from the great Etruscan and Roman civilizations before that, which left an imprint on the entire Western world's alphabet, and laws, and arts, and public works.

There, latently, even in the many of our immediate forebears who had little chance to realize and express the high culture and richness of classical and modern Italy because of their circumstances. There—latently—even in the impoverished and illiterate rural villagers scraping subsistence from an unforgiving land.

The blood is the same. And we share it.

We share something else—our experience in America, our struggle, survival, and success here. We share, reaching the point where we can give full expression to our ancient gifts.

Everyone here tonight understands the distance our people have come in realizing dreams that a generation ago would have seemed too remote even to speak about. Everyone here remembers Momma and Poppa or their parents or even, perhaps, their parents' parents who came to this country.

Some came already educated, highly skilled, even wealthy. But many others—shiploads full—came with nothing but the things they could carry with them. A child in their arms, perhaps. Like Al Checchi's grandparents. Deposited on the shores of a great but strange and hostile city, where they knew no one, could not speak the language, could not see their future.

But they had courage and determination. And the strength of thousands of years in their blood.

We know what they faced. We've heard the stories, seen the pictures, cried at the movies.

We know how some of them were laughed at, how some were ridiculed; we know the prejudice that confronted them.

This is not something we read about in somebody else's autobiography. These are the facts of our lives, pictures in our own albums. Many of you don't have to look too far back to remember all of it—the good and the bad.

I have my own memories.

Of an immigrant father—Andrea Cuomo from Nocera Inferiore—who came here and dug ditches until he could save enough to buy the small grocery store and the rooms above it where I was born.

Five feet, six inches tall, 155 pounds soaking wet, up every day long before dawn to go to the market for the day's produce. Always working, hardly a break or a day off, never a vacation. Saving what he could not for himself but for his children. So they could have the education he was denied. And maybe a "sit-down" wedding for his daughter, Marie.

And of Momma—Immaculata Giordano, hesitant about leaving her mountain in Tramonti, her reluctance confirmed when she first got here . . . and later.

She will never forget when we moved from the rooms above the store to a small house in Holliswood, Queens—then a neighborhood of Anglo-Saxon families . . . no blacks, no Jews, and no Italians. Certainly no Italians who had once been poor and illiterate.

She will never forget the first meeting with her new neighbors, or stop telling you about it. Three distinguished-looking women came down the hill to see her. She was outside sweeping the walk. They were a welcoming team of sorts, but they bore no gifts. She remembers them as "freddo"—cold, aloof. And they said to her, "You must be the Italian woman. Well, we want you to know that you are a part of a very good community. And please remember to keep the tops on your garbage pails."

I remember getting out of law school and finding out that I couldn't even get an interview for a job with a top law firm. The dean of the law school thought he knew why, and suggested that I change my name.

I remember that when I became lieutenant governor in 1979 we took a poll. Only 6 percent of the people interviewed said they knew who I was. But 9 percent of the people—apparently just on the basis of my name—suspected connections with the Mafia.

Many of us have these memories. That feeling that wells up in the chest, the anger that comes to the lips, sometimes even the tears it brings to the eyes.

If that were all there was to our story, it would hardly be worth telling. But there is *more—much* more.

Look around this room. You are executives, professors, scientists, writers, prelates, politicians, men and women of substance and influence, free at last of the outright bigotry and snide condescension that limited the immigrant world of our ancestors.

Standing here, it's hard to believe it was ever any other way.

In this room is the *rest* of the story. A story written from all the acts of simple goodness and pride and courage—all the achievements of the giants on whose shoulders we stand. Of people who conquered prejudice, who fought their way up from poverty, helped win wars, who raised factories, skyscrapers, churches, who never stopped reaching, building, and believing. A story that the National Italian American Foundation tells to the world, helping to write new chapters through its advocacy, and its cultural, educational, and research activities.

It's a good thing the Foundation does: we should do more of it.

We should use our history as a basis for making sure that we Italian-Americans continue to make a difference in this society, that we involve ourselves in furthering those policies which embody what the Italian journey into America has been all about—opportunity, hope, equality, compassion, social justice, freedom.

We should show our gratitude to this magic land that gave us a chance, by helping to widen the circle of opportunity for those still excluded—for Italian-Americans of course. But for all the new seekers—of whatever blood. Of whatever origin or color.

Yes, always we must be proud of our contribution to the mosaic. But also we should help make it a world *wider* than the one that welcomed us.

Make it a world *wiser* than the one that welcomed us.

Make it a world *sweeter* than the one that welcomed us.

We should refuse to let the discrimination that may have wounded some of us keep ricocheting through society, wounding others.

We should affirm in our lives the grandness of the values taught us by the highest and humblest of our forebears, through their lives of courage and compassion.

It seems to me, ladies and gentlemen, that the nights like this one have made this a time of satisfaction for Italian-Americans. But if I may suggest, respectfully, I believe we should commit ourselves to assuring it is also a beginning, the opening of a new chapter in our people's history. One that will make our children remember us, our generation, with the pride, respect, and even amazement with which we remember those who came before us—those who with so very little help did so very much.

John Steinbeck could have had our immigrant forebears in mind when he wrote: "It's a story you can hardly believe, but it's true and it's funny and it's beautiful.

"How can such courage be, and such faith?

"Strange things happened to them, some bitterly cruel and some so beautiful that the faith is refired forever."

And that's our task today.

To re-fire the faith in our story . . . in the American dream . . . in this place that has been for us nothing short of a miracle.

Thank you for allowing me to join you.

Viva America! Viva Italia!

Who Is God?

October 15, 1991

92nd Street y, New York, New York

Here's a presentation I never would have tried if I had realized what was involved. Roger Rosenblatt, a real writer and thinker, and some of his similarly gifted friends, were having a public discussion on religion and thought it would be good to have "the state" involved. I agreed, mostly out of respect and admiration for Roger, without thinking a lot about what was required. At the last minute I discovered I would need to make a direct presentation of fifteen minutes or so in answer to the question: "Who is God?" I was consternated. What I produced was barely the beginning of an answer. Someday, when I'm wiser, I'll try again.

When I was asked a couple of weeks ago to join this distinguished panel to discuss the question, "Who is God?" I told the moderator I didn't think I could add anything to the subtlety, the intelligence, and the splendid articulation that was sure to come from the panel as already constructed.

He agreed . . . I couldn't add anything.

He said he didn't want me for any of those things. He wanted me to supply another dimension. He wanted me to talk about "Who God is in the context of political power . . . or doesn't God talk to politicians?"

That's a nice question. And because I was eager to be here to listen to all the bright people on this stage and in the always extraordinary audience drawn to the 92nd Street "Y," I agreed to come and to offer—briefly—my impressions on that relatively narrow question that touches on government and politics. Not quite so personally, not quite so impressionistically, but I hope nearly as briefly as my colleagues.

I do it certainly not as a scholar, or a theologian, or an apologist, but as an ordinary New Yorker—from Queens, from asphalt streets and stickball, from a poor and middle-class neighborhood—who made a living, helped raise a family, and found his way, somewhat improbably, into the difficult world of politics.

I do it as a person who struggles to keep a belief in God that he inherited. I do it as a Catholic raised in a religion closer to the peasant roots of the simple Sunday mass practitioners than to the high intellectual traditions of the Talmudic scholars, elegant Episcopalian homilists, or abstruse Jesuit teachers.

The simple folk of South Jamaica who came from behind the grocery stores, from the tenements, from the little houses on Liverpool Street, perceived the world then as a sort of cosmic basic-training course, filled by God with obstacles and traps to weed out the recruits unfit for eventual service in the heavenly host. The obstacles were everywhere.

Their fate on earth was to be "the poor, banished children of Eve, mourning and weeping in this vale of tears," until by some combination of grace and good works—and luck—they escaped final damnation. Their sense of who God is was reflected in the collective experience of people who through most of their history had little chance to concern themselves with helping the poor or healing the world's wounds. They *were* the poor, the wounded. Their poverty and their endless, sometimes losing, struggle to feed themselves and hold their families together had varied little across the centuries.

It was a cold voice they heard from God on Beaver Road, next to a cemetery across the street from St. Monica's, where a famous ex-jockey, one of the homeless winos, froze to death sleeping in a large wooden crate. It was hard to see God's goodness in the pathetic faces of the customers in our small grocery store who pleaded with my father for bread, and maybe some cold cuts—till the next relief check came in.

It got harder still, during and after the Second World War, when the best we could say about victory was that the new terror was put down . . . for a while. And a gold star in the window announced that someone's son had been killed, his mother's prayers at St. Monica's never answered. It was difficult to believe God spoke at Hiroshima, either.

Who could blame them for feeling that if God was not dead, he must surely be looking in another direction. Vietnam didn't help. Nor the terrible—terrible—1960s. The sadness of the sixties was memorialized by Simon and Garfunkel: "Where have you gone, Joe DiMaggio—our nation turns its lonely eyes to you. What's that you say, Mrs. Robinson? Joltin' Joe has left and gone away."

No more John F. Kennedy, no more Martin Luther King. No more Bobby Kennedy. Nothing to believe in. Nothing to grab hold of. Nothing to uplift us.

People weren't asking *who* is God? They were asking . . . *Is* God?

For some of us the awful burden of disbelief became intolerable. The absurdity of a world without explanation was too much to live with. Our intellects pushed to find a rationale, an explanation, an excuse . . . *anything* to take the place of despair . . . something larger than ourselves to believe in.

If the answer could not be compelled by our intellect, we pleaded for an answer that, at least, we could *choose* to believe without contradicting that intellect. It had to be more than just a God of prohibition. More than just a God of guilt and punishment. It had to be more than John Calvin's chilling conclusion that God loves Jacob but hates Esau. More than Robert Browning's cold and capricious Caliban. It must be a God like the one that was promised in the ancient books: a God of mercy, a God of peace, a God of hope. In the end, to make any sense, it must be a God of love!

Many of us needed so much to believe in a God that we were in danger—as suggested by the old sinner that Ivan described in *The Brothers Karamazov*—of making one up. But we didn't have to. We simply had to be taught.

We were, by one man: a scientist, a paleontologist, a person who understood evolution, a soldier who knew the inexplicable evil of the battlefield, a scholar who knew the ages, a philosopher, a theologian, a believer. And a great priest.

The Jesuit priest Teilhard de Chardin heard our lament, and he answered us. He reoriented our theology and rewrote its language. His wonderful book *The Divine Milieu*, dedicated to "those who love the world," made negativism a sin. Teilhard glorified the world and everything in it. He taught us how the whole universe—even the pain and imperfection we see—is sacred. He taught it in powerful, cogent prose. He taught it in soaring poetry.

Faith, he said, is not a call to escape the world, but to embrace it. Creation is not an elaborate testing ground, but an invitation to join in the work of restoration. God created the world, but he did not finish it. He left that to us. What an extraordinary reaffirmation of Christian optimism!

Think of it. He left it to us to finish the work of creation. Something larger than ourselves to believe in, indeed! A whole world to work on. There are other places to work on improving the world than in politics and government . . . but surely that is a good one.

So . . . who is God? He is a voice urging us to be involved in actively working to improve the world he created—every way possible, including through government. Because it is a world he loves so much that he made us so we could enjoy it.

This is not exactly an exotic view. Until recently, most Americans accepted the idea that government was created among us—by us—"to promote the general welfare," to protect God's water and soil and air from contamination, to secure decent care for those who cannot care for themselves, the sick, the indigent, the homeless, to help people find the dignity of work. Until recently, our history had been largely one of expanding that concept, reaching out to include those once excluded—women, blacks, the poor, the disabled.

But this belief in benevolent activism—in the commitment of each to the welfare of all, especially to the least among us—is today increasingly attacked and ridiculed and denied. There is a powerful move toward a new ethic for government, one that says: "God helps those whom God has helped, and if God has left you out, who are we to presume on his will by trying to help you?"

Hardly anyone denies the ascendancy of this view. Some applaud it as a smarter way; some reject it as abdication. But most Americans understand that today there *is*, indeed, more money for savings and loans, but less for saving addicts; more money for bombs, but less for babies. More rich, more poor than ever.

We are presented with a choice. Either we swim with the tide and accept the notion that the best way to improve the world is for government to help the fortunate, and then hope that personal charity will induce them to take care of the rest of us. Or we resist, by affirming that _as we hear God_, he tells us it is our moral obligation to be our brother's keeper, all of us, as a people, as a government; that our responsibility to our brothers and sisters is greater than any one of us and that it doesn't end when they are out of the individual reach of our hand, or our charity, or our love.

Believing that we have an obligation to love is not a comfortable position to be in. It can haunt us. It can nag at us in moments of happiness and personal success, disturbing our sleep and giving us that sense of guilt and unworthiness that used to be so strong and that the modern age is so eager to deny. It can accuse us—from the faces of the starving, the dispossessed, and the wounded, faces that stare back at us from the front page of our newspapers, images from across the world that blink momentarily on our television screens.

"I was homeless," it says, "and you gave me theories of supply and demand.

"I was imprisoned and silenced for justice' sake, and you washed the hands of my torturers.

"I asked for bread, and you built the world's most sophisticated nuclear arsenal."

Father Teilhard, in just a few magnificent sentences, captured everything I've tried to say here about who today's—and eternity's—God is. He talked about Christ as the personal embodiment of God.

Describing our opportunities to involve ourselves in the things of this world, he wrote: "We must try everything for God. Jerusalem, lift up your head. Look at the immense crowds of those who build and those who seek. All over the world, men are toiling—in laboratories, in studios, in deserts, in factories—in the vast social crucible. The ferment that is taking place by their instrumentality, in art and science and thought, is happening for your sake. Open, then, your arms and your heart . . . like Christ and welcome the waters, the flood—accept the juice of humanity—for without its baptism, you will wither, without desire, like a flower out of water. And _tend it_, since, without your sun, it will disperse itself wildly in sterile roots."

To some of us that is the echo of God . . . at God's most eloquent.

No, not an easy matter, believing that God commits us to the endless task of seeking improvement of the world around us, knowing that fulfillment is an eternity away. But better than the anguish of futility. Better than the emptiness of despair. And capable of bringing meaning to our most modest and clumsy efforts. A useful consolation for any of us, and especially for a politician from Queens, still struggling to believe.

This talk is basically a summary of what I believed the country had to do about our economy a year before the 1992 election. Looking back on it now, it comes fairly close to the Democratic position as it emerged in the campaign. Many economists, analysts, and public officials had been saying similar things. During the 1992 campaign it became the basis for dozens of appearances I made on behalf of the Clinton-Gore ticket. It also supplied some phrases I would use again at the Democratic Convention which nominated Governor Bill Clinton.

I've been asked to offer a "Democratic viewpoint" on the condition of the country.

That is a daunting challenge.

Not only because I am addressing an audience that, I suspect, wears more elephants than donkeys at election time . . . but because I've been asked to do so in a state which hasn't supported a "Democratic viewpoint" in the White House since it voted for John F. Kennedy in 1960.

My situation here today reminds me of a similar one confronted by another Democratic governor from New York, Franklin Delano Roosevelt.

Roosevelt had been invited to speak at a college in upstate New York by its president—a political enemy of the governor. The college president had a reputation as a brilliant, outspoken educator and also as a forceful, tireless supporter of Republican causes and candidates.

As they approached the speakers' platform together, Roosevelt said to the Republican college president, "Well, I suppose you're still trying to convince everybody around here that most of us Democrats are damned fools."

"No, Governor," replied the college president. "That's why we invited you here . . . so that they could find out for themselves."

Hopefully, that won't happen today.

I'll begin with a story that's making the rounds. It's the story of a U.S. ship and its captain. The radar officer announces to the captain, "Blip on the radar screen, dead ahead, sir."

The captain says, "Tell that ship to turn fifteen degrees starboard at once."

The radar officer sends the signal and the response comes back: "You move fifteen degrees."

The captain's irate, and says, "Tell him again. Move fifteen degrees to the starboard."

And the response comes back, again: "You move fifteen degrees."

The captain grabs the radio himself and says, "This is the captain of the greatest ship on the high seas. Move to the starboard fifteen degrees at once!"

And the answer comes back: "This is the lighthouse. . . . You move fifteen degrees!"

I like the story for the simple point it makes: there comes a time when captains—and countries—need to change course.

I don't believe we have a short-term problem. Neither do most of the businesspeople I've talked to, or the Japanese, or Germans, or Italians, or Taiwanese.

I believe the cyclical calamity called "recession" is a symptom of deeper structural weaknesses in our economy, weaknesses that pose a greater long-term threat to our nation's future than Saddam Hussein.

The recession is taking a terrible toll: Two million jobs have been lost since last July. Nine million Americans are out of work. One in ten Americans are on food stamps.

Banks are being seized in some states.

State and local governments are being battered.

More than thirty states—home to more than 80 percent of the American people—are being forced to cut spending, raise revenues, or do both to deal with the aftershocks of the recession.

As a governor of one of those states, I know firsthand what a punishing experience it has been.

But it's worse than that.

This recession—which Washington first denied, then ignored, then said had ended, and now says will end soon—is not like the recessions of 1930 or 1982.

There is less resiliency in the economy now.

There are fewer options for corrections.

There is a great and continuing overload of debt and bad investments.

Our financial institutions are weaker.

Our competition is stronger.

Our people are not as healthy.

We have more *fundamental* problems.

We used to be a great creditor, seller, lender.

We are now a debtor, buyer, borrower.

We have not maintained our dominant strength in making and selling products. We have not invested enough, especially for the longer term. We have become dangerously dependent on foreign capital.

We have gone from being the world's largest creditor to the world's largest debtor. *We* did that. By fiscal irresponsibility. By neglecting our strengths. By a lack of political will. By losing the old values.

Think about it.

Less than twenty years ago, the United States manufactured about 50 percent of the world's TV sets, 90 percent of the world's radios, 76 percent of the autos, nearly half of the world's steel.

Now we produce barely 6 percent of the world's TV sets and radios combined, 28 percent of the cars, and 20 percent of the world's steel.

Today we send billions of dollars to Germany and Japan and other foreign nations to buy from them the goods we used to make and sell to them . . . and then we borrow back our dollars to fill the hole in the federal budget deficit, paying billions more in interest.

We pay 200 billion dollars in interest to service a 3.5 trillion dollar debt that "conservative" administrations more than trebled in the span of a decade.

Two hundred billion dollars a year to pay off past debt, while Washington pleads it has not the wealth to invest in economic renewal for the future.

Nationally, we have an aging—and, in some cases, crumbling—infrastructure. We lag behind our competitors in research.

Our work force is threatened by nearly a million dropouts a year, and by a desperate shortage of scientists and technically skilled workers.

Thirteen million children grow up trapped in poverty.

Twenty-three million Americans can't read a job application.

More than 30 million Americans have no health insurance. Tens of millions more are a pink slip away from losing theirs. Health care costs are eating up a greater share of our nation's wealth.

Our entire society is threatened by a plague of poverty, drugs, and violence that is destroying hundreds of thousands of our children.

Today, children become familiar with the sound of gunfire before they've ever heard the sound of an orchestra. Not your kids. Not mine. But kids who will be part of the work force of the twenty-first century.

It's clearer than ever—at least outside of Washington—that dealing with these vulnerabilities is not just a matter of compassion, but of common sense . . . and national economic self-interest.

But, for ten years, instead of confronting these challenges, the national government pretended these realities did not exist . . . while shifting responsibilities for others to state and local governments, even as they withdrew federal aid to deal with them.

As a result, after a decade of boasting about "record economic growth," the federal government is broke. The states are broke.

And as taxes rise and services are slashed at the local level, the middle class and the working poor are being squeezed more than ever.

While the richest 1 percent of Americans have nearly doubled their incomes over the past ten years, real wages declined for most American workers. In fact, the average hourly wage for *all* workers has declined 4 percent since President Bush was sworn into office.

Families have managed to keep their heads above water by working longer hours, relying on a spouse's second paycheck, sending the kids to work . . . just to keep up with the rising costs of health care, tuition, and child care.

Now millions of Americans are wondering if that will be enough in the nineties. The inherited expectation that each generation could earn at least the comfort and security of the one before it, and probably more, is a defining American belief.

Lose that vision of the American dream and we lose the nation as we have known it.

We must find the strength to prevent that from happening. But that will require changing course.

It will take more than a tax cut for the middle class, as Democrats have proposed. And more than the capital gains tax cut the president has proposed.

There will be no one-shot, silver bullet solution to our ailing economy. There is no sure way to give the economy a quick, substantial boost.

The best we can hope for would be the confidence that comes from a plausible, total, balanced approach that addresses all the areas in need of national attention.

Last year's budget agreement did not do that.

Nor will the president's capital gains tax cut, which operates from the same naive assumption that has transfixed Washington for the past ten years: "Just free up wealth in the hands of the already wealthy, and they'll convert their windfall into productive investments which, by themselves, will energize the economy and spin off loaves and fishes for everyone."

They called it supply-side.

Candidate Bush had a better name for it in 1980—he called it "voodoo economics." He was right. The supply-side miracle, as you know, never happened. They were off, by over 2 trillion dollars.

While the rich bought clothes and cars from overseas and investors gobbled up junk bonds and bad real estate, net savings declined compared to previous decades, as overall investment and productivity growth lagged.

Commonsense deregulation turned into a license for reckless savings and loans to gamble away taxpayers' dollars . . . leading to the greatest financial disaster in our history. . . .

A 500 billion dollar bill for working America.

We had Golden Calf prosperity that resulted in a kind of "free enterprise for the few."

In the nineties, we must promote a more progressive free-enterprise economy with policies that empower the vast majority of Americans—not just those at the top—to participate, to prosper, to be both workers and shareholders in America's future.

Today, our ability to lead the world—and guard our national security—depends on our economic security.

The penetration of markets is now more important than new military garrisons. The nation needs a new economic growth agenda that responds to a changing world.

We need policies that value both capital and labor, that encourage risk taking and long-term growth over short-term gain, that reward entrepreneurship and hard work, and that invest in *all* the building blocks that support true economic growth.

True economic growth—the type that comes from productivity gains, the type that results in bringing prosperity home to tens of millions of Americans—depends on capital and capital investment . . . that much the supply-siders got right.

But it also depends on: skilled and trained workers; basic research and development of new technology; energy and natural resources; twenty-first-century infrastructure; free and fair trade policies that increase exports; and an involved and rewarded middle class.

If we understand what needs to be done, there are dozens of ways to do it.

Let's begin with capital.

At a time when both our economy and the global economy thirst for capital, we must find ways to encourage long-term investments rather than churning capital for quick, unproductive gains.

In May I called for a federal *net investment tax credit* for new

234

productive equipment. Say, 10 percent on new and additional investments in productive machinery and equipment and pollution control equipment. It would be designed to get us to state-of-the-art technology.

Unlike President Bush's proposals for a capital gains tax cut that would provide an enormous windfall to the richest Americans for *old* investment that is not especially productive economically, this new net investment tax credit would ensure that each public dollar is invested only when it spurs new and additional private investment in *productive* equipment.

Rather than encourage high-debt transactions that reshuffle corporate assets and human lives, a net investment tax credit would spark the nation's entrepreneurial spirit to create new wealth and new jobs.

It would be devised to include the type of equipment that increases productivity in important service industries as well as in manufacturing.

It would be especially useful to entrepreneurs starting up new companies, since all of their purchases of productive equipment would receive the tax credit.

It could help fuel an *investment-led recovery* by giving the economy an immediate spark, and by laying the foundation for long-term growth.

In *the short term*, it would increase orders for new equipment, putting people back to work in factories, while spurring demand in the service economy.

In *the long term*, it would raise productivity by giving private companies the incentive to invest in new, productive equipment and cutting-edge technology.

Another way to encourage long-term investment is by reforming the way we tax capital gains. Reducing taxes on longer-term capital gains and increasing the rate on gains earned in less than a year would encourage new, long-term investment. Such reform should be targeted so that the new low rate—of, say, 10 percent—would apply only to *new* and productive investments, not investments in land, art, or collectibles.

Raising the R and D tax credit to 30 percent and in time—

you couldn't do it right away—liberalizing depreciation schedules would also help to sharpen the nation's industrial and technological edge.

All these devices would provide capital more intelligently and more fairly than the supply-side formula applied so far or the president's blunt transfer of more wealth to the wealthy.

Capitalism begins with capital, but it does not end there. Nor should our national economic policies.

Therefore, in addition to encouraging new capital investments, we must also cultivate all the ingredients that will make America more prosperous and competitive in the years ahead.

That means formulating a technology policy that enables us to catch up to Germany and Japan in civilian R and D, that encourages process technology and helps the private sector develop the commercial applications of basic research.

We cannot be content to let other nations reap the benefits of what we have sowed.

We must build a world-class infrastructure that speeds the flow of people, goods, and services. Germany, France, and Japan are way ahead of us in futuristic high-speed rail systems. We need a national strategy that takes us into the twenty-first century.

We must implement an energy plan that is balanced between supply and demand, an energy plan that is not only pro-growth but also pro-environment. We have one in New York. We need one for the nation.

We must work more aggressively to help American firms find markets for their exports, as we are doing in New York through our Global New York Program.

And we must ensure a level playing field for American companies and American workers.

When I visited Japan in October, I told the Japanese that if we are to avoid new protectionist walls, *we must get a better balance in the accounts.*

We can, by increasing trade and investment. Through consensus and cooperation, rather than litigation or legislation.

I told the Japanese they can help ease trade frictions between the two nations—that will surely escalate in the coming election year—by: Liberalizing their distribution system and the rules for government procurement so that foreign suppliers have a chance to profit in Japan;

By refraining from exporting their restrictive business practices to the U.S.—as they appear to be doing in the automobile and auto supply industries.

Of all the president's countless foreign journeys, few were more important to America than the one he recently canceled—to Japan. Regrettably, when the trip suddenly loomed more challenging than a photo opportunity, the president declared he needed to spend more time at home.

His timing was off. So are his priorities.

Having demanded more of ourselves—and foreign powers—we must strengthen our own team at home. We must do more to develop our most precious resource—human capital, skilled, educated, motivated, healthy human beings . . . the work force of the twenty-first century.

This country must take a fresh look at the work force, which has been largely ignored over the past ten years. We must begin with our children. And we should start early, by fully funding WIC and Head Start and expanding pre-K programs.

Educational *goals* must be clearer. *Standards* must be higher. We must be more intelligent in assessing whether those standards have been reached. Teachers and parents must have more say about how schools are run. Smaller classes. More computers in the classrooms.

We must make better use of choice in public education. In a world where our competitors are sending their children to school from 200 to 243 days a year—and we, only 180 days—we need to move toward longer school days and longer school years.

And instead of cutting college aid and job training, Washington should join the states, to promote skills training, literacy programs, apprenticeships for those not bound for college, and greater college opportunities for those who are.

American workers ought not to be blamed for the nation's lagging productivity growth. If you find the wealth to educate them, train them, motivate them—if you give them a stake in their labor and our future—American workers will lead the world.

•   •   •

But with the federal deficit hanging like a gray cloud over our future, where will the money come from to do all these things? Where did the money come from when the hurricane struck?

When we went to war?

When Washington bailed out the savings and loans?

Where there is a will there is always a way to the wealth. The American people do not believe we are spending 1.4 trillion dollars as efficiently as we can—not when we've learned about all the waste in the Department of Energy, in HUD and the Pentagon.

Look again at the military budget, now that communism has crumbled.

Look again at reducing non-means-tested spending. We're spending too much on wants and not enough on needs.

Do a better job at collecting our own taxes, and go after the tens of billions of dollars that foreign corporations owe the U.S. Treasury.

Make better use of pension funds.

And if new revenues are needed after all that, instead of taxing the middle class and the working poor—whom we've soaked for the past ten years—look to people making more than 250,000 dollars, Americans whose wealth has doubled in the past ten years, and whose federal tax burden is one of the lowest in the industrial world.

I understand the political reluctance to act. It will be difficult to free up the wealth to do all that we have to do. Some people will get less. Some people will be asked to give more. Not everyone will agree.

Politicians will have to spend some of their political capital. And that's one kind of spending politicians don't like to do.

I know. I'm a politician.

But it will cost this nation a great deal more if we continue to do nothing.

Let me sum it up this way.

Today we are better at making war than progress, better at thumping our chests than racking our brains, better at inspiring people in other parts of the world than uplifting ourselves.

We've won the Gulf War, but we have not overcome the gulf crisis in our own country.

There is still a gulf between us and our competitors.

Between those assured of health care and those who must beg for it.

Between our ability to build smart bombs and our ability to produce smart students.

Between America as it is and America as it should be.

We've shown how tough we can be in protecting our interests overseas. Now we need to show how tough—and how smart—we can be in protecting our interests at home.

I believe we can avoid the lighthouse rocks.

But before the captain can turn the wheel, he must recognize that what's out there is more than just a blip on the radar screen.

Thank you.

NAACP ADDRESS*

DECEMBER 11, 1991

NEW YORK HILTON HOTEL,

NEW YORK, NEW YORK

In my first political speech, given in 1974 (see page 3), I said Democrats must be the ones to heal the hurt caused by divisiveness. In 1991 I believed that the country was going through another particularly dangerous period of racist sentiment. I gave this speech urging our federal government to recognize its obligation to help reduce the problem by working to bridge the chasm between the lucky and the left out in America. In effect, it was the notion of "Two Cities" that I had talked about in my 1984 keynote in San Francisco, and a number of times thereafter.

It is appropriate that we hold this celebration in New York.

It was in this state, in 1909, that the idea for a national, biracial organization to right social injustices was first formulated.

It is certainly appropriate, too, that the honoree be Mr. Benjamin Hooks. His long, diverse, and productive career makes him a worthy recipient of this year's award. Not just because of the many hats he has worn throughout his professional life . . . as a public defender, pastor, judge, businessman, FCC commissioner, and as a fifteen-year executive director of the NAACP, but for the many talents he brings to his work—formidable forensic abilities, an unrelenting tenacity, a proud and deep respect for his heritage.

•   •   •

*A speech given at a dinner honoring Benjamin Hooks.

It's been said that behind every great man is a good woman.

In Ben's case, she has been beside him, ever since they first met at an ice cream stand in Memphis, forty-two autumns ago.

As an advisor, confidante, and constant companion through the late hours, victories, and setbacks, Frances has been an essential part of her husband's success.

"Marriage," said the playwright Ibsen, "is something you must give your whole mind to."

He could have added . . . heart and soul, because it also takes fidelity, devotion, and a certainty about the course you've chosen.

Those characteristics describe Benjamin and Frances's marriage.

They can also, it seems to me, be applied to the NAACP and its long, faithful pursuit of social justice in this country.

Like a committed partner, the NAACP was there through good times and bad, in sickness and in health, relentlessly devoted to moving this nation towards equality, opportunity, freedom, and justice for all.

Wedded to the idea that we are all indeed equal in God's eyes— and before any law that respects that God—the NAACP has been a guiding light to this nation, not just for the black community, but for all Americans.

It has withstood all the assaults, all the pain, all the disillusionment, all the despair of the long, agonizing struggle. It has stood up to the white-sheeted face of hate and cleansed the stain of "separate but equal" from the nation's soul.

It has persevered through the mocking insults at the lunch counter sit-ins, and the torments and tirades of the Freedom Rides.

It was not cowed by the specter of the lynch mobs; by the rocks of ignorant, misled enemies; by the harsher weapons of the criminal bigots; by the murders of Martin Luther King, Jr., and Medgar Evers, of Goodman, Chaney, and Schwerner, of Viola Liuzzo, and all the other unheralded martyrs.

The NAACP survived it all, and kept the dream alive.

You helped push open the doors to integration.

You led the way to passage of the Civil Rights Act of 1964. The Voting Rights Act of 1965. The Fair Housing Act of 1968.

With great leaders like Ben Hooks and Roy Wilkins, the NAACP has built up more grass root chapters than any civil rights organization in America. And it built the platform which launched Thurgood Marshall to the Supreme Court—a justice whose legacy of opinions will shine like the Northern Star, giving direction and guidance to American jurists well into the next century.

It's difficult to communicate the spirit of the civil rights movement to those who came later or were too young to remember it. It was many things.

Despite the turbulence of that era, the movement brought people together: Christians and Jews, blacks and whites, young and old, northerners and southerners, united behind a coalition of conscience, in pursuit of a common vision of justice and equality in America.

It became recognized by good people as a good cause for the whole community.

It is history well worth remembering.

Especially today when organizations like the NAACP are accused of being a "special interest."

As if you were lobbying for oil rights or leniency for corrupt savings and loan executives. . . .

As if freedom and equal justice were not the most general of all the nation's interests.

It would be a mistake to think the fight is over.

The truth is that the ugly and dangerous instinct still lives among us . . . the instinct to stigmatize, to stereotype, to scapegoat; to malign people because of the tint of their skin, the God they pray to, or the place their parents come from.

The truth is we need the strength and the wisdom of the NAACP now more than we have in a long time. A lot of people need you.

Despite the blood, the sweat, the lives lost to remove the legal barriers, we still have a long way to go to make the dream real for all our people.

We have not yet arrived in the land of milk and honey.

Not just because we have a White House that threatens to take away with one hand what they offer with the other.

Or a Supreme Court that reads the words but doesn't hear the music.

But because of fundamental problems ignored and neglected by Washington for more than a decade.

The policies of the last ten years have widened a great chasm in our country, between the wealthy and the struggling middle class; between the privileged few, their heirs, and tens of millions of Americans who have fallen into an abyss so deep they can hardly see the light.

Today, unemployed auto workers wait on unemployment lines with nearly 9 millon fellow Americans. Young executives who once thought life was going to be peaches and cream now worry about being able to pay for meat and potatoes.

More than 30 million Americans with no health insurance pray, "God forbid someone in the house gets sick: it could wipe out all we have." Tens of millions more are a pink slip away from similar nightmares.

Twenty-three million Americans, unable to read a street sign, a job form, or the label on a bottle of poison.

Homeless mothers beg for change on street corners.

Our children are having children. And in Washington, D.C., Chicago, Detroit, and LA, children are emptied out into streets, surrounded by drug dealers, violence—all kinds of disorientation. Some of them learn to recognize the noise of gunfire before they've ever heard the sound of an orchestra.

These failures affect the whole nation's people.

But it is also true that the African-American community feels a disproportionate share of the pain.

Today, nearly one in two African-American babies is born into poverty.

Today, African-American boys are more likely to end up in prison than in college.

Today, young African-American men are more likely to be killed in the streets of some of our cities than American soldiers were in the jungles of Vietnam.

From 1980 to 1990, Washington ignored the struggle of the middle class and neglected the needs of the poor. "Let them figure out how to pick themselves up by their bootstraps, and if they have no boots, that's none of our business."

Now we get a thousand points of light.

But the results are the same. The states and the cities have been abandoned to deal with national vulnerabilities on their own.

And the cumulative weight of that burden is crushing these local governments, forcing service cuts, higher taxes, and a retreat from progress made over the last sixty years.

Nationally, we have retreated—not just from civil rights, but from the entire cause the civil rights movement helped inspire.

It's been a retreat from help for the middle class, from equality for women, from the fight for social justice, from the rebuilding of our cities, from the retraining and education of the millions of unemployed and poor, from the plight of entire areas of this country that are desperately trying to restore their economies.

It has left us asking a fundamental question: Are we going to grow together or grow apart?

Regrettably, over the past ten years, national policies have pushed America apart, instead of helping Americans grow together.

Think about the fight over the Civil Rights Bill, which Ben Hooks and the NAACP worked so hard to secure. What began in Washington as an effort to restore rights revoked by the Supreme Court descended into an ugly and divisive debate about so-called "quotas."

The new civil rights law had a simple goal: protecting every American against intentional discrimination on the basis of race, religion, sex, or disability. However, the federal administration could only find two words to describe the proposed law: "quota bill."

Even though there was nothing in the bill about quotas. Even though Democrats and Republicans—and leaders like Ben Hooks—have long opposed quotas. Even though quotas were—and remain—illegal.

With all our domestic ills, why so much emphasis on quotas?

Because the White House is concerned about fairness? Really?

Have they made the tax system fairer?

Was the census count [of 1990] fair?

If they were so concerned about fairness, why were they so quick to lift sanctions against South Africa, and now so unwilling to deal with the consequences of their embargo on Haiti?

•   •   •

I don't believe the debate was about quotas, or fairness, or justice. Quotas were being discussed because "quota" is a buzzword for race.

Like Willie Horton was about race. Like the white worker's hands in the North Carolina TV ad were about race. Like the photo of the "welfare mother" and her child in Mississippi was about race.

Why use race?

Because whether we like it or not, elections can be won in this country just by insinuating that "those African-Americans" are asking for too much, that those "others" are asking for more than they deserve.

That's what David Duke is.

Behind the cosmetic surgery and the code words lies a history haunted by the white sheet, the bloodhound, and the noose.

The president and his party will do everything they can to disavow David Duke. But the sad truth is David Duke is the child of their politics. David Duke is the son of the Republican party. David Duke and the people who invented "Willie Horton" are political and philosophical first cousins.

Duke is dangerous. So is his message.

This nation must not be tempted into accepting cynical political strategies that suggest our problems are caused by minorities, by immigrants, by the poor, by "others" who are demanding too much.

That is a message that builds no bridges. It heals no wounds. It cannot elevate us; it can only reduce us.

We have resisted this destructive force before. Now we must do so again. Not only because such scapegoating is an assault on our compassion. It's an affront to our common sense . . . and our intelligence.

Scapegoating diverts and distracts Americans from the real issue: what must be done to expand the economy, so our people don't have to fight each other for a smaller piece of the pie? Instead of continuing tactics that can only tear us apart, we must create a successful free-enterprise system for the *many*—not just the few.

We must grow together or we will fall together.

•   •   •

We must begin by admitting the obvious: the nation is headed for the rocks and we need to chart a new course.

That course should encourage our people to reassert all the basic values and strengths that made us economically strong in the first place: the eagerness to work, to compete, to achieve; the courage to overcome odds; a sense of responsibility; a sense of right and wrong, of what we owe to ourselves and those around us.

Those values, those instincts, are there—in our people—as they always have been.

As they were in my parents who came here seeking only one thing—the chance to earn their own bread. Who were given the chance to work, to produce, and did, and achieved security—and dignity—if not affluence.

It wasn't easy, but they prevailed. Their grandchildren will, too.

And it will be done through the free-enterprise system.

But government must help, not by handouts, but by providing our people the tools they need to succeed in our complicated free-enterprise economy, and by making the necessary *public* investments that the private sector cannot—or will not—make.

I have proposed a comprehensive investment-led economic growth strategy that addresses all the ingredients we need to grow.

It was good enough for the CEOs of the Fortune 500 who applauded it last month in Charleston.

And it is fair enough—and smart enough—for the practical, the pained, the middle class, and the poor.

It calls for new federal incentives to encourage private investment in our economy.

For a *technology* policy that enables us to keep up with Germany and Japan.

For a national *energy plan* that is pro-growth and pro-environment.

For a *world-class infrastructure* that takes us into the twenty-first century.

For more help from Washington to help the states and cities mired in fiscal distress: for community development block grants to spur economic development, federal economic opportunity zones, loans to minority entrepreneurs.

It calls for government to help American firms find markets for their exports, and to ensure a *level playing field* for American companies and American workers.

In addition to freeing up capital, it also calls for freeing up hearts and hands and minds.

That means developing the work force.

By the next century, 80 percent of the net additions to the work force will be African-Americans, Latinos, immigrants, and women.

But at the moment, these are the most vulnerable parts of our population. It's clear we must do more to ensure that they will participate productively.

Of course no one—least of all the people on welfare—wants to see people on welfare forever. Of course we don't want to create a never-ending dependency.

But in order to break the cycle of dependency, there must be jobs available and people trained and fit to do them. So we need health care treatment, pre-K education, Head Start, tuition assistance for needy middle-class and poor students, job training, day care, and literacy programs.

American workers can lead the world if we educate and train them, if we motivate them by giving workers a stake in their labor and our future, if we give them the security that comes with health insurance and parental leave, if we treat them with fairness and dignity.

These aren't giveaways or concessions to liberal sentimentality, or exercises in compassion—they are investments in our future. The whole nation's future.

But with the federal deficit hanging like a gray cloud over our future, where will the money come from to do all these things?

Where did the money come from when the hurricane and the earthquake [in San Francisco, in 1989] struck?

When we went to war?

For the savings and loans?

Where there's a will, there is always a way to the wealth.

We must find the will to reverse the policies that have made the distance between the richest and the safest of us, and the poorest and the most vulnerable of us, wider and deeper and more perilous.

That have made that distance a sea of hopelessness, fear, and anger.

The time has come to channel our anger towards the policies that deprive people, not towards the people that they deprive.

We must resume our journey as a whole people, as a whole community.

We must, again, overcome the narrowness, the shortsightedness, and even the meanness that made the existence of the NAACP both inevitable and essential.

If we need any more inspiration, we should keep in mind one of the descriptions of the NAACP that came out of the civil rights movement: "The NAACP's quiet, effective struggle is like the power of the sun. True power never makes any noise. The sun is powerful. It doesn't argue with the nighttime; it just smacks the nighttime right out of the sky."

That's you—Ben Hooks, the NAACP—all of you.

May you continue to light the way, and may we resume our climb to the top of the mountain . . . together.

Thank you.

This event at the United Nations, which occurred a half-year before the historic environmental summit in Rio de Janeiro, was an unusual opportunity to talk to a group of world leaders on this vital subject. It is another example of the extraordinary benefits that flow from being at the center of the world in New York.

The address focuses on a pervasive political dilemma: the apparent clash of competing interests. Too often political contestants assume irreconcilable polar positions, both sides overlooking the truth that lies somewhere between them. One of today's struggles is between those who say that their economy cannot afford to do what must be done to preserve the ecology and those who say we cannot afford not to. The solution will come as we find more ways to make environmental protection economically feasible . . . and even attractive.

There is another aspect to the environmental issues that intrigues me. Commitment to preserving the planet comes as close to a purely selfless concern as we get in our political life. For all the work and sacrifice that we make to keep our waters clean, these efforts will probably not add a single fish for me to catch from a single lake during the remainder of my life. It doesn't work that way. We save the planet for the benefit of generations to come, who will not even know our names. There's something especially rewarding about that, especially in a society that appears to be hungry for "basic values."

How wonderful the music; how it soars—how it lifts us above the difficult distractions. How perfectly it describes the subject that brings us here, something larger, more important, more beautiful, more right than most things most of us are forced to deal with in the course of our everyday activities.

Through all the ages, humankind's first preoccupation has been the struggle to understand, and to cope with, our place in the universe. At one level, we concern ourselves—beyond mere survival—with the preservation and enhancement of the world's life-giving elements.

At our very best, we think of ourselves as being assigned to the task of perfecting the work of Creation, and that requires preserving the purity of the elements we start with.

It is indeed a grand aspiration, but it is not more than we are capable of, or should commit ourselves to. In the end, it is as simple as accepting the miracle of air and water and earth as demanding our attention—and even our reverence.

At a time—like most times—when the world is dragged down by meaner needs and narrower concerns, it is good that the United Nations convenes this conference.

I congratulate you all, and on behalf of 18 million vitally interested New Yorkers, I *thank* you all, for the good it is certain to accomplish.

The timing of the conference, I think, is exquisite.

So long as the intelligence and processes that put this miraculous universe together elude our perfect understanding, we cannot say for sure what will be 50 or 100 years from now.

But it seems increasingly likely that a century or so from now, historians will look back on this era as one when global and biospheric changes of an order of magnitude never before experienced perceptibly threatened the balances that sustain life on this planet.

And they will be able to judge, by then, whether we who saw the warning signs, responded to them with wisdom and strength.

The warning signs are everywhere.

The notion of the skies closing in on us and choking us, and sea levels rising to inundate us, is no longer thought of as science fiction, or the apocalyptic musings of remote academicians.

Greenhouse gases in the atmosphere are building at an increasing rate, stratospheric ozone is being depleted, sea levels are rising, forests are being destroyed, and landscapes are degrading. Climatic instability and all the other dangerous effects of imbalance become less improbable every day . . . and the potential for devastation grows as the world's population grows.

There were one billion human beings on this planet in 1800. Two billion in 1930; 4 billion in 1975; 5.3 billion today. It is estimated that a billion more people will be added to the world's population in just the next decade. At the current rate, the earth will be home to 10 billion people by the year 2025.

And unless there is a new—even unprecedented—worldwide political enlightenment and statesmanship, the problems associated with population growth will be compounded by the growing *poverty* of two-thirds of the world.

Today in the developing countries, 40,000 children die every twenty-four hours, simply because of contaminated water.

And all these problems are exacerbated by the enormous international debt that hangs like an albatross around the neck of the developing world.

UNCED has the difficult mission of finding the way to balance two fundamental necessities: the need to promote economic progress and prosperity, especially in developing countries; and the need to do so in a way that protects and enhances our global environment upon which all life depends.

Obviously, we begin by rejecting the notion that we must *choose* between the environment and economic development.

Norwegian prime minister Gro Harlem Brundtland is right: "The environment is where we all live; development is what we all do in attempting to improve our lot within that abode. The two are inseparable."

That must be the first predicate of this conference.

The challenge and this conference come, as Dickens put it, at the best of times, and the worst of times.

The best of times because, finally, we are beginning to understand and recognize the one most important political idea that we live with today: No man is an island. No woman. No state. No nation. No continent. Interconnectedness, interdependence, means that all the parts and all the players, everywhere, touch and move and react to one another.

We Americans must deal with this new truth.

And so must the rest of the world. It is easier now because the end of the cold war has taken down ideological and military barriers that divided so many nations against each other, allowing for a new era of cooperative action in dealing with global problems.

At the same time, however, it is difficult to deal intelligently with our interconnectedness, in this erratic world. In many ways this is the worst of times: because much of the world is forced to respond to other immediate concerns that distract us and diminish our resources.

Even here where we meet—in this blessed and powerful land—poverty, drugs, AIDS, an aging population, endangered children, suffocating debt demand our attention in an often preemptive way.

Our own internal weaknesses are turning Americans inward.

That reality is complicated by two other forces . . . one arising from the nature of today's politics, the other from human nature.

Politically, our whole thrust—at least here in America, with elections every two or four or six years—has been towards short-term solutions. Politicians are given only brief tenures, and that discourages the development of long-range policies. Most politicians are inclined to be different from scientists, who, as C. P. Snow once observed, "have to think of one thing, deeply and obsessively, for a long time."

If politicians think of anything obsessively, it is apt to be what they can do quickly in order to get reelected.

This tendency becomes a worse impediment to serious and sustained long-term action because of a concomitant human instinct. Unlike C. P. Snow's scientists, most human beings will resist contemplating unpleasant possibilities that they think are remote.

That reluctance could become for us one of the deadly sins.

This conference seeks to improve on that element of our human nature. It is predicated on the belief that we are capable of something better, nobler . . . smarter. It says we can open our minds to the frightening prospects and marshal the energy and the will to change our habits so as to *avoid* calamity.

Surely, this conference will tell us the first thing we have to do is to understand and admit the problem. The truth is most people have neither the knowledge nor the comprehension to accept and deal with the harsh realities that you will deal with in this conference.

Worse than that, there are also significant voices inside this country—and inside the administration in Washington—that still refuse to concede that global warming is a real, potentially devastating problem . . . despite all the evidence, and the expressed opinion of the rest of the world.

Indeed, some in the United States argue we cannot *afford* to negotiate ways to reduce the threat: "We do not have the wealth. The costs will crush our economy."

I've heard those voices.

They often belong to the same people who say we need a 300 billion dollar defense budget.

Or to the people who say we have not the wealth to fight contamination of the planet, but we can find upwards of a trillion dollars to bail out our corrupted savings and loans.

These are wrong judgments.

With CFCs floating up to the sky, burning holes through the ozone, letting in the sun's harmful rays, which can burn holes through your skin.

With acid rain fouling our waters and killing our lakes.

With tropical and boreal forests being endangered.

With whole species of life facing extinction.

It is absurd for this powerful nation to say that we cannot afford to curb the flow of greenhouse gases . . . when they're building up like a blanket in the atmosphere, threatening eventually to melt the ice caps, to flood our coastal regions, to turn the world's breadbaskets into deserts and convert the planet into a cosmic hothouse!

The threat was not caused by nature, alone.

Nor by the wrath of an angry God.

Human beings—many of them Americans—created the threat; we must defuse it . . . and I am one of those who believe we can.

253

• • •

I hope you will not regard it as presumptuous of me to give you some other thoughts on what I believe this convention must do and communicate in order to prove that we can. They are more than my own personal points of view: they represent a consensus of the many excellent experts on the environment I am privileged to have advising me in my work as governor. Here they are:

The world needs a global effort to protect our environment and to promote sustainable economic development . . . and it needs the full cooperation of the United States to make that happen.

And so I urge President Bush to lead the American delegation to the Rio summit to demonstrate in the strongest way possible—through his own personal involvement—the United States' commitment to work with the other nations of the world, to promote sustainable development and to protect the planet we share.

Having admitted the full scope of the problem and enlisted the world's leaders to respond to it, it seems to me that, as Prime Minister Giulio Andreotti and the Italian government have suggested, we will need a new international "rule of law" to deal with all these environmental issues.

That effort should begin with an *international convention on climate change,* including a protocol to stabilize and reduce carbon dioxide emissions and other greenhouse gas emissions—a program with specific goals and specific timetables and a specific commitment to assist nature in absorbing carbon emissions by planting trees.

We should set as our minimum goal the reduction of carbon dioxide emissions by the year 2000 to at least the levels of 1990. A global climate change convention would provide a basic framework for altering patterns of abuse and for protecting our common home.

British prime minister John Major was correct when he wrote recently, in discussing the Rio summit, that the rich nations of the world must provide clear evidence that we are willing to put our environmental house in order.

The United States, as one of the world's richest nations—and the largest contributor of greenhouse gases—has a special responsibility. Today, the U.S. uses twice as much energy to achieve roughly the same standard of living as Western Europe and Japan. This is wasteful and unnecessary.

The United States must develop a comprehensive national energy policy that integrates energy, environmental, and economic development concerns . . . as we have done at the state level in New York. That policy should recommit the U.S. to a strong national energy-efficiency program, and encourage the exploration of renewable forms of energy.

Then, in addition to the subject of climate change, all nations, including the United States, should ratify the UN *Convention on the Law of the Sea*—one of the most comprehensive pieces of international law on the environment ever negotiated.

The Convention contains a common set of rules for management and protection of our oceans and marine resources. Fifty-one nations have already ratified the Convention. Only nine more are necessary for the Convention to go into effect.

Third, we should commit ourselves to enacting a *convention to protect biological diversity.*

Today, 20 percent of all species in the biosphere remain unexplored. The "undiscovered species" offer the promise of new, miraculous discoveries that could unlock the secrets to life and death.

We must preserve these gene pools, protect the food chain, *and* ensure that those nations that are stewards of this biotic wealth share in the commercial wealth derived from its use.

We also need a greater flow of capital, ideas, technology, and goods from North to South.

It is not fair or realistic to ask nations struggling to develop an economy that will sustain their population—nations poorer than most of the rest of the world—to do what must be done to protect and enhance the environment without help from the more fortunate of us.

The developing world's debt burden is unsustainable. We need to reexamine the entire debt structure that is strangling growth in developing nations and that undermines the environmental progress of all nations.

The industrialized nations should explore developing international and bilateral programs, such as "debt for nature" swaps, which provide an economic self-interest for "steward nations" to protect these irreplaceable resources.

It may take a decade of negotiating protocols to realize our common objective, but we should embark upon this journey in Rio.

Having outlined a new rule of law, we must also strengthen international mechanisms for the management and protection of the environment. The UN Environment Programme should be strengthened. All three of these proposed treaties need a secretariat. The Programme has only 200 professionals worldwide. That's inadequate. The nations of the world should earmark resources for a UN Environment Fund to help establish UNEP's role and promote environmentally sustainable economic and social conditions.

The UN should establish a program to assist developing countries in meeting the energy needs for their expanding populations.

We should also consider some of the following options:

• Establishing an energy-efficiency center within the UN;

• creating regional centers under UN auspices for research, training, and joint procurement of energy-efficiency and renewable resources;

• using resources of multilateral lending institutions to fund energy-efficiency measures.

All this must be done by you and the other world leaders of thought and opinion in the field of the environment. But because, as I have noted, much of the world does not know or understand the issues we discuss today, we have another important mission, and that is to *educate* the people.

The people don't fully understand terms like "ozone depletion" and "global warming." If they did, more of them would be pushing their leaders to respond, *now*. The *people* must understand the threat, because the ultimate political force is the *consensus* of the people clearly expressed.

That's why it's important we get into the schools, to reach young people early on, to influence the way they think and live.

I'm proud to say that here in New York City, the board of education is creating a special "environmental high school," which will serve as a model—a testing ground—to teach our young people about developing, preserving, and improving the world they will inherit.

Changing the way our children look at the world is our best hope for carrying through the long-term changes that are needed.

I have already taken a great deal of your valuable time. Let me try to sum up.

With the end of the cold war, the nations of the world now have a new chance to realize more of our vast, untapped human potential. We have the opportunity, as a planet, to rechannel our wealth away from expensive instruments of destruction, and towards the things that promote human dignity and safeguard the environment.

The United Nations should lead that effort.

Together, with the nations of the world—including the United States of America—we should lift our sights . . . not just to save our civilization, but to improve it, to elevate it to a new level.

We can.

By opposing aggression, as we did in Kuwait; by preventing barbarous violations of basic human rights; by reaffirming the role of international law as an antidote to world chaos; by promoting the reduction of the absurd proliferation of nuclear weapons worldwide; by promoting democratically elected governments, especially by working together to strengthen the newly emerging democracies of Eastern Europe and the former Soviet Union.

And by working toward one great, integrated global economy: one that sustains our planet—that protects the air, the oceans, the earth, the heavens, and the life all around us.

And an economy that, at the same time, gives the mass of suffering humanity—especially in the southern half of this world— a chance to live in dignity and to realize the kind of opportunity that much of the industrialized world is blessed with today.

•   •   •

Just a generation ago, one of America's great national symbols, the bald eagle, was on the verge of extinction in the continental United States, a victim of what Rachel Carson called "a chemical barrage . . . hurled against the fabric of life."

But, fortunately, Rachel Carson's warning helped educate an entire generation to the delicate ecosystems that support us all. Today, the bald eagle has returned, in New York and in the rest of America.

That lesson is a reminder of what we can achieve when we approach our environment with reason and humility, and a sincere willingness to do what must be done. Frankly, I think one of the most important lessons we can teach our children is that our own survival is interwoven with the survival of all God's creatures.

For that reason, protecting our environment can be an essential instruction in fundamental values. Democratic governments like ours in New York and the United States are not allowed to promote any theology, religion, or even formal philosophy.

What then are our ultimate values?

What do we say to our children?

What do we say to human beings about the way they ought to behave? Without being accused of teaching religion?

There is one area where the assertion of what could easily be accepted as a "moral value" is allowed. It is in dealing with the environment.

When we act to protect the air, the water, the earth, the sky, and the life that passes through it, we're not doing these things for ourselves or even our own families. We're protecting generations that we will never know. And generations that will never know us.

It is the ultimate selfless act.

All our efforts to preserve and enhance our environment demonstrate our profound reverence for "the great web of being," for the generations before us who planted and preserved the earth, and for the generations to come.

All the life that surrounds us, the magnificent links of creation, reaching forward, beyond us, to places and to dreams we ourselves will never reach.

It is a kind of magnificent statement about our human obligation to one another.

An act as intelligent as any prayer ever uttered: as beautiful as any faith ever held.

That is our work today . . . and in the days ahead.

The upcoming Earth Summit in Rio de Janeiro presents the nations of the North and South a unique opportunity to pursue that common goal, together.

Protecting the planet we share, for ourselves, and for generations we will never know, could set the tone for the kind of synergism our world will need to prosper into the twenty-first century . . . a world that must be freer, more secure, more prosperous—more healthy—than the one we know today.

We look to you to advance that effort significantly in this conference. We trust our nation's leader will join you!

Good luck.

The Empire State, like the rest of America, was built mostly by immigrants. Today New York is moving into a new era, infused by energy from yet a new wave of immigration. At a time, in the early 1990s, when other parts of the country were deriding the immigrant influence, I wanted to give another view. The new immigrants from the Caribbean, Asia, and Latin and South America are replenishing New York's work force and middle class. Most of them are coming to our state with families . . . literate, educated, able to be immediately productive. They represent all the traditional values and strength brought by people, like my mother and father, who came from Italy and pursued the American dream, which they then passed on to me in spectacular fashion. I welcome these new seekers and builders to our state.

In New York, most of us have always preferred to think of ourselves as a mosaic that creates beauty by the harmonious arrangement of different fragments, instead of a melting pot which would boil away differences, producing some bland new stereotype. Now our mosaic grows more lustrous.

Today, the Big Apple is moving towards a new era of strength and progress, propelled by a concerted new program called the *New New York* Plan. It is one of the most ambitious economic development plans undertaken in our city and state history.

It calls for new capital investments in the infrastructure that supports business in New York, for a revitalization and expansion of our transportation infrastructure, for developing areas of the city that hold great and as yet untapped potential for jobs and housing and commerce. I could speak about it at great length.

Today, however, I'd like to speak for a few minutes about another aspect of the *new* New York that is of vital interest and concern to you. It's that aspect which, from its founding, has always kept remaking New York, keeping it ever new: its people. The ever-changing mix that constitutes the splendid diversity of the family of New York.

Throughout our history, wave upon wave of immigrants—English and Irish and Scots; Germans, Italians, and Poles; people from Eastern Europe and Asia—most of them sailing in steerage, some of them brought here in chains from Africa.

And today—I need not tell you—the renewal and remaking of New York continues.

Now the immigrants land not at Ellis Island but at Kennedy Airport, on flights from the Caribbean, Latin America, Asia, any of the 165 countries last year's immigrants came from.

Over 110,000 immigrants came to New York last year. Indeed, since 1980, New York has been the destination for over 1 million immigrants. It is estimated that today one in three residents of this city was born in another land.

Immigration is the history, the story of America, and, in a special way, of New York. In fact, the reality of immigration is so important to an understanding of what America really is that, without it, our nation has no history at all.

The historian Oscar Handlin has said that he "once thought to write a history of immigrants in America." "Then I discovered," Handlin said, "that the immigrants *were* American history."

And so, having to defend immigration—as an American and especially as a New Yorker—is a little like having to convince people that breathing is good for them.

Still, at times it is necessary to say the obvious—because people forget. And it doesn't take long . . . a generation, two, three . . . and suddenly the children and grandchildren and great-grandchildren of immigrants can look at the new arrivals, the new seekers, and see not one of *us*, but one of *them*.

Of course we have the great statue in the harbor, Lady Liberty—lifting her lamp "beside the golden door," in the words of the New

York poet Emma Lazarus. And we have all the beautiful, uplifting poetry written to celebrate our national commitment to diversity— a commitment that is engraved on the Great Seal of the United States in the words, *"E pluribus unum."*

The prose, unfortunately, has not always matched the sublime poetry.

There have been periodic calls throughout our history to slam the golden door shut. Those who came here and made it have occasionally said, illogically, "It's ours. It belongs to us. We have to keep *them* out." And that sentiment at times in our history has been translated into laws that defined *them* and either excluded them or severely limited their access.

"They are criminals," it was said, "drunken and licentious." Or, "They're lazy." Or, "inherently inferior." Or, "They couldn't be loyal." "They're anarchists and papists and subversives." "Their language is different and their food and their music, their morals and their manners. They could never be real Americans. They'll ruin everything."

In Abraham Lincoln's day, the nativists wrapped themselves in the flag and called themselves "the American party." But leaders like Lincoln saw them for what they were and called them something else: "Know-Nothings." Support for exclusion, he said, was nothing less than "degeneracy."

And he warned: If "the Know-Nothings get control, our Declaration will read, 'All men are created equal, *except Negroes, and foreigners, and Catholics.'* When it comes to this I should prefer emigrating to some country where they make no pretence of loving liberty . . . where despotism can be taken pure, and without the base alloy of hypocrisy."

Lincoln warned us of the shortsightedness and dangers of the politics of exclusion. And group after group came, justifying his faith in the American experiment and disproving the nativists.

They came and pledged allegiance to America.

And they kept that pledge.

They raised families and toiled and sacrificed.

With their sweat they pushed back the frontier and built the railroads. They raised up great cities like this one, and tunneled subways beneath it. They spanned the harbors with bridges. They worked in factories or started small businesses. They patrolled the streets and put out the fires. They danced and sang and prayed and—when called—fought and died for this place, America.

They *made* America. They made it the freest, richest, most powerful country in the world.

Today, America has its troubles. A severe and prolonged national recession. Mountains of debt. Huge social problems—poverty, unemployment, homelessness, illiteracy, inadequate access to health services.

It's a difficult time. The American people are angered and frustrated—by losing a job, by not being able to get ahead, by the sinking feeling that elements of the American dream are out of their reach, by diminished prospects for themselves and their children.

People are always eager to blame someone for hard times. They do it in all recessions.

Certainly they did it in the Great Depression.

In 1932, people blamed the rich, the stockbrokers, the mighty industrial barons, the bankers and landowners. The powerful officials and politicians who failed them.

Some of that is happening now. But something else is happening that makes *this* different from the depression.

This time, the powerful—instead of confessing error and pledging to correct it—are deflecting the blame from themselves to the *powerless:* to the poor, to the child who just had a child, to the new immigrants.

You've heard it.

Immigrants, some are saying, are the cause—or at least *a* cause—of the problems.

In the early days of this presidential campaign, some candidates tried to resurrect the perennial anti-immigrant specter by talking about "the unraveling of America" and about "taking America back."

It is the same nativist sloganeering and parochial fearmongering that's been aimed at every group of new immigrants throughout our history.

And even the governor of our largest state, California—an excellent man, Pete Wilson, said not long ago that one of his problems is the immigrants. They have too many people coming into their state. They don't think they can afford them.

I will assume that there is some foundation in fact in the governor's mind for that conclusion in California. But it's a regrettable conclusion to have to reach even if there is a plausibility to it.

That's sad to me. Really sad.

I was born just a few miles from here, across the river, in South Jamaica, Queens, of immigrant parents. Everyone in that neighborhood came from somewhere else.

I thank God this country didn't say to them, "We can't afford you. You might take someone's job, or cost us too much."

I'm glad they didn't ask my father if he could speak English, because he couldn't. I'm glad they didn't ask my mother if she could count, because she couldn't. They didn't go to school a day in Italy. I'm glad they didn't ask my father what special skills he brought to this great and dynamic nation, because there was no special expertise to the way he handled a shovel when he dug trenches for sewer pipe. I'm glad they let him in anyway.

I thank God this city's public school system didn't say to my parents, "We don't have the time or the inclination or the resources to teach your son, Mario, how to speak English. It's taking him too long."

I thank God for a government that was wise enough to see that they were our future, and strong enough to help them without stifling them, to provide them with an opportunity to earn their own bread with dignity.

And so, the revival of anti-immigrant sentiment in America, however motivated, is sad to me personally. And millions like me. But it's much more than that.

It can be *dangerous*. Police agencies have noted a dramatic increase in bias-related crime. Bias violence—some of it directed at immigrants—has more than doubled since 1984. A recent report by the U.S. Civil Rights Commission cites a national rise in anti-Asian violence. But I'm sure many of you who work with immigrants don't need a report to convince you of this ugly reality among us.

We need a bias-related crime bill in New York. I've tried year after year to convince the legislature of the need. I won't give up until we pass a law which says that violence motivated by bias is a special degradation of a civilized society, deserving special punishment.

There's another word besides "sad" and "dangerous" to describe anti-immigrant sentiment: stupid.

That's especially true here in New York.

Let me tell you why. In New York today, we are getting stronger and stronger through immigration. The newer generation of immigrants to New York are, in large measure, a ready-made middle class.

Many of today's immigrants arrive with more education than immigrants did sixty years ago, many with medical, engineering, and other advanced degrees, with knowledge and skills we need. Twenty percent of the immigrants in New York's work force are in white-collar and professional positions.

Many other immigrants take jobs in the hotels, hospitals, restaurants, and factories on which we all rely. It is hard to imagine, for example, how New York's health care system would continue to function without the immigrant doctors, nurses, technicians, and food services staff.

In fact, immigrants are credited with saving several industries in New York, such as garment manufacturing, which would have left New York had immigrants not provided a new source for labor. Likewise, thousands of Dominican and Korean immigrants have given new life to the fresh produce and grocery industries.

Immigrant entrepreneurs have started thousands of new businesses. In New York today there are over 40,000 firms owned by immigrants, firms that add jobs and three and a half billion dollars to the economy each year.

New immigrants have rented and purchased thousands of homes and apartments all over the city. Their presence is attracting new investments to New York. In Flushing, for example, Sheraton has built a new hotel to cater to the thriving new businesses, banks, and stores created by immigrants. A hotel, as you know, means jobs—hundreds of jobs.

Immigrants are also credited with rebuilding New York neighborhoods such as Elmhurst, Washington Heights, Sunset Park, and Flatbush. And new immigrants are likely responsible for the increase in subway ridership during the 1980s.

It's all part of a pattern that's been recognized by experts in recent decades.

In the 1970s, New York faced difficult times, and the influx of immigrants did much to rejuvenate the economy here. Experts estimate that three-quarters of the jobs added from 1980 to 1985 were filled by immigrants. And consider this: New York is the only major northern city which did not lose population in the 1980s. In fact, immigrants helped stop an eight-year pattern of population decline in this state. From 1980 to 1987, 375,000 native-born New Yorkers left the city. But 575,000 immigrants replaced them, and prevented a massive decline in population.

One expert who has studied this subject in depth says there is simply no way that the economy in New York could have grown at the pace it did during the 1980s without immigrants.

Study after study confirms something similar.

In a 1990 survey of thirty-eight leading economists conducted by the Hudson Institute, two-thirds of the respondents said they thought *increasing* the level of immigration would have a positive effect on the economy.

A U.S. Department of Labor study in 1989 said that immigrants neither take jobs from nor depress the wages of native-born workers. In fact, they create jobs for U.S. workers because of their propensity to start new businesses.

The President's Council of Economic Advisors issued a report last year which states that the long-run benefits of immigration greatly exceed the costs.

And our host today, Mitchell Moss, who knows what he's talking about, has written this: "Among the most valuable of New York's assets is the area's diverse and growing immigrant population. Just as refugees from pogroms and potato famines helped in earlier eras to reinvigorate New York's economy, so today are newcomers from Hong Kong and Haiti, St. Petersburg and Santo Domingo. They represent an enormous infusion of talent and they enrich immeasurably our connections to the global economy."

These are all economic arguments. I make them in some detail because the anti-immigrant arguments of today are often cast in economic terms, saying in effect, "We simply can't afford any more immigrants. They will eat our bread."

In New York, we simply cannot *afford to lose what they bring.*

Here's another example. At the New York Public Library last week, there was a ceremony to honor the city's high school valedictorians. Ninety-six of the city's best students attended . . . and guess what? Almost half of those valedictorians were born in another country. Think about it. Are these the immigrants we cannot afford?

And the contribution of immigrants cannot be measured solely in economic or scholastic terms. Different as they may be from the immigrants of my parents' generation, the new immigrants bring with them the same old-fashioned values.

The eagerness to work, to achieve. Discipline. Commitment. Ambition, healthy, stimulating ambition. The willingness to sacrifice for the next generation. A belief in family and responsibility. Respect for their obligations. Faith in something larger than themselves . . . All positive things we need to be reminded of.

And they remind us again of the beauty and profusion of God's Creation, and how ingenious the human family is in expressing it— in language and food and fashion and music and culture.

And so, the people of New York should not buy into the anti-immigrant syndrome. And there's some indication that they don't. A poll by the *New York Times* last year found that two-thirds of the respondents felt immigrants work harder than people born in the United States and do not take jobs away from the native-born.

For all these reasons, New York remains what it has always been: the golden door—open, welcoming, willing to help the immigrants and in turn be helped by them.

One concrete sign of that is a guidebook we've put together for new immigrants in New York. Called *Getting Started*, it contains valuable information about the vast array of programs and resources available to new New Yorkers to help them adjust to the challenges of life in New York.

Permit me just two final thoughts on immigration—one national, the other closer to home.

American immigration policy is of course set by the federal government, not by the states. I supported the Immigration Act of 1990, landmark legislation that reformed and updated our immigration laws.

It was not perfect. It was, however, an honest attempt to be fair to all the legitimate and sometimes competing forces with an interest in American immigration. It was reasonably realistic about America's capacity and America's need.

I believe we should watch the effects of the 1990 law closely, study its impact, and be willing to revise the law more frequently than we have in the past, to keep it as fair and equitable as possible . . . to Americans, to those wishing to come to the United States, to the countries from which our immigrants come.

As a governor I also urge Washington to live up to commitments it made in the 1980s to help states with the costs involved in the assimilation of aliens who moved from illegal to legal status, and of refugees.

The federal government has not lived up to its original agreements.

The legalization program has never been fully funded. Under the administration's proposed budget, 800 million dollars promised to the states will once again be withheld. New York State alone will be left with close to 90 million dollars in cumulative unreimbursed costs.

By failing to take responsibility for incarcerated illegal aliens, the federal government has cost New York State alone several hundred million dollars, with a national impact of close to one billion dollars annually.

President Bush's budget contains unprecedented reductions in federal funding for refugees. The national appropriation was reduced by 45 percent. New York's State's allocation would fall from 62 million dollars to 40 million dollars.

The federal government, through cuts and failures like these, is fostering resentment against immigrants and refugees by forcing states and local governments to spend their shrinking resources to fill the gaps created by Washington's abandonment of its responsibilities.

That's wrong. And I know you will join me in saying so.

Thank God, here in New York there are those willing to work to fill the gaps. Dozens of groups and thousands of individuals like many of you here today who work day in, day out to ease the way for immigrants, to steer them through an often intimidating maze of bureaucracy, to counsel and assist them.

The *Immigration Hotline* of the *Victim Services Agency* in Jackson Heights, whose staff we acknowledge today with certificates of appreciation, is a fine example.

The hotline each year offers counseling, information, and referral to more than 36,000 immigrants . . . in eleven languages. I want to say publicly that we know you're there, we know what you do for new New Yorkers, we know what you do for the city and state.

And we know how many of you there are, in organizations like the *Chinese-American Planning Council*, *HANAC*, *Citizen's Advice Bureau*, *CARECEN*, the *Korean Association*, *Emerald Isle*, *NYANA*, the *Center for Immigrants Rights*, *CAMBA*, and many, many others.

On behalf of the people of New York, I thank you.

I thank you for your patience in listening.

I thank you, particularly, for everything you bring to New York, everything you do for New York, for all the brightness and charm you contribute to this miracle of a place. It is an honor and a privilege to live here with you.

Thank you.

Nominating Speech,

Democratic National Convention

July 15, 1992

Madison Square Garden,

New York, New York

Shortly before the Democratic convention in 1992, Bill Clinton asked me to nominate him. I was honored by the invitation but concerned about my ability to prepare because I was then heavily involved with state problems. In fact, there were only about ten days before the convention. I was not able to free up much time, so preparing the speech became a matter of finding space at night and on the one weekend I had before the convention.

The objective was to portray Governor Clinton as the kind of person America needed as president and his prescriptions as the right ones for what was ailing the country.

The speech took all the time I had—including the two hours between rehearsals at the TelePrompTer on the day it was given when I changed significant portions of it. In the end I was satisfied that I had adequately described both the message and the messenger.

It was a different kind of challenge than the keynote of 1984, which allowed me to describe my personal views of things without reference to any specific candidate or even platform. Fortunately, there was enough coincidence between my views of the issues and our candidate's, so I could endorse him comfortably. That surprised some people who had been taken in by the "label game" and thought that somehow we were ideologically incompatible.

In the end he was nominated, and I eventually had the honor of having participated in the election of a president of the greatest country in the world.

Tonight, I will have the great privilege and honor of placing before you the name of the next president of the United States of America, Governor Bill Clinton of Arkansas.

It is not a matter of our wanting Bill Clinton. It is more than that. We *need* Bill Clinton because he is our only hope for change from this nation's current disastrous course.

Eight years ago, in San Francisco, some of us tried to convince America that while President Reagan was telling us we were all one "shining city on a hill," there was *another* city, where people were struggling, many of them living in pain.

And we tried to tell America that unless we changed policies— unless we expanded opportunity—the deterioration of the other city would spread.

We Democrats failed to reach enough Americans with that message, and now the nation has paid the price.

We cannot afford to fail again.

For the first time in their lives, millions of Americans who took for granted the basic right to make a living with one's own hands and mind and heart have been denied the dignity of earning their own bread.

Today, a fifty-year-old father lives nearly in terror at the prospect that if he is laid off—as so many around him have been—in addition to losing everything else, he will lose his health insurance, too.

"What if I'm struck by cancer?

"What about the mortgage?

"What about my son in college?

"And my daughter who's graduating high school?

"How will they get an education?

"And will they find a job even if they get an education?"

How could it have happened?

In a country where the executives of companies that fail, the presidents and chairmen of companies that make profits by trading solid American jobs for cheap labor overseas, make 5 million, 10 million, 15 million dollars a year?

How can our middle-class workers be in such terrible jeopardy?

A million children a year leaving school for the mean streets, surrounded by prostitutes and drug dealers, by violence and degradation.

Some of them growing up familiar with the sound of gunfire before they've ever heard an orchestra . . . becoming young adults, only to be instructed by the powerful evidence of their surroundings that there is little hope for them—even in America.

Nearly a whole generation surrendering in despair—to drugs, to having children while they're still children, to hopelessness.

How did it happen, here, in the most powerful nation in the world?

It's a terrible tragedy.

Not only for our children, but for all of America.

They are not my children, perhaps. Perhaps not yours, either. But they are our children.

We should love them.

But even if we could choose not to love them, we would still need them to be sound and productive. Because they are the nation's future.

It would be bad enough if we could believe this is all the result of a terrible but only a temporary recession. But this is more than a recession. Our economy has been weakened fundamentally by twelve years of conservative Republicans' supply-side policy.

In fact, supply-side was just another version of the failed Republican dogma of sixty-five years ago—then called "trickle-down"— which led to the Great Depression.

And it has failed again!

It operated from the naive Republican assumption that if we fed the wealthiest Americans with huge income tax cuts, they would eventually produce "loaves and fishes" for everyone.

Instead, it made a small group of our wealthiest Americans wealthier than ever, and left the rest of the country the crumbs from their tables.

Unemployment. Bankruptcies. Economic stagnation.

Today, a 400 billion dollar annual deficit and a 4 trillion dollar national debt hang like great albatrosses around our nation's neck, strangling our economy, menacing our future.

We became a great nation by making things and selling them to others.

But today, we buy from Japan and Germany and other nations the things we used to make and sell to them: cars, radios, televisions, clothing—giving them our dollars for their goods.

Then at the end of the year, because we spend more than we collect in taxes, we borrow back those dollars, paying billions more of our dollars in interest, increasing our debt—decreasing our ability to invest—perpetuating a mad economic cycle that threatens to spin us out of control.

In no time at all, we have gone from the greatest seller, lender, creditor nation, to the world's largest buyer, borrower, and debtor nation.

And that, ladies and gentlemen, is the legacy of the Bush years.

The slowest economic growth for any four-year presidential term since Herbert Hoover.

An economy crippled by debt and deficit. The fading of the American dream. Working-class families sliding back down towards poverty, deprivation, inexplicable violence.

After twelve years, Americans are disillusioned, angry, and fearful.

The people showed it with the quick embrace they gave to the sudden appearance on television of a provocative, wealthy businessman who said he'd like to be president.

Before he told anyone what he would do or how he would do it, he used one word and applause broke out all over America—"change!"

Of course, the American people want change—of course we want something better than George Bush and the politics of decline, decay, and deception.

And beginning with this convention, we must demonstrate to all the American people that change for the better is at hand, ready, able, and eager to serve . . . in the person of Governor Bill Clinton of Arkansas.

And this time, we cannot afford to fail to deliver the message—not just to Democrats, but to the whole nation.

Because the ship of state is headed for the rocks.

The crew knows it.

The passengers know it.

Only the captain of the ship—President Bush—appears not to know it.

He seems to think that the ship will be saved by imperceptible undercurrents, directed by the invisible hand of some cyclical economic god, that will gradually move the ship so that at the last moment it will miraculously glide past the rocks to safer shores.

Well, prayer is always a good idea, but our prayers must be accompanied by good works.

We need a captain who understands that, and who will seize the wheel . . . before it's too late.

I am here tonight to offer America that new captain with a new course . . . Governor Bill Clinton of Arkansas.

Bill Clinton understands that a great political party must apply the best of its accumulated wisdom to the new configurations of a changing society. He cherishes the ideals of justice, liberty, and opportunity that Robert Kennedy died for.

But he knows that these ideals require new implementations—new ways to provide incentive to reward achievement, to encourage entrepreneurship.

Bill Clinton believes—as we all here do—in the first principle of our commitment: the politics of inclusion, the solemn obligation to create opportunity for all our people.

For the aging factory worker in Pittsburgh; the school child in Atlanta; the family farmer in Des Moines; the eager immigrants, sweating to make their place alongside of us, here in New York

City, and in San Francisco; the bright, young businesswoman in Chicago.

From *wherever*, no matter how recently, of *whatever color, whatever creed, whatever sex*, of *whatever sexual orientation*, all of them, equal members of the American family and the neediest of them—because of age or illness or circumstance—entitled to the greatest help from the rest of us.

Surrender that Democratic principle and we might just as well tear the donkeys from our lapels, pin elephants on instead, and retreat to elegant estates behind ivy-covered walls, where, when they detect a callus on their palms, people conclude it's time to put down their polo mallet.

Bill Clinton believes that the closest thing to a panacea that we have is described by a simple four-letter word—work!

He has been living that truth all his life.

So, Bill Clinton believes that what we most need now is to create jobs by investing in the rebuilding of our cities; shoring up our agricultural strength; investing to produce well-trained workers, new technologies, safe energy; entrepreneurship; laying the foundations for economic growth into the next century, pulling people off welfare, off unemployment, giving people back their dignity and their confidence.

And unlike the other candidates, he has a solid, intelligent, workable plan to produce those jobs.

President Bush disagrees with Bill Clinton. He says we cannot afford to do all that needs to be done. He says we have the will but not the wallet.

Bill Clinton knows that we have the wealth available. We've proved it over and over, when the dramatic catastrophes strike.

Remember the savings and loans? Governors and mayors had gone to Washington to plead for help for education, for job training, for health care, for roads and bridges.

"Sorry, there is none," said the president. "We're broke. We have the will but not the wallet."

Then Americans discovered that wealthy bankers—educated in the most exquisite forms of conservative, Republican banking—through their incompetence and thievery, and the government's neglect, had stolen or squandered everything in sight!

We heard no moralizing about values then from our Republican leaders.

Instead, *mirabile dictu*—all of a sudden—the heavens opened, and out of the blue, billions of dollars appeared.

Not for children. Not for jobs. Not for the ill. But hundreds of billions of dollars to bail out failed savings and loans.

Billions for war.

Billions for earthquakes and hurricanes.

Bill Clinton asks: if we can do all this for these spectacular catastrophes, why can't we find the wealth to respond to the quiet catastrophes that every day oppress the lives of thousands, that destroy our children with drugs, that kill thousands with terrible new diseases like AIDS, that deprive our people of the sureness of adequate health care, that stifle our future.

America needs Bill Clinton, too, because he understands we must deal with what could be, eventually, the most lethal problem of all: a degraded environment . . . one that kills life in our lakes with acid rain, allows cancer-causing rays to pierce a deteriorated ozone shield, and threatens to convert the planet into a cosmic hothouse.

Bill Clinton made clear how well he understands that when he announced Senator Al Gore would be the next vice president of the United States of America.

America needs Bill Clinton for still another reason. We need a leader who will stop the Republican attempt—through laws and through the courts—to tell us *what God to believe in*, and how to apply that God's judgment to our schoolrooms, our bedrooms, and our bodies.

Bill Clinton knows the course from here, past peril, to a new era of growth and progress for this nation that will enable us to share our power and our abundance with the world community.

•   •   •

He was born and raised with all the personal attributes needed for leadership. God-given intelligence. Vitality. And an extraordinary strength of character that allowed him to survive the buffeting and the trauma of a difficult youth.

He was born poor in Hope, Arkansas.

The accents, even the colors may have been a tint different, but the feelings were the same that many of us experienced on the asphalt streets of some of the nation's great cities: the same pain, the same anguish, the same hopes.

He has lived through years of hard challenges since then.

And with each new challenge, he has grown wiser and stronger, as he demonstrated with his remarkable resiliency in the recent, bruising Democratic primaries.

Bill Clinton has always been driven by the desire to lift himself above his own immediate concerns: to give himself to something larger than himself.

His entire adult life has been devoted to helping others through public service.

And for eleven years now, he has been the governor of his beloved state, protecting Arkansas from a federal government that has been depriving the states and cities for over a decade; balancing eleven budgets in a row; doing the things that governors and presidents are supposed to do: enforcing the laws, providing education and opportunities for children and young adults, expanding health care, attracting new jobs, and reaching out to heal wounds caused by 300 years of unfairness and oppression.

He has done it so well that the nation's other governors, both Democratic and Republican, have repeatedly acknowledged him to be a national leader.

All this time, Bill Clinton has worked to relieve other people's discomfort because he remembers his own struggle.

That's why we need Bill Clinton. Because Bill Clinton still remembers . . . because he is equipped to break the awful gridlock in

Washington and to deliver effective government . . . because he will remind this nation that we are too good to make war our most successful enterprise. Because he does not believe that the way to win political support is to pit one group against another.

He does not believe in the cynical political arithmetic that says you can add by subtracting, or multiply by dividing; but instead he will work to make the whole nation stronger, by bringing people together, showing us our commonality, instructing us in cooperation, making us, not a collection of competing special interests, but one great, special family—the family of America!

For all these reasons, we must make Bill Clinton the next president of the United States of America.

A year ago, we had a great parade in New York City to celebrate the return of our armed forces from the Persian Gulf.

I'm sure you had one, too.

But as joyous as those parades were, I'd like to march with you in a different kind of celebration, one, regrettably, we cannot hold yet.

I'd like to march with you behind President Bill Clinton through cities and rural villages where all the people have safe streets, affordable housing, and health care when they need it.

I want to clap my hands and throw my fists in the air, cheering neighborhoods where children can be children, where they can grow up and get the chance to go to college, and one day own their own home.

I want to sing—proud songs, happy songs—arm in arm with workers who have a real stake in their company's success, who once again have the assurance that a lifetime of hard work will make life better for their children than it's been for them.

I want to march behind President Bill Clinton in a victory parade that sends up fireworks, celebrating the triumph of our technology centers and factories, outproducing and outselling our overseas competitors.

I want to march—with you—knowing that we are selecting justices to the Supreme Court who are qualified to be there, and who understand the basic American right of each individual to make his or her own moral and religious judgments.

I want to look forward and feel the warmth, the pride, the profound gratitude of knowing that we are making America surer, stronger, and sweeter.

I want to shout out our thanks because President Bill Clinton helped us make the greatest nation in the world better than it's ever been.

So step aside, Mr. Bush. You've had your parade!

It's time for change—someone smart enough to know, strong enough to do, sure enough to lead.

The Comeback Kid. A new voice for a new America.

Because I love New York, because I love America, I nominate for the office of the President of the United States, the man from Hope, Arkansas, Governor Bill Clinton!

This speech was my eleventh State of the State. Its principal emphases were similar to those that characterized President Clinton's first presentations to the country a month later. I called for massive investments in New York's infrastructure, high-tech centers, health system, and education. Further governmental reform was on my agenda, as it has been each year of my administration. Our state legislature, like the Congress, makes changes slowly.

There was one major difference between my approach and the president's. He asked for tax increases at the federal level to help reduce the huge projected deficit: I continued to hold the line on our major tax rates, having already reduced them substantially during my governorship. The truth is that our state taxes had been increased so dramatically during the so-called Rockefeller years from the late fifties to the early seventies that we have had to struggle to reduce them since then because of their adverse effect on our competitiveness with other states. Federal tax rates, on the other hand, were slashed drastically during the early Reagan years, helping to create a staggering national debt.

The reference to the New York Proposition near the end of the speech was the second such formulation of our state's underlying values, and would be followed by several more in later addresses.

Before anything else, I am sure I speak for all New Yorkers when I express to President George Bush— and his family—our respect and gratitude for his service as our president, and wish him and Barbara Bush a long and happy life together.

At the same time, we extend our congratulations, our pledge of support, and our prayers for success as he assumes leadership of the nation . . . to President-elect Bill Clinton . . . and to Hillary Clinton.

The national recession has battered our state and much of the rest of the nation. For the first time in their lifetime, some of the people of this state are not able to earn a living—denied the one staple that has always before nourished the American dream: a job.

The people are hurt, concerned, and angry.

Everywhere in the nation we hear their unconditional demands for those of us in public office to change our ways—to control taxes, to produce more jobs. To find less expensive ways to provide better health care.

And they demand that we make government more accessible and more accountable.

We have a head start in New York.

We've disciplined our finances. We are putting an end to the thirty-four-year-old practice of spring borrowing. We have improved our overall efficiency.

And we've controlled spending. Instead of raising our tax rates to balance our budget when times got tough, in recent years, as some other states did, we've found ways to cut 7 billion dollars in anticipated spending over the last two years alone.

As a result, spending from taxes has grown less here than the national average since 1983, while leaving basic institutions in this state stronger than those in most states in the country.

And there's more we will do—debt reform, for example. Comptroller Regan and I have agreed on a plan to give the people more say on how much debt we create, stopping back-door financing altogether. And I'm sure that before the end of the session you'll agree.

But we have to do still more.

We have a new administration in Washington and the worst of the recession appears to be behind us, but national economic growth will be slow.

Your fiscal staffs have already agreed with us that this year our still lagging revenues will fall far short of the current statutory spending commitments. And so, in order to avoid huge tax increases that could slow our recovery, we will once again have to make dramatic cuts. It will be difficult, because our previous cuts have brought us so much closer to muscle and bone.

But the truth is there is no real alternative, if we are not only to balance our budget but also to help reignite the engine of our economy. And that must be our goal: you and I must help create a *new prosperity* for New York, growing out of good jobs for New Yorkers.

It is how we became the Empire State—and it is how we will reach those heights again.

We are vividly aware over the last few years we've lost hundreds of thousands of jobs, many of them lost to America altogether by our faltering national competitiveness.

But we must be just as aware that we have all the advantages needed to create extraordinary *new* economic strength in the global marketplace.

Think of it:

This state is the center of the richest markets in our hemisphere.

We are tied to the powerful emerging *European* market by proximity, by history, by mutuality.

Our trade relations with Japan and the rest of Asia are growing.

We already have the most extensive infrastructure in the country, a powerful network of high-technology centers, America's strongest system of higher education and the most productive work force in the United States of America, ample energy—and a history of providing opportunity to generation after generation.

Now, to build on this strength, and to stimulate the economy, we need to generate good, solid jobs that will enhance economic strength, spinning off still more permanent jobs. And we need to do it *right now*—particularly in the construction industry, where some trades are experiencing 60 percent and 70 percent unemployment.

In my time as governor we have committed massively to the rebuilding of this state. And now *we must do more*—and we will— with one of the largest and most productive building programs in the history of this state, or any other.

I propose over the next five years to invest over 25 billion dollars in projects to match the needs and opportunities of every region in the state . . . creating more than 300,000 jobs in the process!

Three hundred thousand jobs . . . people, earning their own living instead of being on welfare or unemployment. Three hundred thousand . . . creating permanent strength that produces even more jobs for years to come!

Now, there are too many specific projects for me to describe each one fully here. But they stretch from one end of the state to the other: including railways, roads, bridges, parks; construction for the state and city universities, for court facilities, for schoolhouses, construction for our airports, for our libraries, for our hospitals.

Another of the state's greatest strengths, which I think has not received the attention it deserves, is our growing mastery in high technology.

Again, we are leaders here and not followers.

At the turn of the century, *General Electric* created the nation's first industrial research laboratory in the country. They did it in Schenectady. Since then New York has produced nearly a thousand industrial research-and-development facilities.

This year we celebrate the tenth anniversary of our *Centers for Advanced Technology*—the first program in the nation to use state funds for private research and development—we did in fields like bio-technology, advanced materials, ceramics, robotics, optics . . . creating new ideas, new companies, new jobs. We're going to celebrate this year with a ten-point plan that will be the cornerstone of an even more dynamic *new* emphasis on technology in this state.

Our plan includes an ambitious collaboration between the public and the private sectors to bring the government "on-line"—a network to link every branch and every level of government. Making it possible for a doctor in Watertown to evaluate an X ray with a specialist in Buffalo, at the same time, and without either of them leaving the office. Giving a student in Elmira instant access to the same research material and at the same as a student in Scarsdale.

Making it as easy and automatic as it should be for New Yorkers to find the services and information they need from their government—a permit, a certificate, a license. Moving closer to the day when our people will no longer feel that state government means waiting on line.

Emerging technologies also offer an answer to our current energy and environmental challenges—from complying with the pro-visions of the *Clean Air Act* to reducing our dependence on fossil fuels. This year, we will combine all of the tremendous expertise and intelligence of our high-tech business, science, and academic sectors to help identify the most promising of these technologies—and turn them into practical products and productive jobs.

These are only small pieces of the broad, exciting high-tech program I propose. I urge you to study it all. It's all set out in the book. The future is high-tech, and we will be in the forefront, thanks to the programs that we have already established and those that we will propose to you this year.

In recent years—barely noticed by the general public—we have begun to tap a rich new vein of opportunity.

Our exports to countries like Japan, Italy, Canada, and Argen-tina—and investments by those nations in our own economy—have grown dramatically. Our *Global New York* initiative, only two years old, has helped more than 3,500 businesses break into or expand sales to international markets.

And we already surpass every state in the nation in foreign investment in critical areas like banking, and finance, and retail.

I propose that during the next three years we help thousands more companies increase their export sales by at least a half-billion dollars. And I've concluded that I made a mistake—one among a number, I'm afraid, in my early years as governor—in not traveling more on trade missions than I did. Our missions to Israel and Italy this year and to Japan the year before were even more productive than we had hoped.

And so, this year, I plan to go to Mexico, and to Asia and Europe again—at no expense, incidentally, to the taxpayers.

To make the most of all our possibilities for economic growth, we need one thing perhaps more than any other: a healthy, productive work force. Today, as you know, companies across the state are struggling to avoid layoffs and workers are praying that they keep their jobs—because decent health care simply costs too much.

Internationally, one of the most serious threats to the compet-itiveness of this country is the skyrocketing cost of health care. New York already leads the nation with reforms—controlling costs, improving access, and tackling public health crises from TB to AIDS. But still there is a great deal more to do.

My proposals are in the book, but health care is such an urgent and complicated issue that I believe it merits special treatment—by you and by me—and deserves, therefore, a special message, which I will send to you within the next few weeks.

We must also make sure that our strong work force is replenished by New Yorkers who have all the skills that the tough new market-place demands.

In addition to top-quality higher education, we must see to it that our elementary and secondary schools give our children the best start possible.

At the moment, we have some of the finest public schools in the country. I note with pride that the United States Education Department recently declared *Voorheesville Elementary* a *Blue Ribbon School*—an honor it now shares with the Voorheesville Middle School and High School. Congratulations to all of you in Voorheesville. But we also have hovels called schoolhouses . . . schools in desperate need of the most basic assistance. And we have students graduating illiterate, if they haven't already dropped out.

All of this while some other school districts squander their money outrageously, with salaries as high as two hundred thousand dollars a year for a superintendent, and annual pensions even higher. In one well-publicized disgrace, there was a nine-hundred-and-sixty-thousand-dollar going-away gift to a BOCES superintendent who was retiring . . . the same year that we told other school districts all over this state that we did not have the money to afford them fairness!

This is a travesty.

Last year—before the revelation—I asked for $200,000 to audit BOCES organizations like the one in question. You thought it wasn't necessary.

This year I will use my executive powers to conduct my own salary investigations. I will report to the people every substantial public salary affecting taxpayers in the state, including every one in the entire education system. And then, instead of settling for episodic explosions of indignation, together you and I can cure some of the outrageous unfairness.

Nowhere, nowhere, do we need change more than in our education system. It is responsible for nearly 30 percent of the entire budget—and an immeasurable part of our future. We must correct our school aid formula. To the extent that you can understand it, it is palpably unfair to our middle-class and poor communities.

We must pursue vigorously the good ideas proposed by Commissioner Sobol and the Regents in the *New Compact for Learning*, ideas like allowing individual schools to make more of their own decisions, getting parents more involved, making sure our students are mastering the skills they will need for tomorrow. We should expand the idea of choice everywhere in our public school system.

We also need to help young people prepare for the marketplace through new apprenticeships and our *Career Pathways* initiative, being led for us by Lieutenant Governor Lundine.

There is another way we can help unlock opportunity in New York: by increasing the assistance to local governments and reducing the burdens we place on them.

When I took office, as governor, the highest personal state income tax rate was 14 percent. It's now less than 8 percent.

When I took office, as governor, the state sales tax rate was 4 percent. It's still 4 percent.

When I took office, we were the fourteenth highest-taxed state in terms of state taxes—today, we are twenty-fourth. Twenty-three others demand more of their taxpayers than we do.

And so we have made considerable progress, and I do not intend to reverse it. I will not raise our broad-based tax rates this year.

Local taxes, on the other hand, have continued to grow, damaging our taxpayers and discouraging business. And they have continued to grow despite the fact that over the last ten years, we've increased the portion of the state budget that goes to those local governments from 60 percent to 68 percent, while assuming 80 percent of local long-term Medicaid costs. That means we picked up for them over this period more than 6 billion dollars.

This year, I want to do more.

We must pass Medicaid takeover and "wrap-up" insurance. And we must offer relief from scores of other laws that require localities to spend money.

The proposals I submit to you on these subjects, together, would save local governments and school districts billions of dollars in the next several years.

Today I'll add a pledge you've not heard before: this year I will not propose any new, unfunded, state-mandated programs for local governments. I call on *you* to join me in that promise.

Here's another good idea for local governments. The property tax represents the single largest source of local revenues. And yet, as you know, it is a tax that often imposes an unfair burden on those who can least afford to pay it. No tax is pleasant, but there *is* another, fairer way to pay for schools: why not allow school districts to change from real estate taxes to local income taxes, if they and their constituents choose to?

And we can make responsible progress with entitlements, as well. Entitlements, as you know, are the fastest-growing programs in the budget. Medicaid is an entitlement. So are public assistance and tuition assistance for higher education. And these are just to name a few.

So this year, in another unprecedented change, I will not add any new entitlements nor expand eligibility to any of our existing ones. And I ask you to pledge to do the same.

Another part of our responsibility—beyond producing jobs and a new prosperity for the state—is to help those who have not yet shared in our prosperity. But we impair that purpose if our public assistance programs don't run efficiently, or if they tend to encourage a cycle of dependency. Or if they are unfair to our taxpayers.

We are national leaders in reforming the welfare system. We have been for a long time. Our *Child Assistance Program*—the CAP Program—helps make sure that child support is paid, and it gives mothers a real incentive to find a job. As the only program of its kind in the United States of America, it recently received a national *Innovations in Government* award from the *Ford Foundation*. I congratulate everyone involved, from the people who planned the program to those who make it work, at all levels of government.

Like our new *Working Toward Independence* program, CAP increases work opportunities for welfare recipients. Both programs work. And so, both will be expanded this year.

Despite these successes, it appears to me that we are not making the progress that we should for some of the people in greatest need—all of those trapped in concentrated pockets of poverty that are scattered across this state. This is partly because these people are tangled in a complex web of social, economic, and medical problems, and many of the programs we offer go after only one strand of that web at a time.

As part of the *Decade of the Child*, therefore, I propose an initiative called the *Neighborhood-based Alliance* that will help us make a difference by focusing our resources on fifteen target neighborhoods—in places like Central Islip and Bed-Stuy, in Newburgh and Washington Heights, and in Port Henry. In each of these neighborhoods, we will combine the power of a number of our best programs, including our economic development zones, our *Gateway* initiative, community policing, community schools.

The result? A neighborhood in which a little girl could get a measles vaccine in the same building where she goes to school—and where her father, at night takes English lessons after work. In which her mother could get a low-interest loan to open a shop nearby—and feel safe walking home because the police on the beat know her name.

This is a good idea. Please help me get it done.

The recent [presidential] election produced an unprecedented expression of disapproval, not only of prevailing economic conditions, but disapproval as well of the way elected government conducts its business.

But despite that, this state has not moved forward with badly needed reforms.

Let me ask all of you out there, right now: Do you agree, whether you personally like term limitations or not, and you may not, do you agree that there are many people in this state who would like a chance to vote on the question of term limitations?

Do you think the people would like the chance to vote for limits, new, tougher limits, on the amount lobbyists and special interests can contribute to my campaign, or to legislators' campaigns, to win our favor?

And whatever your personal position on the issue, or mine, do you think that most New Yorkers would like a chance to vote on the death penalty and life imprisonment without parole?

Then what are we afraid of? We should support a constitutional convention—and we should do it this year.

I will continue to propose a package of important electoral reforms, some of which would be the subject of a constitutional convention, and I will explain to the public as well as I can that in 1997—if we don't do it before then—they will be *guaranteed* the chance to vote themselves a constitutional convention, *whether we like it or not*, and I will tell them that they should be ready for that chance.

But it would be better if we did it before then.

I've outlined the entire agenda in the book before you now.

So putting New Yorkers to work, creating a new prosperity, reinventing and reforming the government, all of that seems a healthy agenda for this year.

But to understand the full scope of our challenge: We must keep in mind that there is something more at work in New York— and in America—that is more profound than people's concern over a feeble economy and their resentment over government's imperfection. Something surely affected by these difficulties but that goes beyond them.

Many New Yorkers—many Americans—are asking, "What has happened to our families? What produces this grotesque violence? The drugs? The loss of respect for authority, for discipline, for a sense of obligation? Where did people get the idea that they could choose not to work and still share freely in the fruits of *our* labors?

"Why are we fighting one another in the streets of our cities?"

People everywhere are asking, "What has happened to the American Proposition, the values we hold, at our best, that allow us, despite our differences and our tensions, to go forward, *together?*"

This question of traditional values was raised in the recent presidential election but was eclipsed by other issues. That's too bad, because it is a fundamental question. And a significant one.

And so, we must do more this year than make a budget that

balances. *By the contents* of our budget and the other bills we pass, we must make clear what defines us as a people. What basic values and ideas tie *us* together—loosely enough to allow us a full measure of individual freedom but firmly enough to make us one united powerful people.

This is the place to do it—here in New York—because this is where much of America was born. And this is the time to do it, as our new president is about to lead us into a whole new era.

Now, of course, making sense of this extraordinary democracy has never been easy. It has always required an improbable level of agreement, in a highly diverse and stratified society. But it has worked here in America—and especially here in New York, because of a handful of crucial ideas that bind us all together . . . ideas that unite the elderly white couple living on social security in Plattsburgh with the black or Latino children of Syracuse or Buffalo or the Bronx . . . principles that link the Adirondack logger with the New York City conservationist . . . values that join the struggling young entrepreneur in Rochester with the unskilled worker seeking training in Freeport.

What we need now is to rearticulate them, commit ourselves to them again, and then put them to work in the everyday business of governing—and living.

That's what my message seeks to do.

All the ideas, all the programs, all the policies I offer you in the printed message reflect those values and principles specifically. Indeed, I summarize all of them for you with just four words that I believe capture this basic *New York Proposition*.

The first: *opportunity*. That's the heart of what I've spoken of already today.

For ten generations, immigrants came to this place for opportunity, to find work. Historically, the principal source of this nation's, and this state's, power has been an economy that allows people to achieve security and comfort, perhaps even affluence, by putting themselves to work productively.

New Yorkers all understand this, we all agree. The word "work" for us is like a talisman. The magic path to the American dream.

The second word is *liberty*. It means many things: the right to pray to any God, or to no god.

The idea that a person should not be denied opportunity because of gender, or color, or creed, or nationality; should not be denied because of so-called disability, or age; should not be denied because of sexual orientation.

Liberty says that a person should not be denied because of a quota that in the name of justice does injustice.

In New York, we believe that liberty also means a woman's right to choose.

And liberty is the freedom to feel safe in one's own neighborhood—or any other—protected by the power of government.

In the words of Dr. Martin Luther King, Jr.: "The law may not be able to make us love one another—but it should be strong enough to keep us from lynching one another." And so while we continue our attempts to conciliate contending groups like those in Bensonhurst or Crown Heights, we must also provide all the legal resources, all the legal procedures needed to keep the peace . . . including weapons like a law on bias-related violence.

Now we have got a lot of ideas on how we can help. They're all laid out in the book.

Our third principle is *responsibility*. It means our basic duty to comply with the law. It means the obligation to work if you can. It means the understanding that if you bring a child into the world, you should care for it . . . and for the parents who brought *you* into the world.

Responsibility is also government's obligation, while living within its means, to fulfill its duty to help those who have no one else to care for them. And because the earth is ours to use, but not to waste, responsibility means preserving the planet for the generations to come.

The last word is *family*, and it describes the simplest, most logical, most intelligent rationale for coming together in this disparate society: The need to share benefits and burdens for the good of all. Reasonably. Honestly. Fairly.

Out of compassion, but not *just* out of compassion, out of an enlightened self-interest as well. Because we cannot make it as a people if we lose a generation of our children to drugs, or to AIDS, or to inadequate education, or if we are locked in combat with our neighbors in the streets of our cities.

We cannot make it without understanding and believing in the idea of family.

Because business cannot survive without labor. Because no man is an island, no state or nation either.

Opportunity. Liberty. Responsibility. Family. *The New York Proposition!* I believe this is what we are at our very best. Indeed, I believe this is what America is at its very best.

Opportunity. Liberty. Responsibility. Family.

You and I are charged with the duty to get this state as close to these ideals as we can. Of course we have problems, serious ones, but I don't think we can claim that they are unsolvable.

The hard truth is, if you and I did not succeed, it would not be because of a God who denied us natural resources, nor forebears who squandered our blessings, nor a people unable or unwilling to do their part. If we failed, it would be rather because we—the leaders chosen to show the way—had failed the people who chose us . . . by refusing to face our problems honestly and refusing to make the hard judgments they require.

We must not let that happen.

I have given you solid proposals that will put our people to work and that will leave our state stronger and more prosperous than it is today.

I know you will not approve of my proposals without change. But I ask you to work *with* me with a full heart, cooperatively, avoiding the governmental gridlock that our people so despise, in order to give New Yorkers the progressive government and the new prosperity that they deserve.

I assure every one of you that I will devote every ounce of strength I have to that mutual effort.

Thank you.

Whatever else can be said about this short tribute to the memory of Robert Kennedy, it is an appropriate final piece to the collection of thoughts and words bound together in this volume. The first of the speeches I included was written in 1974, while the memory of Robert Kennedy's wonderfully uplifting rhetoric was perhaps more vividly alive than it is today. I called upon the liberal elements of the Democratic party to recognize the need to keep all the economic classes together—especially the poor and the middle classes—because it was right and because it was practically necessary.

This idea of a unity shared by all Americans was at the heart of Robert Kennedy's message. He delivered it with a power that might have swept him to the presidency and world leadership—had it not been for the inexplicable act of violence that struck him down. A generation later, as my tribute reveals, we are still begging for the fusing of interests that will finally allow this nation to realize its full potential. Now there is a new inspiration . . . another bright, strong, young voice calling on America to lock arms, and to march forward together toward a better nation and a better world . . . President Bill Clinton. I present this speech here with the profound hope that with his leadership, Robert Kennedy's dream of sweetness, sanity, and strength will finally have its day.

Thank you, Robert Kennedy, Jr.

"The last campaign," that brief and finally heartbreaking eighty-one days in 1968. . . .

And it *was* the last in the sense that one of the most valuable lives of our era came to an end—tragically and much too soon.

We went to the cathedral and wept, because we would never hear the voice again.

We wept for another reason. We knew that we, *too,* had been wounded. All of society had.

In the agony of our grief, it was hard to believe that not everything had been lost on that night in the Ambassador Hotel.

The last of four strong brothers reminded us that though Robert Kennedy was gone, we had not lost "what he said, what he did, and what he stood for." He told us that if we remembered those things, Robert Kennedy would live with us still. But he told us, too, that remembering wasn't enough.

To do him justice, we would have to commit ourselves to living his mission, to carrying on his *work*.

When I look at the America we face today, I have to confess the commitment seems to live more in the poetry of our aspirations than in the prose of the realities we have created.

I'm afraid that not enough of us have filled the twenty-five years since then with the kind of thinking and action that would have brought us closer to Robert Kennedy's goal.

Despite the best efforts of the extraordinary family he left behind, and other good people, I think Robert Kennedy would look at America today and regret that in a quarter of a century we had done so little to reach the dream.

The real irony remains that the things that Robert Kennedy believed, said, and died for have not *failed* in the last quarter of a century—the real irony is that they *never* had their day.

The problem is *not* that these ideas became part of our public agenda and were found too costly or inconvenient or impractical. The problem is *not* that they were tried and found wanting; the problem is that *we never even tried them*, before now. And today, our new leaders face problems so big and so daunting that there will be a temptation not to try anything that seems so daring.

The temptation will be to hang up the memory of Robert Kennedy respectfully in a little gold frame and dust it with incense from time to time, as we chant familiar words of praise.

It would be wrong to honor Robert Kennedy with poetry alone. We must understand that his greatest gift to us was the *prose*, the facts, the details, his practical proposals as much as his soaring aspirations.

It's right to have memorials, but we need more than sweet reminiscence. We should be going back into the annals of the Kennedy years, taking his speeches, analyzing them, figuring out why people loved this man.

Then we should try to do what he was not given the chance to do.

What *was* it about him? I think I understand one thing about him. He had at least one powerful fundamental idea. "Remember," he said to us, "this is a disparate place."

There's tremendous variety here; there's an awful lot of elbowing for space. There are all kinds of forces, some of them competing with one another. You have to put it all together, you have to find a synergism. Something that brings all the classes together.

For a decade and more in America, we have witnessed some of the most effective, most unnerving political maneuvers ever recorded— politicians who won, over and over, by doing just the opposite, by using tactics of fear and division, pitting one part of our people against the other. Trying to frighten people out of their belief in fairness.

We've witnessed campaigns conducted in code—by making an issue out of welfare, or using the image of Willie Horton, or proposing to "take America back" from the latest seekers who hoped to join us here.

When people start talking in code, you can be pretty sure there's a war on, and in this case the war was against the poor and the voiceless—against the new immigrant, against the child who just had a child, against the sick old man with no home to go to—as if they were somehow the *source* of our troubles instead of the casualties.

What happened in the 1980s was a deliberate, relentless campaign to drive the middle class toward the right by frightening them out of their better instincts. It didn't seem to matter much that with the heavy hammer forged out of the coalition of the rich and the middle class, the poor might get beaten into oblivion. And that's what happened.

Things might have been different if Robert Kennedy had been here to help. He had the one powerful idea. Years before, he had said to us, "Look. You've got to keep the middle class and the poor together. They have to understand their relationship to one another. That they need one another.

"You have to reach every one of the enlightened affluent. Everyone has to understand his and her relationship to one another."

No man is an island. No woman. No class. No city. No state— no nation either. You have to keep people *together*.

The way you do that is not just by appealing to the noble sense of charity, generosity, compassion. That's easy. Robert Kennedy was brilliant at that. *Anybody* can play the part of the lover; it's the easiest thing in the world to say, "You must love one another." We know that by instinct.

But sometimes it's too hard to do; sometimes it costs you too much.

If loving you means I have to let you move into my neighborhood and spoil it, if loving you means I have to give up the money I need to educate my child, if loving you costs me too much, then . . . "the heck with it; I won't do it."

And so what Robert Kennedy taught us was: "Now, look; it is not just that you love them—that's the natural instinct—but it is also good for *you* to be good to them.

"In this case, compassion and common sense come together."

He was right.

This country cannot make it unless we rescue those people who have been left behind.

The work force of the twenty-first century will be so diminished, we won't be able to compete in a global economy unless we rescue those children from AIDS, from crack, from violence, unless we pull them out of the prisons and put them into the laboratories, unless they become our work force.

What would we do otherwise? Hire the Mexicans or the Taiwanese? Move *everything* somewhere else?

Bobby Kennedy lived a real life, a blessed life, rich in many ways, but a hard life, too, a terribly challenging one. He felt the exultation, but he knew the agony that invites despair as well.

Bobby Kennedy understood the romance, but he was brilliant at the sweaty reality of things, too. And because he lived it all and understood it, he could explain it all—like no one since.

No one since has been able to put the poetry and the prose together the way he did.

After the assassination, Norman Cousins wrote that "none of the attempts to define the meaning of his life said it better than the quiet presence of hundreds of thousands of people who waited in lines in New York City through most of the night and day for a chance to file past a flag-draped coffin. . . .

"Robert Kennedy's meaning for these people was *hope*. He had recaptured hope in situations where it had been broken down so often it had nearly ceased to exist."

Twenty-five years later, we owe it to his memory to find that hope once more, and nourish it, and make it bright again. To make sure that the "last campaign," no matter how long it has been delayed, is not a lost campaign after all.

Let's listen to his speeches again. Let's read them again. Let's study his words again, let's remember what made him so effective, and let's for once—just once—try applying his ideas, and seeing what happens.

Surely it would be a better world, and then, by having made his words real, we will have given Robert Kennedy the best memorial of all.

There are periods in our history when the disorder and level of incivility frighten us and make us wonder what we are as a people. The grotesque explosion of violence in our streets and homes, added to the uncertainty produced by lost jobs and a vulnerable economy, created such a period in the early 1990s. This speech and the State of the State that followed it sought to raise the fundamental question of how we can reorient our society by a clearer affirmation of the best of the nation's fundamental principles. It argues for a rejection of reactionary attempts to erode the essential protections of the First Amendment. It also tries to remind us that the ultimate answer will lie not with government ordering the people to be rational, but with the people choosing to make right decisions. It reminds me of some wonderful lines from Emily Dickinson, ". . . Thyself may be Thine Enemy—Captivity is Consciousness—So's Liberty."

It's a pleasure to be joining you here today—a group of tremendously accomplished individuals representing one of our state's most powerful industries, and an important part of New York's economic base.

You are, in fact, much more than that. As the fourth estate, you are the Inspector General Supreme of the government and other institutions, and in that capacity you protect our cherished liberty. You are also—like it or not—one of the greatest influences on our people's thoughts, judgments, and actions.

I'd like to talk to you today about both those roles.

Every age has its disorder and even its crises and calamities, but it does seem that our current situation in this country is so disorienting as to frighten even the historians among us—an ugly litany proves this is no exaggeration.

• We have five percent of the world's population and consume fifty percent of its cocaine.

• Twelve thousand times a year, an American dies because someone else chooses to pull the trigger on a handgun.

• So many of our children are lost to stray bullets in the drug war that we no longer find the stories shocking.

• The suicide rate is at an all-time high.

• So are our bias-related crimes, our divorce rate, our rate of abortion, and the harshness and volatility of our politics.

In this atmosphere, it's no surprise that the people seek strong solutions and beg for strong leaders.

That has always been true at time like this, and it has always been dangerous, because occasionally, the people settle for the wrong expressions of strength.

One example of this urgent desire to wrestle our society back into some kind of more comfortable order is the current movement among usually liberal officials to reimpose what's known as the "Fairness Doctrine." The campaign is championed by some of our brightest and most capable leaders in Congress, including Senator Hollings and Congressmen Dingell and Markey. I admire their impulse to help heal an ailing world. But I disagree with their remedy.

I haven't changed my mind since the last time Congress took up the fairness issue in 1987, when I found myself in the unfamiliar position of agreeing with President Reagan's veto of the bill. Then, as now, what these Congressional leaders hoped to legislate was a society in which broadcasters who presented material on one side of a controversial public issue were obliged to balance it out—to create a sense of fairness—by offering the opposing view as well.

That is, without question, a laudable journalistic standard, but it should not be the subject for government regulation. If the central concept of our constitution is liberty, perhaps its most important working principle is this: that the people, who will always remain the ultimate authority, must have freedom of expression.

From the beginning it has been clear that this extraordinary gift—the right to speak, to advocate, to describe, to dissent—is not just a wonderful privilege, it is vital to what makes this democracy the miracle that it is. The Founding Fathers knew all about oppression, and they believed that one of the best protections against it would be the guarantee of free expression. So—with a bluntness and plainness that emphasized its fundamental significance—they made it a part of the document that rules us.

Listen to the language they used, its sureness, its clarity: "Congress shall make no law respecting an establishment of religion, or prohibiting the free exercise thereof; of abridging the freedom of speech, or of the press."

The Founding Fathers gave that power not tentatively, not embroidered with nuances, not shrouded and bound up in conditions, but plainly, surely, purely.

People were to be free to say what they wanted, when they wanted.

To be accurate or not.

In good taste or bad.

To give no side of an issue, or only one side.

All in the name of freedom.

Then, nearly a century and a half after the nation was born, came the advent of broadcasting, and eventually the electronic media. This was a new way of communicating, an awesomely powerful one that was not nearly well enough appreciated.

In the beginning, the government was concerned by its implications, and secured this great new force with both hands. In this early and naive stage, the government believed that there were just so many roadways through the air that could carry these marvelous new communications, and, fearing they could be monopolized and wielded as an instrument of destructive distortion, the government invented the "Fairness Doctrine" to demand that something close to the whole truth would be told.

America's leaders dared to impose a standard or "right conduct" on the broadcasters that would be unthinkable for the print media. Imagine ordering *The National Review* to pair every article on the beauty of free trade with another on the merits of protectionism! Or requiring *The Nation* magazine to counterbalance an editorial on Nicaragua by printing a defense of the Contras!

Can you imagine a federal agency ordering Oliver Stone to

produce a more "balanced" film on the Kennedy Assassination, or forcing theaters to offset the movie *JFK* with alternative portrayals of those tragic and infinitely disputable events of thirty years ago?

Isn't it clear that if there had been a "Six o'Clock News" in Thomas Jefferson's day, the First Amendment would have referred to the freedom of the media, not just freedom of the press?

I think so.

It seems to me, the reasoning that persuaded the Founding Fathers to leave the balancing and the filtering to the people, instead of the politicians, applies perfectly to electronic broadcasting as well.

There are people of good will on the other side who say the scarcity argument is still a good one. But whatever validity that argument had in 1949, when broadcasting was limited to the A.M. band, has been long since washed away by the tide of advancing technology. What could "scarcity" possibly mean in a country now equipped with more than 10,000 radio stations, 1,800 television stations, and more choices on cable television than there is programming to fill them?

Today, the case for scarcity is that access to the airwaves is still limited—to the rich—because it takes a lot of money to buy network time, or take over a cable station. As if it didn't take a lot of money to buy a major newspaper or a full-page ad in *Fortune Magazine*.

Realistically, there is no more danger of inordinate private control of the broadcast media than of the print media, and diversity of viewpoints is virtually assured by the explosion of outlets for informational program. In fact, as all-talk formats have proliferated on radio, TV, and cable, including dozens of local and national call-in shows, it is now possible for individual citizens to broadcast their views directly, for free, to vast, sometimes even international, audiences.

In the end, although the "Fairness Doctrine" was constructed as a way to ensure a healthy diversity of opinion in the public arena, I suspect that it chilled as much dialogue and debate as it encouraged. Why should the owner of a broadcast station bother airing *any* side of a sharply controversial issue and risk an entanglement with the government—one that would surely involve a bunch of paperwork, might involve fines, and could easily produce a bill from the lawyers? Who would want to bother convincing some bureaucrat that he or she had given fair hearing to one—or a dozen—"competing points of view"?

While the "Fairness Doctrine" was still on the books, organizations all across the political spectrum sensed this skittishness on the part of broadcasters, and deliberately used the threat of "Fairness Doctrine" litigation to scare station owners away from airing any viewpoint the organization opposed. In fact, before the "Fairness Doctrine" was repelled, the FCC compiled more than sixty reported cases in which broadcasters killed a piece of programming for fear of triggering "Fairness Doctrine" obligations. Who knows how many other incidents went unreported altogether?

With all these strikes against it, how can the "Fairness Doctrine" manage to revive itself, over and over, like some anticonstitutional Rasputin? Because those who believe in its virtues are driven by one essential observation—an overriding concern that I confess I share.

They fear your power. So do I.

They fear that the powerful portrayal of views and ideas they think are noxious will hurt this society.

Now that fear has extended to new and even greater concerns than your political opinions. The American people are so traumatized by the terrible syndrome of drugs-guns-violence, and all the accompanying ugly disarray, that they are desperate for strong new responses. In their eagerness they see the electronic media as the principal means of displaying this chaos, and they conclude that because you display it you encourage and disseminate it.

I believe there is no question that the media's unbridled recreation of all of this madness induces a certain amount of irrationality, especially among our children and vulnerable adults. And I am not surprised that the idea of restricting violence with tough new governmental regulations starts to sound appealing, if for no other reason than that it would give us a sense of doing something strong about a problem that seems hopelessly out of control.

But acting on that impulse would be applying the wrong kind of strength, however well intentioned. It would mean seizing an important part of our freedom and delivering it to a government we already distrust; substituting the opinions of faceless and unaccountable bureaucrats for our own judgments about what is valuable or interesting or entertaining.

And even if we could raise up a cadre of governmental brahmins whom we would trust more than ourselves, what rules would they apply in censoring our radio and television—not to mention, eventually, our printed media? Would the New York Police Department be okay because its violence seems to have a moral? How about Schwarzenegger? Or operas? Is *artful* violence okay, but poorly done violence not okay?

Even if you could make it past the test of common sense, I don't believe any significant regulation would make it pass the test of constitutionality—although that question should be left to the courts. In the end, government regulation simply does not represent the least intrusive means to the end we all desire, which is a culture that could find some other way to worship at the altar of liberty than by making human sacrifices.

Where does that leave us?

From Attorney General Janet Reno right on down, it seems that every politician and community leader and minister and priest and teacher and parent—and most of the rest of America—wants to do something about the violence in our culture. And a lot of us would like to cut down on the sex and profanity and disrespect, the cynicism and the emptiness, too.

I—and I expect most of you—are saying that governmental regulation of the media is not a useful strength here.

What choices are left?

Well, maybe instead of regulation by government, we should consider trying a little regulation by ourselves. Can't the rest of us work little harder at living out—and displaying—the message that violent solutions diminish us as human beings?

Can't we work harder at delivering more constructive messages?

Shouldn't we, especially the parents among us, be doing more to reject the violence and filth we see around us?

Can't we keep our children from watching and being contaminated by the poisons of television the way we keep them from the bottles marked with a skull and crossbones?

What do we teach our children when we refuse to pressure our legislators to ban assault weapons, instruments explicitly designed to kill the largest number of people in the shortest period of time? And if you need more controversy, should government really be telling our children that the best way for society to handle brutality is through brutality—with the death penalty?

Another alternative: Some important voices in your industry have suggested some kind of "self-policing." Warning labels are already in effect, and control chips are being talked about. Ideas like these might help, but they won't be enough on their own, because we function in a profit-driven, free enterprise system, a system that imposes on you an overriding obligation to produce dividends for your shareholders—no matter what.

This suggests still another possibility.

Perhaps the most efficient way to improve the quality of radio and television, as well as movies and popular music and advertising, would be the purest kind of legitimate commercial persuasion, a real campaign by the consumers: "We won't buy your action-adventure killer robots or your lemon-fresh soap or your cold-filtered beer if you keep purchasing garbage and pouring it into our living rooms!"

But I can tell by looking at you that you're certain that will never happen. Because while I'm up here telling you, "The people should put a stop to it!" *you know that the people started it!* You're giving the people what they want.

The executives of radio and cable and television aren't jamming sex and violence and profanity down our throats—the American people are choosing it from a menu called the program guide! The American people, not the producers, boost the ratings of the overheated, made-for-TV movies about other people's adultery.

We're the ones with the appetite for endless reenactments of the real live blood and terror of police work.

We're the ones with the bloodlust, the taste for seeing people get blown away. Make it fast and plentiful, or maybe slow and intricate this time, but I love to see the killing!

If America contains this extraordinary contradiction—this desire for what disgusts us, this disgust for what we desire—perhaps the best thing that could happen to this country right now would be to find a way to test what we really believe as a people; to see if we're serious about wanting more civilization in our civilization.

Perhaps we should have a kind of grand referendum, a coast-to-coast cooperative campaign led by the President and the wonderful Hillary, enlisting every thoughtful American, embracing every worried parent to demand that we aim for a higher standard in what the cables and airwaves pump into our lives, in what we see at the movies or buy on a compact disc; a campaign that includes young people and government officials and corporate executives and our great spiritual leaders. Jesse Jackson is already paving the way with his efforts to help school children reject violence and seek higher standards in their own lives. His leadership is helpful. Now it should be extended to the whole community. If you don't like this filth, say so, loudly, *now!*

If such a campaign is conducted, it could help push us—through our own good instincts—to the kind of civility and sensibleness and feeling of community that has been eclipsed by the dark images coming from our television screens. . . . And if it didn't, it would nevertheless serve a purpose.

Because if the campaign fails, it will tell us something we need to know: that unlike every generation of Americans who came before us, we lack the simple decency to try to leave a better world for our children; that, in fact, we don't give a damn about the filth and the fury. We like our mayhem, and we cherish our guns. As a nation we were born in violence and we will live with it . . . and all our protestations are mostly pretense.

That kind of look in the mirror on the morning after might shock us into a *real* commitment to change things.

* * *

America is wandering a little. . . . Now, we—the people—on our own, without a censor's sharp pencil pinching and prodding us, must choose the right path. It will be what we say it should be, not what the radio and television say, not what the politicians say. We will say what we choose for ourselves.

With all the talent your industry possesses, surely you can help set us on a better road. If you *think about it,* I believe that the choice you *will* make is to find ways—and to help the people find ways—to take us down the better path.

And for that I thank you.

STATE OF THE STATE ADDRESS

ASSEMBLY CHAMBER, STATE CAPITOL

ALBANY, NEW YORK

JANUARY 5, 1994

The 1994 State of the State was different from my previous ones mostly because it made a more concerted effort to elevate specific ideas over style. It was my most vigorous attempt to produce a speech that was "More Than Words." Shakespeare helped by offering the nice line "Action is eloquence." To emphasize the urgency of my proposals for more effective crime fighting, and greater job opportunities—including for people on welfare—I used the line at both the beginning and the end. The public response was the most gratifying I had received in years.

In this place, from this podium, many speakers have articulated our dreams and obligations as a people, often quite poetically. But this is not a time for sweet recitations.

Shakespeare said it best: *"Action* is eloquence."

And this is surely a time for action, action as clear and direct as the challenges and opportunities that confront us.

It is tragically obvious that the thing that must concern us first—and most—at this moment, is the people's safety. We are threatened by one of the most grotesque explosions of criminal violence in our lifetime. The urgency it creates leaves no time for academic debate over whether we should emphasize law enforcement or deal with prevention instead. We need to do both . . . right now!

We must be clear that there is no single magic answer.

Surely, we need tough new laws. We need stronger enforcement. But we also need to create the kind of life that will prevent our young people from turning to crime in the first place. How can we continue to argue with the necessity of pulling guns out of the hands of criminals?

Let me say it again: assault weapons are specifically designed, not for hunting or sport, but to kill the largest number of people in the shortest period of time.

Why would any society that has seen these instruments used to kill innocent people over and over declare them legally acceptable? I ask you one more time to raise the voice of reason in New York—ban assault weapons, now! That is only one of several new criminal laws that I propose. Some of the others call for more severe punishment. Let me tell you about one of them.

I believe felons whose repeated acts of violence make it clear that they are incorrigible should be put away, never again to terrorize our people.

In baseball, it's three strikes and you're out; in dealing with violent crime, it should be three strikes and you're in—*permanently*! I recommend that we impose a life sentence without parole on anyone convicted of a third violent felony.

Among the other items on my agenda, I will insist that we place sharp new limits on the granting of parole. And I will ask, once again, that we pass a bill that condemns unequivocally another category of detestable crimes, those motivated by bias and hate, because of race or religion or gender or color or age or disability or sexual orientation. It's time to put an end to bias-related violence.

You and I have passed tough laws before. But the truth is, too many of them have become empty threats that fail to deter criminals because we have not enabled our police and the rest of the criminal justice system to enforce these laws effectively.

Here are two things that will help:

• I propose for New York City and other urban areas a program I call "GRIP," the Gun Retrieval and Interdiction Program. GRIP will provide special squads of police and prosecutors whose sole focus will be getting illegal guns and dealers off the streets and putting the cases through special court parts on a fast-track basis.

• For troubled neighborhoods upstate, from Albany to Buffalo, my budget will include funds to begin another new initiative, Operation Firebreak. Operation Firebreak will make available a team of at least one hundred state troopers to wipe out growing dens of drugs and guns and violence upstate. It represents the same kind of concentrated police action that shattered a drug ring in Schenectady so dramatically last November.

I have invited you to consider and act on my entire legislative agenda on guns in a special session on January 17—the day we set aside annually to honor an extraordinary leader lost to us by criminal gunfire, the Reverend Dr. Martin Luther King, Jr.

We need all these strong new measures, strongly applied. We cannot permit any longer the awful irresponsibility and irrationality we are victimized by at this moment. But the recent summit held by African-American leaders on the fate of some of our most disadvantaged children told another truth. We need to do much more than to imprison violent criminals.

If we condemn our children to dirty streets filled with degradation and violence, if they have no good reason to believe that they can earn for themselves—with their own honest efforts—a full and rich life, aren't we *inviting* disaster?

The children in our troubled neighborhoods need a lot from us. Perhaps most of all, they need the feeling that they're not despised, the feeling—if this is not too much for our frightened hearts—the feeling that they are loved, and that they are important to us all. They need streets without drug dealers, schools that excite their interest in some promising work or career. They need a real sense that they can dream and aspire as you and I did, and that if they study hard and apply themselves, they can get a good job and succeed, as you and I did.

That's what our decade of the child must do.

We need to encourage the kind of healthy, vibrant neighborhoods where young people can find better alternatives than fighting gang wars and dealing drugs. Our Neighborhood-Based Alliance Program already serves many of those communities where drugs and crime and poverty strike hardest. This year, we will expand the services they offer. We will open community schools in every location and add special initiatives to combat youth violence.

To help us detect and prevent problems like lead poisoning and child abuse, we will open more in-school health centers. To give young girls better avenues to dignity than having a baby while they're still too young, we'll expand our successful Adolescent Pregnancy Prevention Program.

No doubt it's a hard time in America and in New York, and surely there is no simple solution. But I believe that one thing comes closer to being a panacea than any other. Most of all, what our children *will* need—and what many of their parents need *now*—is the chance to *work*, to earn their own dignity and their own fulfillment with a job.

Providing those jobs has been—and must remain—our continuing focus. A powerful, job-producing economy made New York the *Empire State* and the nation's most exciting generator of opportunity for seekers from all over the world.

Today, we are striving to regain that position. We're doing it, not reactively or sporadically, but with a specific strategy and plan. The premise of that plan is that our economy will be built on our ability to make the highest quality goods and services, and to sell them to the rest of the world.

Here are the elements we need to do that: We need high-tech capacity—in fiber optics, telecommunications, biomedicine, biogenetics, robotics, optics and imaging, advanced materials, computers and other high-tech areas.

We need superior higher education and skills training. We need markets. And we need the stimulus of road, bridge, and building development that both constructs the physical foundation for our future economic development and at the same time produces hundreds of thousands of jobs immediately.

There is another element that the plan requires, *perhaps the most vital of all:* the same basic values that made our parents and grandparents the world's greatest makers and builders.

A fiery hot ambition. A respect for hard work and making it on the merits. A sense of responsibility to one's parents and to the children one brings into this world. A belief in something larger than ourselves—our community, our country. And all of these elements must operate in an environment that is aggressively hospitable to the businesses that will create jobs and opportunity for our people, keeping those businesses competitive by reducing taxes and fees, and by avoiding excessive regulation. . . . This is *not* a vision—this is a plan and it is already producing results.

Look closely at the most recent economic statistics: new job growth for the first time in years, business and consumer confidence on the rise, new business incorporations are up, and so is personal income. Of course, the struggle is not over. The recession still hurts. *But we are clearly on our way back.*

All across the state, companies big and small are producing the exciting new products and ideas created by our high-tech capacity, our superior work force, and our powerful infrastructure, and selling these products and services to markets all over the world.

• During the Midwest floods last summer, it was a product from New York's Corning Incorporated that preserved emergency communications for three states—when every other telecommunications link went down.

• In Somalia, a new Kodak product allows army field doctors to send medical images to the United States by satellite, *instantly,* so they can consult with doctors here.

• When Michelangelo's delicate frescos in the Sistine Chapel were threatened by the heat and humidity caused by two million visitors a year, Carrier Corporation in Syracuse came to the rescue with a climate control system custom-designed for the job.

Now, in this session, we must amplify our message to every corner of this nation and beyond. "New York State believes in business, and if you're prepared to create jobs for our people, we'll do everything we can to make it worth your while." To reinforce that message, I am recommending some bold, simple measures to prove we mean it. With your help, this year we will lighten the load of taxes, fees, and regulations on New York businesses.

• First, in a step that should produce jobs by benefiting every business in every corner of the state, I propose that we cut the business tax surcharge.

• Second, to support travel and tourism—an industry that employs one of every nine New Yorkers in the work force—I propose that we phase out the State Hotel Occupancy Tax.

I will call on you to encourage a new surge in real estate development by lifting the gains tax for builders who can get their shovels in the ground by the end of next year.

I believe we should give small businesses a break for performing the service of collecting our sales taxes. We should reduce their costs through a sales tax vendor allowance. And I propose that we eliminate the Petroleum Business Tax on diesel and residual fuel for farmers.

We must also reduce business fees, and eliminate them wherever possible.

I propose that we cut corporate filing fees.

And I propose that we eliminate the permit and fee to pay wages by check.

I also urge strongly that we wipe out several onerous environmental fees.

And I will call for a *moratorium* on all new business fees. No new taxes. No new business fees.

We must also eliminate unfair regulatory burdens, especially on our smaller businesses.

I will require all agencies in charge of substantial business regulations—including the Departments of Health, Labor, and Taxation and Finance—to conduct a top-to-bottom review to eliminate unnecessary or outdated regulations.

And I will appoint special representatives—what I will call Business Ambassadors—to serve as the voice of the business community within each of the key state agencies, to make sure state government gives New York companies a fair hearing. The comprehensive improvements I'm proposing will give New York businesses the flexibility and strength they need to create new jobs.

At the same time, we will help speed them to the future with five new Centers for Advanced Technology at universities around the state. With the help of local executives, we will work to promote a new high-technology corridor at the heart of Long Island, supplying the capital and expertise to create a home-grown Silicon Valley. In Rochester, to encourage local start-up firms, we will establish a high-tech business "incubator."

And we will begin planning for a Buffalo metro-medical corridor, building on the strength of the Roswell Park Cancer Institute, where we have just committed to invest $240 million more. We will move forward with major recommendations of our telecommunications exchange, and we will expand our efforts to bring the latest in agricultural technology out of the laboratory and into the hands of our farmers.

To help build the roads and bridges and schools and research centers that will make our state still stronger in the future, we will accelerate our New, New York Building Program. These crucial public building projects will supply more than three hundred thousand jobs over the next few years, all across the state.

It's a huge program. You will recall that President Clinton asked Congress for sixteen billion dollars as a stimulus for the whole nation's economy. His request was rejected. But our New, New York provides twice that sum—thirty-two billion—for our state alone.

We are also building on our strength in transportation through an ambitious strategy developed through the leadership of Lieutenant Governor Stan Lundine. We will establish a high-speed rail corridor between New York City and Albany, extending westward eventually to Buffalo. Then, we will develop the *first* intercity magnetic levitation train system in the world. Eventually, Maglev would mean not only swifter, safer transportation but thousands of jobs for our people as well.

Our economic development plan strengthens the entire state. It will touch *every* region.

In the end, however, the work we do to cultivate our economy adds up to nothing if we are not preparing our *people* to seize its challenges and reap its rewards. To give our people the best skills in the most promising industries, I am proposing a major commitment to strengthening our work force training system and our education system.

President Pat Swygert's Moreland Commission has already set us on the high road to real reform in education.

We will introduce a whole new approach to the way schools are run.

Let's try this: Let's put education in the hands of the people who care most and know best. Let's allow individual schools to scrap virtually every educational mandate handed down by the state, except a clear standard of high-quality education. Let the schools determine, on their own, how and what to teach.

We will call these new institutions, these liberated institutions, Twenty-First Century Schools.

 My budget will also increase support for our Pre-K and Community Schools Program, and expand our highly successful Career Pathways reforms to more locations. We should move forward with another new idea: Excelsior High Schools. Each would be affiliated with a SUNY campus and would serve juniors and seniors with exceptional gifts in math, science, and technology. I want to initiate the first of these schools this year.

I will also call for a special summit on education to help us put into practice other ideas for reform, such as expanded public school choice and longer school years. All these initiatives to cultivate the strength of our people will help give us the powerful economy and the jobs our children will need.

And here's a place where the rest of the nation is following our lead, and we should stay ahead—welfare reform.

We've had great success with CAP—the Child Assistance Program—a national model for welfare reform that declares unequivocally that work is better than welfare, and which rewards parents for escaping welfare by allowing them to profit from work.

Now, we must do for everyone on welfare what CAP is doing for single parents and their children—help them regain self-sufficiency, dignity, and hope. In effect, we want to save people from the system, wherever and whenever we can.

First, I propose that we institute a new state Earned Income Tax Credit that will help nearly 1.3 million poor working families keep their heads above water. Next, we must turn the welfare system inside out. Staring now, that's exactly what we'll do, with an initiative called "Jobs First."

Traditionally, when you walked into a welfare office in New York or in any other state, you'd be handed a form to sign yourself up for welfare.

Our "Jobs First" philosophy says that's the *last* thing that should happen to you.

- *First*—before welfare—we should help you find work.
- *First*—before welfare—we should help you get job training.
- *First*—before welfare—we should determine if a one-time cash payment would tide you over, pay the rent, let you hold on to your car until you can find another job.

Jobs should come first. Welfare should come only as a last resort.

I propose that we expand our Working Toward Independence Program. Through this initiative, home relief recipients are required to work off their grants if they can't find a private-sector, paying job. Last year the city of New York and the counties put 25,000 welfare recipients into some form of work program. They should do more and we will help them do it.

I also recommend that we expand our contract with America Works. America Works is a New York company we've collaborated with since 1988. They help us find job placements for New Yorkers on welfare—and we pay *only* for results. When we are able to take people off welfare and put them into long-term, stable jobs, *then* we pay America Works.

What's more, when we provide financial help and technical expertise to New York companies—when we're giving the companies something—we should ask for something. We will encourage these companies to hire people on our welfare rolls.

Finally, we will step up our effort, already one of the most aggressive in the nation, to combat fraud and misuse of the welfare system.

These are just some of our proposals to rescue our neighborhoods from violence and put all our people back to work.

Of course, as you know better than anyone, we are working to serve the people of New York in dozens and dozens of other areas, including health care reform, that I have not had time to discuss today: working to pass a civil rights bill; looking after our parks; "reinventing" DMV; reforming our democracy.

You will see in the message that no part of our mission is neglected. Many times in the past, New Yorkers have endured uncertainty and harshness and hardship.

You and I began our work together facing hard times. Do you recall? In 1983, at the start of my first year as governor, an earlier recession had left us with what was then the largest potential budget deficit in our state's history. At the same time we were attacked with the sudden appearance of a diabolical new drug called crack. Crack caused madness, violence, and death. We had never seen anything like it.

And then we were visited by the terrible tragedy of AIDS. All at once!

We had to fight back. We had to make tough decisions, many of them politically unpopular. We did it.

By 1987 we had brought the unemployment rate to its lowest point since 1970, taken steps that would bring our top tax rate to its lowest level in thirty years, and begun the most massive rebuilding New York had ever seen. By 1989, we had created over a million jobs. We had created a whole new, exciting state-of-the-art network of high-tech concentrations called Centers for Advanced Technology. And we had created a whole new transportation manufacturing industry.

How many people understand that? How many people remember that in the campaign of 1982, I objected to buying subway cars made outside New York because I believed we could make our own right here. At that time we had *no* train car makers in this state. Today we have three of the four largest United States manufacturers of subway trains. And a fourth, Bombardier, is now looking for a location in our state.

Today, we can make every new subway car we need right here in New York. What's more, we have the country's two largest bus manufacturers. We had neither of them in 1982; a whole new manufacturing industry, with thousands of jobs . . . just as promised!

We can do that kind of thing over and over in this state.

We have produced two budget surpluses in a row. Job growth has begun again, and I predict real, tangible, continuing job growth all through 1994. Together you and I have been building the foundation for a better New York. Now we should commit ourselves to finishing the job of building the future.

What will New York look like in that future, as we open the door to a new century of possibility? . . . I think I know. New York will be a thriving economy of agile young companies charging into the future, driven by evolving technologies. . . . It will be neighborhoods that belong to their residents again.

There will be a new generation of young New Yorkers with the wisdom to overcome racism, divisiveness, and discrimination.

There will be Excelsior High Schools—like the great schools we now have—Stuyvesant, Bronx High School of Science, Brooklyn Tech. They will be all over this state, training gifted young scientists and mathematicians.

There will be a high-speed rail system whisking passengers from New York City to Buffalo, a "people mover" at last linking the airports in New York City, and building begun on our ambitious

Maglev system. There'll be a high-tech corridor on Long Island that is the envy of the nation, but only the first among equals in New York State.

There'll be a state government so technologically advanced that you can do most of your business with a telephone or an ATM card.

There will be thousands and thousands of people for whom being on welfare is only a distant memory; a sparkling new state constitution—adopted after a people's convention—revitalizing the democracy of this state.

And in the next presidential election, New York State's presidential primary will have moved up to March, giving us the strongest voice in America in deciding who will lead the country.

Our future will have not one New Yorker who wakes up worried about the family's health insurance.

And we will be breathing cleaner air, and continuing to enjoy the protected lands of the Adirondacks and the Catskills, still and forever wild.

We have everything we need to make all of this real—high-tech, markets, infrastructure, transportation, schools, a beautiful piece of the earth . . . and the toughest, strongest, brightest, sweetest people in America.

We have no excuse for failing.

If we work really hard, we will be able to make enough of our enormous potential that our grandchildren will remember us with the same respect and amazement we feel for the generations who build this great state and country the first time.

So let us be truly eloquent—let's act, and let's do it now!

Thank you, good luck, and God bless us all!

Here it is again, as it was in the beginning, the simple notion that returns in every careful analysis of our current situation—we can't make it through the shoals and falls of this turbulent current without lashing ourselves together. Elsewhere, I refer, as others have, to the need to recognize our interdependence, our interconnectedness, and the need for synergism. Here the point is made in terms of the idea of basic "democratic values" and especially the value of community. Soon, I believe, all of these statements will crystallize into a national consensus producing a crusade to implement the simple truth that to make ourselves better, we must act as a family would.

And so, the circle closes.

It's difficult to believe that I could add anything to a discussion on the "moral state of the union" when you have such an impressive panel of real experts on hand.

But I hope I can offer one useful perspective—the view of a person who has spent the better part of two decades in public service, in the trenches, struggling to help the people articulate what we believe, and if we can keep the order straight, then help them decide what we should *do* about what we believe.

This is a strange time for a country founded by the most optimistic people history ever produced. Every age has its frightening disorder, and even its crises and calamities, but it does seem that our current situation in this country is particularly disorienting.

An ugly litany shows this is no exaggeration:

• Twelve thousand times a year, an American dies because someone else chooses to pull the trigger on a handgun.

- We have five percent of the world's population and consume 50 percent of its cocaine.
- We have lost so many of our children to stray bullets in the drug war that we no longer find the stories shocking.
- We see more and more crimes motivated by prejudice and hate.
- The suicide rate is at an all-time high.
- And so are the rates of divorce and abortion.

The litany could go on . . . but the point, I think, is made. And what do most Americans feel when they encounter a list like that? Pain—sadness—bewilderment. Disgust, perhaps, for some people, probably a sense of numbness for many others. Many Americans believe that many Americans have lost their moral bearings.

But a significant number of Americans seem to feel these problems are someone else's fault, or someone else's responsibility, or both. Either it's not happening to them, or when it does, it doesn't count. We hear comments like these:

- "What am *I* supposed to do about those kids shooting each other in Brooklyn or Roxbury or East L. A.?"
- "Look, *my* kids aren't on drugs . . . okay, maybe a little pot now and then."
- "What do you want me to say? My second wife and I just couldn't get along."
- "Hey, *I'm* not prejudiced."
- "There's nothing wrong with me and *my family*. Our values are perfectly all right."

Maybe, *maybe* we can use parachutes like these to jump clear of the plane before it crashes.

But first we should be sure that our parachutes have no holes.

Let me give you some other facts of the time:

- Twenty-three million American adults can't read well enough to make out the label on a bottle of poison. But now we see a trend toward *abandoning* the public schools that were made fully accessible to all children only about forty years ago.

Instead of abandoning the public schools, we should be improving them!

• In the richest nation in human history, twenty percent of our children grow up in poverty. For African-American children, the number reaches forty-four percent.

And although white Americans enjoy the highest standard of living on Earth, our brothers and sisters who are born Latino or black, live, on average, at a *Third World* standard.

• In many places—including, tragically, my own state—*assault* weapons remain legal, despite the fact that they are expressly designed to kill the largest number of people in the shortest period of time.

Now, I do not understand what has created this consternating confluence of violence and self-debasement that *is* worse than it has been. Is it that expressions of disorder and deviance have been exacerbated by the explosion of lethal technology? That attitudes of children and vulnerable others have been rendered callous or brutal by the hypnotic effect of six and a half hours of callousness and brutality every day on television . . . all made worse by the drug madness?

There's more. What of *this* attitude?

• Reduce the deficit? Of course! But have *me* pay more taxes? That's class warfare!

• Means test for Social Security? That's heresy!

• Drug treatment, more money for early education? $16 billion for jobs, especially for inner city children? We can't afford it!

If these are not moral failures, in the end, I think, they all reveal something else: a failure to appreciate where our own best interests lie.

I have a simple opinion.

If we hope to reestablish our strength, confidence, and balance as a nation, we need to orchestrate a fundamental shift in our perception of the good. We need to help people see that their *self-interest* is not identical with their *selfish* interests; *that self-interest is inextricably linked to the common good.*

Of course there are many among us whose commitment to something larger than themselves is inspiring. There are people of all kinds, volunteering to help others one way or another. But we are not as good at doing it all at once and together, through our government.

It's something we seem to remember automatically in moments of obvious crisis—the Great Depression, World War Two. We saw the same spirit after the explosion in 1993 at the World Trade Center, when tens of thousands of people were plunged into a hell of smoke, darkness, fear, and uncertainty and responded with such a miracle of bravery and intelligence and calm.

But the importance of the collective good is an insight that seems to be elusive in the face of more insidious dangers—like the vapors of despair and disintegration that creep in under our doorsills today: the loss of a generation of children, the growth of an underclass, the disconcerting vulnerability of our middle class.

Individualism is fine. Tocqueville was right, it's very American. But individualism that forbids a higher degree of communal participation than we have now impedes us. If we want to be better at moving forward toward the light as a society, we need one thing more than any other: a new sense of *National Community*. And we need to persuade the people that "community" is much more than a pretty idea to be tricked up and trotted around the ring once or twice every election year.

As one who has spent some time in government and politics, I can tell you one thing with certainty—you get a lot further by appealing to people's practical self-interest than by any appeal, no matter how stirring or eloquent, to altruism or morality alone.

So we should remind people that community is much more than nice; it is absolutely *necessary*. Without a restoration of community—a willingness to share—we *cannot hope* to conquer the huge and sobering problems that confront us as a nation.

These are problems so big they almost defy understanding; problems we created because we refused, before now, to insist on our common interest; problems that will devour our future if we simply leave them to be dealt with through the uncoordinated personal initiatives of 250 million Americans.

Without a new sense of national community, we will grow defenseless against politicians who offer wedges instead of solutions, who seek to divide us against one another for their momentary gain.

Without community, we will move deeper and deeper into the dark woods of "either/or," in which every public issue becomes a battle of good and evil, in which compromise and rational discussion become quaint impossibilities.

Without community, without an articulate sense of our *common* interest, we will donate to the infinitely articulate voices called the special interests the strength and the wealth of this nation.

Without a sense of community—without a restoration of those powerful unwritten codes that prevent more lawlessness than the law ever could alone—we will begin the steady march, ironically, toward a society in which we are forced, bit by bit, to give up our freedoms, so that "someone from the government" will take care of those scary kids on the corner.

Without community, we can say a swift good-bye to the tradition of American prosperity. Because *we cannot make it as a nation* if we lose a generation of our children to drugs, or AIDS, or inadequate education—even if they're not your children, or mine. We *cannot survive* without their talent and intelligence and energy. We cannot afford to jam our prisons and leave our laboratories half empty.

We cannot make it if we fail to rescue those who've been left behind.

Those of us who are comfortable may run away from the consequences for awhile. We can move to pretty, impenetrable suburbs or marble fortresses with doormen who look like Swiss Guards. But eventually, we will run out of places to hide, and then we will understand what we might have understood before: that no man is an island. No woman. No race. No neighborhood. No state.

For all our macho individualism, *we cannot make it as individuals alone.* In this complicated, uneven, and totally interconnected democracy we will each find our individual good in the good of the whole community.

And again, if we fail to reach this new understanding—and to reach it soon—I am afraid that America may start, in fear and exasperation, to make some regrettable choices. If we fail to come together as a community, we will get just what we deserve:

• As a people, we'll get so frustrated with the violence and filth that pours out of our TVs and radios that we will agree to let *Congress* decide who and what should be on the air and when—and let the *First Amendment* go hang itself.

- We'll choose to set a timer at the limits of our charity, and kick people who cannot find work off welfare categorically when the bell goes off—rather than insisting that our political leaders design a constructive, intelligent system to lead struggling people back to self-sufficiency.

- We'll choose to slam the gate unconditionally on the latest generation of immigrants who seek to share with us in the promise of America—immigrants whose predecessors built this country the first time, over ten generations—thereby bolting the door against the very people who seem endowed with all the qualities we say we are losing: fiery hot ambition; a respect for hard work, and responsibility, and making it on the merits; a passionate dedication to family.

- Perhaps worst of all, we'll choose leaders who mistake harshness for firmness, and severity for strength. Leaders who disguise reflexive scapegoating as reasoned analysis, and persuade us that *we have no better choice*. Leaders who suggest that they have swift, clean, satisfying alternatives to the slow, messy miracle that is our democracy at work.

In effect, the people are already shouting, "For God's sake, do something!"

Now, before those voices switch from urgency to recklessness, before "do something" becomes "do anything!," we must respond with a substantive, curative strength; a holy, uplifting strength of constructive discussion and intelligent new consensus.

The strength of a great nation coming together one more time.

Any great change of course requires two things: the *will* and the *direction*. Today, sixty percent of Americans routinely tell the pollsters that we're "on the wrong track" as a nation. Surely that is proof that we have the *will* to make a change.

Finding the *direction* will be a little harder.

Because before we can decide which way to turn on any of the massive public issues that confront us, *we need to decide what we believe together as a people, what we really value*. Surely most of us would include the values we think of as quintessentially American: the *opportunity* to go as far as your talents will take you, without respect to birth or background; the *liberty* to believe what you want to believe, and say so.

And perhaps we will find that our common values are not so far from the ideas articulated so beautifully by thoughtful people like you here today—that great rights imply great *responsibilities*, That individualism has its value, but its limits, and that *community* in the end will set us free.

But whatever we conclude, the most important truth is that we need to come to these positions together—openly, publicly, deliberately, democratically, in every debate on every major public issue. That process will take extraordinary leadership from the people, who will have to decide that they care about their democracy again, and from the politicians, who will have to be willing to discard their traditional positions and allegiances, and lead the people toward the truth, no matter how risky politically.

And perhaps most of all, it will take the insight and tenacity and moral leadership of people like you—people who can lead us to a new frontier of understanding because they have staked out the territory *already*, with sharp minds and generous hearts.

Thank you for that.

The speeches collected here show a man whose remarkable ability to weave the competing concerns of head and heart into a coherent political philosophy has allowed him to become one of our more skillful practitioners of the art of governance—and one of the most compelling speakers of his generation.

Now serving his third term as the fifty-second Governor of New York State, Mario Matthew Cuomo began life in the struggling neighborhood of South Jamaica, Queens, at the height of the Great Depression. Born on June 15, 1932, he was the third surviving child of Andrea and Immaculata Cuomo, recent immigrants from rural Italy. On the savings wrung from his father's wages as a ditch-digger, the family opened a tiny grocery store, and Cuomo spent his first years behind the counter and in a few tenement rooms upstairs.

Though he could barely speak English when he entered the New York City public schools, Cuomo graduated summa cum laude from St. John's University in 1953, and tied for top-of-the-class honors at St. John's University School of Law in 1956, where he later served as adjunct professor.

For more than a decade he fought as an advocate for the ordinary citizen, but did not gain prominent public notice until 1972, when, at the request of New York City Mayor John Lindsay, he stepped in to resolve a bitter dispute over proposed public housing in the community of Forest Hills. His subsequent book, *Forest Hills Diary: The Crisis of Low-Income Housing* (Random House, 1974), captures both the political and philosophical dimensions of the controversy.

Cuomo continued to practice law until, in 1975, he was appointed by Governor Hugh Carey as New York's Secretary of State. In 1978, he was elected as Lieutenant Governor and went on to win his own race for the governorship in 1982. This fierce campaign became the subject of his second book, *Diaries of Mario M. Cuomo* (Random House, 1984).

In 1984, Governor Cuomo gained national attention through two landmark speeches, both included in this volume: the keynote address at the Democratic National Convention in San Francisco, which helped define the political landscape in the 1980s, and, later that year, a statement at the University of Notre Dame on the unique challenges and obligations of the Catholic politician.

Reelected in 1986, he won again in 1990, with the biggest margin of victory and highest percentage of the vote of any candidate who ever ran for a third four-year term as Governor of New York. The same year, he served as co-editor for *Lincoln on Democracy*, a volume that brought together for the first time all of Abraham Lincoln's speeches, writings, and correspondence on this defining theme of American history.

In these pages, as in his public presentations, the voice of Mario Cuomo is warm, inspiring, often funny, but in the end, uncompromising: a clear, wise, insistent appeal to what Lincoln described as the "better angels of our natures." Over and over, he asks that we consider our responsibilities to each other and to ourselves—asks that we reject the destructive simplicity of political labels and sloganeering, but take up the idea that in this democracy of the very fortunate and the deeply deprived, we learn to share benefits and burdens for the good of all.

Married since 1954 to the former Matilda Raffa, the Cuomos are parents of five children: Margaret I. Cuomo, M.D.; Andrew, married to Kerry Kennedy; Maria, married to Kenneth Cole; Madeline, married to Brian O'Donoghue; and Christopher. They are grandparents of Christina Cuomo Perpignano; Emily Carrie Cole; and Amanda Matilda Cole.